A Covenant with Power

A Covenant with Power

*America and World Order
from Wilson to Reagan*

Lloyd C. Gardner

OXFORD UNIVERSITY PRESS
New York

Library of Congress Cataloging in Publication Data

Gardner, Lloyd C., 1934–
A covenant with power.

Includes index.
1. United States—Foreign relations—20th century.
2. Liberalism—United States—History—20th century.
I. Title.
E744.G3425   1984   327.73   83-13149
ISBN 0-19-503357-4
ISBN 0-19-503009-0 (pbk.)

Printing (last digit): 9 8 7 6 5 4 3 2 1
Printed in the United States of America

TO THREE GREAT TEACHERS
David Jennings
Ben Spencer
and the memory of W. Roy Diem

Acknowledgments

Books grow in different ways, of course. This one resulted, in part, from outside stimulus, and in part from a desire to rethink earlier positions. Several people may not recognize their contributions, but they are there. These include Richard Immerman, William Stueck, Michael Schaller, Michael Kren, John Rossi, and David Schmitz. I am especially grateful to Thomas Knock of Princeton for sharing his ideas with me about Woodrow Wilson. At Rutgers several colleagues do double duty as friends and sources of information. These include Michael Adas, Sam Baily, Warren Susman, and Warren Kimball. The last two read the entire manuscript, and kept pulling me back to a clearer definition of the problem. Walter LaFeber, who first urged me to produce a "think-piece" on Wilson, never admits to being bored by my demands on his patience and gifts as a critic, through which, amazingly we remain not only on speaking terms but great good friends. Thanks, as always, to Thomas McCormick and William Appleman Williams. Some of these essays were first delivered, in primitive form, as lectures at Adelphi University, and Free University of Berlin, Lafayette College, New College in Sarasota, Florida, Ohio Wesleyan University, and New College, Oxford. Finally, a special word of gratitude to Sheldon Meyer, whose confidence in American historians must be unmatched among publishers, and to his colleague, Leona Capeless.

East Brunswick, N.J.   L.C.G.
September 1982–March 1983

Contents

Introduction

That was the one thing he was obsessed about: staying young. To him, a closed frontier was like a hardened artery, and too much government, too much system, too much political theory, was a kind of senility. It was what made him hate socialists: "a bunch of goddamn zombies," he called them. "Dead before they're born!"

> Novelist Robert Coover,
> quoting "Uncle Sam" in *The Public Burning*,
> 1976—The Bicentennial Year

Woodrow Wilson spoke of making the world safe for democracy. Our task today is to make the world safe for liberty. . . . Making the world safe for liberty, . . . does not mean establishing democracy everywhere on earth.

> Richard M. Nixon,
> *The Real War*, 1980

Q. Is there a danger that if we do not deal with the world problems that here at home we would become so frustrated that we would retreat, not into the old-time isolationism but into a kind of chauvinism that would make the whole question of world order really impossible?

Secretary Kissinger: It is a big problem. There is such a tendency in America; but at least part of our chauvinism is disappointed idealism so it's always a question of whether one can evoke the idealism.

> Henry Kissinger, 1974

It is vital to us that democracy be allowed to succeed in these countries.

> Ronald Reagan on
> Central America, March 1983

Yearning as well to see the collapse of European hegemony, and the rotting timbers of monarchy and mercantilism replaced with sturdy republican institutions, the makers of the American Revolution brought forth—as Lincoln would say at Gettysburg—a *new* nation, dedicated to advancing liberal ideology throughout the world. America was the last, best hope of mankind. Surrounding Lincoln was the evidence of the terrible burden thus imposed on American leaders, but a new world order did not become an urgent necessity until the twentieth century.

Cracks in the makeshift imperial system invented by Europe and forced upon the areas outside the metropolis to resolve disputes between nations in the industrial era had become apparent even before the Great War began in 1914—as had other signs that the social contract within each might not stand up to the heavy stress caused by working-class demands for economic democracy. America was least affected, perhaps, by these disturbing portents, but worry about what industrialization and corporatism did to liberal ideology and political institutions required going beyond what had sustained the Founding Fathers or Abraham Lincoln in their time of trials.

Merely shoring-up the original assumptions of the liberal state would not suffice, at least not for long. A much bolder approach was needed. Somewhat surprisingly, the pivotal figure in this search became Woodrow Wilson. With minimal political experience, Wilson entered the White House in 1913. Intellectually, however, he was well aware of the reasons for growing pessimism. "The old sort of growth is at an end," he wrote in 1897, "the growth by mere expansion. We have now to look more closely to internal conditions, and study the means by which a various people is to be bound together in a single interest."

But how much time was left for "study"? Wilson was no radical. Even as he moved to implement what many impatient "Progressives" regarded as a mildly reformist "New Freedom" program, the rasping sounds of the old order splintering apart in Mexico reached American ears. Wilson was quick to observe that the Mexican Revolution was a "wedge" in domestic politics. Unsure of his next steps in responding to this challenge, he knew one thing: the real danger was not the loss of investments, but that the wedge would be driven deeper and deeper. He saw into the future, and what the consequences would be if the Mexican Revolution did *not* succeed.

Either Mexico would become a battleground where "liberalism" would lose out to reaction, or it would become the opening skirmish in a worldwide "civil war." Europe's distraction in the Great War gave Wilson a respite, an opportunity to rethink the problem of world order, and to consider how the "old" liberalism might be transformed into a "new" liberalism to save the past and protect the future.* His critics often missed the point. Wilson's idealism was not revealed in a foredoomed effort to impose on the world an abstract set of principles, but in his conviction that the American Revolution could be inverted. Now, instead of America as exemplar to the world, the reverse would have to happen. To achieve such an end justified taking necessary risks. By 1916, when, having left the New Freedom behind, Wilson began seriously to consider a covenant with power, the Progressive movement was deeply divided, with many seeing the preparedness campaign as a final surrender of liberalism to capital and the corporation.

Not Wilson. He saw the danger, but believed that it could be, must be, transcended by making the covenant serve liberal purposes. Wilson imagined that a league of nations, by thwarting would-be perpetrators of war and revolution alike, would allow individual nations breathing room to overcome the constrictions of the modern age, space to solve their internal problems, safety in which to deliberate without fear of external disturbances to domestic tranquility. The President's original drafts of the covenant of the League of Nations faithfully incorporated this vision.

It slipped away at Paris. Faced by the spokesmen of victory on the right, and the prophets of revolution on the left, Wilson's grip on events loosened. The tight bonds he had wrapped around ideology—the American Expeditionary Force, the economic force of American loans—parted, leaving Wilson with the frayed strands, useless to his purpose. Forty years after he asked Congress for a mandate to make the world safe for democracy, a decade after the Second World War, American leaders were still puzzling over Wilson's unhappy experience, and still undecided about the nature of America's destined role in the preservation of World Order.

---

* It is not possible to eliminate all the confusion about the term *liberalism*. In this book it is used several ways, to describe the views of 19th-century thinkers who were opposed to feudalism and aristocracy and favored, therefore, limited government. It is also used to characterize those who, in the early decades of this century, believed that government intervention had become absolutely necessary, paradoxically, to preserve individualism. As I suggest, Wilson is an important transition figure, but liberalism will still mean many things to many people after him. Wide differences separate those who saw themselves as liberals in the early days of the Cold War and those who espoused restrictions on presidential war-making powers during and after Vietnam. The reader will appreciate the difficulty, it is hoped, and tolerate the sometimes unstated nuances necessary in any discourse on the topics discussed.

"The United States," Henry Kissinger, a "realist" intellectual would argue in *Nuclear Weapons and Foreign Policy* (1957), "requires a twentieth-century equivalent of 'showing the flag,' an ability and a readiness to make our power felt quickly and decisively, not only to deter Soviet aggression, but also to impress the uncommitted with our capacity for decisive action." Such attempts to resolve the tension in the old Wilsonian world-view made, and then unmade, the careers of many of the "Best and Brightest" in a generation of "action intellectuals."

The Soviets had become maddeningly successful opportunists, as portrayed in their models, scavengers in the inevitable debris that piled up on the outskirts of modernization theory. They were disease carriers, who would, if left unchecked, endanger the health of the global community. The only remedy was to be found in convincing the Russians (as old Europe had convinced the French a century and a half earlier) to abandon their perverse, and ultimately suicidal, aspirations for a "revolutionary" *dis*-order, and settle for what the rest of the world desired—a return to legitimacy.

Kissinger's efforts to rework American internationalism into a conservative, straightforward *Realpolitik* approach, faced many obstacles, not least the absence of an American conservative tradition. John Kennedy tried. He and his advisers took the central thesis of *Nuclear Weapons and Foreign Policy* and openly avowed their determination to ensure American arms superiority at every step up the escalation ladder. The covenant with power was risky, they said, unless one had total command. Vietnam thus became the ultimate test of national will and credibility, a war that would determine the final outcome of the American Revolution.

No one expected that the Vietnam "conflict" would last longer than the revolutionary war for independence, and leave the nation more divided than the civil war. After Kennedy's death, it was "All the Way with LBJ." Never did a campaign slogan foretell such a cruel irony. Lyndon Johnson simply could not go all the way. Bombing targets had to be personally approved by Johnson, but his grip proved no tighter than Wilson's hold over the Allies at Paris. Each night he went to bed fearful that a mistake would be made, a tragedy caused when a pilot strayed into China's airspace, or when someone in the State Department misread a signal between Hanoi and Moscow, anything that might make it a wider war, a trigger for a nuclear holocaust.

And so the war dragged on, a netherworlds struggle waged against phantoms that could kill without ever being seen. At home, the center shrank, until there was only LBJ. Once sure that quantitative measurements promised victory, his advisers departed one by one, even Secretary of Defense Robert McNamara, who as president of the World Bank undertook a search for Wilson's original vision. In 1968 Americans elected Richard Nixon in the first of a series of "protest" elections. But neither political party could successfully translate this growing unrest into a cohesive alignment of interest groups and ideologies that could replace the worn-out New Deal system. Nixon *almost* pulled it off. He and Henry Kissinger both sensed that, perhaps for the first time, Americans were open to reconsidering their role. Thus Kissinger would observe, "History has, I think, placed me in a key position at a time when we are moving from the relics of the postwar period toward a new international structure. . . . We are at the beginning of building a consciousness of the global community that must come after us."

Ultimately, they failed. The attempt at a conservative vision was defeated, but not by Watergate. Never fully confident in their post-cold war world-view, nor in the ability of American institutions to adjust, nor willing, finally, to take risks as big as Wilson's gamble, Nixon and Kissinger left a vexed nation with a confused covenant with power they called *détente*. Jimmy Carter could not do much with it, and Ronald Reagan did not want to try. He preferred the Kissinger of *Nuclear Weapons and Foreign Policy* for a guide, and hired Alexander Haig to supply the rhetoric of *Realpolitik*.

Onlookers in the Nixon-Kissinger years, a group of former "liberals" found Washington much more congenial under Reagan. These neo-conservatives, as they called themselves (political labels were now hopelessly confused as well), had fretted that America's retreat from power since Vietnam threatened the liberal state at home. In that belief, at least, they were true Wilsonians, as well as in their fear that a self-contained liberalism was a contradiction in terms. Against this view arose other voices, including those of other former cold warriors, who warned that American over-interventionism had subverted the legitimacy of the world order.

At the point where these views meet, at that place is the nexus of the predicament Wilson foresaw; only now we confront it on the rim of extinction.

A Covenant with Power

1

Woodrow Wilson and the Liberal Covenant with Power

During the Vietnam War both Lyndon Johnson and Richard Nixon invoked the Wilsonian creed to bear witness to their concern for the cause of humankind. "Woodrow Wilson once said," Johnson observed, " 'I hope we shall never forget that we created this nation, not to serve ourselves, but to serve mankind.' " Richard Nixon stared directly into the television camera to ask his countrymen in their homes to see the world as he saw it—from behind Wilson's own desk. It was necessary to invade Cambodia, he said. The struggle in Vietnam was not an isolated guerrilla war. Americans were not there because they coveted any material advantage. They were there for the same reason Wilson had asked for war in 1917, to serve the cause of liberty and freedom. Was the world to suffer once again because of the shortsightedness of those who believed the nation could turn its back on such an obligation?

Wilson's example was also used, however, by Jimmy Carter. As he pondered what to say in his inaugural address, Carter read the speeches of earlier Presidents. "I was touched most of all by Woodrow Wilson's. Like him, I felt I was taking office at a time when Americans desired a return to first principles by their government. His call for national repentance also seemed appropriate, although I feared that a modern audience might not understand a similar call from me."*

---

* *Keeping Faith: Memoirs of a President* (New York, 1982), p. 19.

No President left a fuller record of his thoughts than Woodrow Wilson. None probed deeper into the challenges facing the liberal state in the modern era. As these statements suggest, however, Wilson left behind an ambiguous legacy. What still eludes his successors is the process by which Wilson came to believe that the "new" liberalism could make its peace with power. The American example, he would say in 1916 in defense of his military preparedness campaign, had promoted the "sovereignty of self-governing peoples" and spurred "the fine impulses which have built up human liberty on both sides of the water." America now had a duty to take such action as possible, maintaining its self-respect, to see that its example was not neglected or thrust to one side. "Those are great things to defend, and in their defense, sometimes, our thought must take a great sweep, even beyond our own borders."

When Wilson launched the preparedness campaign behind this rationale, the Vietnam War was still fifty years in the future. But his generation had witnessed the transformation of the American republic into a fully industrialized Great Power. It had fought its first "colonial" war and put down a "national liberation movement" in the Philippines. It had intervened to protect "friendly regimes" in Panama, Santo Domingo, and Haiti. Worried intellectual leaders had much to ponder about what the changing environment of industrialism and imperialism had already done to damage the belief in limited government and liberty that Wilson proposed to defend with arms if necessary.

There was no denying that the smokestacks and assembly lines had altered the political climate, had remade America as they had remade Europe, into a society increasingly dominated by corporate bodies: the giant manufacturing concerns, the great banking houses with their world-spanning power and influence, and the burgeoning communications monopolies. Set against these—yet integral to them— were the newly created "peasant" class in the South and West and the Permanent "labor" ranks being recruited every day in larger numbers from the shiploads of arriving European immigrants. Things had worked out almost exactly the opposite of what had been predicted in Richard Cobden's day. Expand international trade, the English liberal thinker had said, and war would become obsolete—as obsolete as European feudalism. Instead nation-states had become empires, reaching to control trade outlets and building armies and navies to protect them against interlopers.

The "Long Depression" (1873-96) had raised the most serious doubts that the liberal theory worked in practice, or that the liberal state could defend itself against its enemies—external or internal. Much of Woodrow Wilson's academic career was given over to the study of this problem. In 1889 he called attention to the danger of importing social disorder and disease from Europe. There was a modern lesson, he believed, in the contrast between the inauguration of George Washington and the outbreak of the French Revolution, between ordered change and the "ineffectual turbulence" let loose when the mob stormed the Bastille. The descendants of those rioters were now coming to America, more all the time.

But a worse spectacle appeared on the western plains. There a native-born demagogue, William Jennings Bryan, had seized hold of the Democratic party. "Any man," Wilson wrote of the presidential candidate of his own party, "who expects to bring the millennium by a sudden and violent effort at reform is fit for a lunatic asylum." But if the only answer to the so-called Populist revolt Bryan now led was a Republican imitation of European "social imperialism," then the vital institutions of the liberal state as it existed in America were indeed in deep peril. Wilson did not oppose annexation of the Philippine Islands, but he could not believe that these tiny pinpoints far off in the Pacific offered an answer to fundamental issues.

Neither did he think that Theodore Roosevelt's efforts to arouse the martial spirit and hitch it to Progressivism would pull the country together. Worst of all, TR might actually succeed for a long enough time to destroy what was left of liberalism. Wilson entered the White House in 1913—after an election that saw the two "corporatist" candidates, Roosevelt and Socialist Eugene Debs, do amazingly well at the polls. Roosevelt's huge personal following accounted for his million-vote lead in the election over President William Howard Taft, the Republican candidate. But what accounted for Debs's doubling of his vote from four years before, unless it was the legitimacy TR gave to "corporatism" as the answer to traditional liberalism's apparent failure?

Wilson's Presidential campaign stressed market expansion, an "old" liberal remedy, not government interventionism as preached by either TR or Debs, or as described by John A. Hobson as a corrective for the maldistribution of wealth that produced an aggressive foreign policy. "Imperialism," wrote Hobson in a book that would later also describe Wilson's attitude, "is the endeavor of the great controllers of industry to broaden the channel for the flow of their surplus wealth by seeking foreign markets and foreign investments to take off the goods and capital they cannot sell or use at home."

Down to 1916, however, Wilson remained a believing Cobdenite. It preyed upon his mind, in fact, that the "special interests" Hobson identified in *Imperialism* (1902), choked off foreign trade and were largely responsible for the slowness of American businessmen to seek foreign markets. "It is amazing to me—it has been amazing ever since I was a thoughtful man—that the businessmen of America have concerned themselves so little with the commerce of the world, as distinguished from the commerce of America." He deduced several things from this failure, ideas that he thought would stand well with the electorate. If business could be made less reliant upon the domestic market, business would be less demanding of government protection. And, therefore, the ties between government and business could be cut off at the root.

Lowering the tariff, though it might seem old-fashioned, still had considerable potential, he thought, in an age of "socialist inquiry," as historian Frederick Jackson Turner put it once. It could correct the abuses of monopoly and privilege. Wilson never entirely lost this faith. But a "new" liberalism gradually emerged as Wilson observed the events of the Mexican Revolution, and he gained a point of view that would take him closer to Hobson.

At first Wilson seemed to relish the opportunity to use Mexico to revitalize the principles of the "old" liberalism. Here was a classic example of the perversions wrought by the "special interests" in the era of "Dollar Diplomacy." Having dealt with them at home by legislation to lower the tariff, he would now apply the political Cobdenism of free elections to their ugly growth abroad, thereby liberating the creative powers of capitalism.

For forty years and more, Mexico's "developers" had enjoyed a bonanza; most of the country's natural resources and much of its good land were owned or controlled by Europeans or citizens of the United States. All this had occurred under the regime of one man, Porfirio Díaz. In 1910 Díaz was forced into retirement; but his reformist successor, Francisco Madero, simply could not meet the expectations of the "radical" countryside, or win the support of metropolitan elites. His death in early 1913 under strange circumstances was already being openly discussed in American newspapers as the result of collusion between the American embassy and General Victoriano Huerta. They conspired, it was said, to restore the *ancien régime*.

Mexican conspiracies—and American participation therein—were hardly unprecedented. In James K. Polk's day conspirators were heroes of Manifest Destiny. But that was all changed now. Newspaper reporting on foreign affairs was no longer a recitation of thrilling deeds set in exotic locales. The world was suddenly topsy-turvy. John Reed, who would soon have Wilson's ear on Mexico, celebrated instead the insurgents' struggle against Huerta. Lincoln Steffens, who had exposed the shame of American cities, had become excited about the adventures of Pancho Villa, who had dared to lay hands upon the foreigner.

But beyond a journalistic new frontier was the reality of social upheaval, the first serious challenge to the established world order. As such it could not be contained in Mexico, could not be regarded, say, as Pulitzer and Hearst looked upon Cuba, a storybook revolution peopled with evil Spanish generals and TR's brave roughriders. And ending happily. The common people in Mexico, Woodrow Wilson could write his future wife, hated the privileged classes. "Therefore," he concluded, "the alliance of the church is necessarily with the 'cientifico' class, who are, *as with us*, owning and running everything, the reactionary class. Hence the wedge in our own domestic politics." It was the wedge that bothered him.

It bothered a lot of people. If the Mexicans could allow the Pancho Villas to run around shooting foreigners and stealing their property, and if American journalists continued to send back euphoric dispatches praising such activities, well, where would the Mexican Revolution end? Wilson was no friend of disorder and chaos. But as his letter to Mrs. Galt suggests, he thought the only way to remove the wedge was to bring the "special interests" under control. And the only way to do that would be to seek the proper remedy: free elections.

The main problem, he thought, was how to introduce a benign American influence without playing the game of the "special interests." Wilson's proposed solution became a favorite theme, not only in this era, but down to Vietnam. The idea was for all the contending forces to accept a truce, and proceed, under Washington's good offices, to hold elections. These completed, the United States would throw a protective shield over the winners. In April 1914, convinced that the liberal forces in Mexico, or those he supposed to be liberal, the Constitutionalists, could not persuade Huerta to yield, nor by themselves overthrow the putative dictator, Wilson sent military forces to occupy Vera Cruz and Tampico. Ostensibly undertaken to protest an insult to the flag, and the arrest of a few American sailors, Wilson admitted some months later at a press conference that the real objective had been to topple General Huerta.

Without a magnifying glass it was difficult for many to see how Wilsonian naval demonstrations and landing parties differed very much from those dispatched by European rulers to chasten a local upstart, or as forerunners of the colonial administrators already under way from the metropolis. Huerta did go. But the Constitutionalists wanted none of Wilson's "moral" interventionism. Their reaction was so negative, in fact, that any thought of a follow-up action had to be put aside. Thus when Secretary of War Lindley M. Garrison suggested that the opportunity presented itself to impose a protectorate, Wilson recoiled violently, as if finally aware of having stepped across the line on a narrow path paved with good intentions. No conceivable circumstances, he replied to Garrison, could lead him to permit such a thing: "All the world has been shocked ever since the time of the revolution in France that Europe should have undertaken to nullify what has been done there, no matter what the excesses committed."

That was still a long way, certainly, from recognizing that the Mexican Revolution could not be channeled into safe Jeffersonian lines—at least not by such methods. Yet what Wilson now learned from his special agents and from writers like Reed and Steffens convinced him that he must not intervene prematurely, before the Constitutionalists had had an opportunity to work out their program. Every nation had an absolute right of self-determination, he told the Jackson Day celebrants in Indianapolis on January 8, 1915:

> It is none of my business, and it is none of your business, how long they take in determining it. It is none of my business, and it is none of yours, how they go about the business. The country is theirs. The government is theirs. The liberty, if they can get it, is theirs, and, so far as my influence goes while I am President, nobody shall interfere with them.

In the original drafts Wilson made of a covenant for the League of Nations at the end of World War I, the President set forth protection of the right of self-determination as the key responsibility of the proposed international security organization. What happened to that injunction helps to explain the ambiguity of the liberal position, an ambiguity Wilson could not overcome in the end.

Though he had told his fellow Americans that Mexico's right to self-determination was absolute, and though he also intended such statements as the Jackson Day message as a warning to Europeans to stay out of Mexico's affairs, leaving Mexico alone was the farthest thing from his mind. Wilson now imagined himself a mediator, acting on behalf of the various factions in the revolution, and as a buffer between them and the ever alert and ever avoracious "special interests." Indeed, if there was no room for such a mission, if America could not thus "serve" the world, liberalism (old or new) was a defunct theory.

Only a week after Huerta finally resigned, Secretary of State William Jennings Bryan—the once abhorred Populist leader— informed the Constitutionalist leader, Venustiano Carranza, that the United States was the only first-class power Mexico should be concerned about. All the others would take their lead from Washington. Should the Constitutionalists ignore liberal principles in dealing with foreign citizens—and their property—or even if they permitted depredations against the Catholic Church, the United States would not be able to grant the new government diplomatic recognition. Mexico's real friends would be rendered incapable, he said, of providing support for the revolution. And it would inevitably fail.

An impasse resulted. Wilson granted Carranza *de facto* recognition in the fall of 1915, but never allowed the Constitutionalist leader to forget that he was still on probation. In the State Department, meanwhile, feelings about the Constitutionalists were of an altogether different nature. Having to confront outraged propertyholders and corporation lawyers who had nothing to say in favor of the Carranzazistas no doubt shaped the Department's views, but it was not to be expected that such men would look kindly upon any disturbance that might alter a perfectly satisfactory status quo. Carranza's repeated threats to regulate and tax foreign property were viewed in much the same manner as the War Department might look upon military preparations in a rival industrial power: with fear and loathing.

Wilson soon had his hands full simply keeping tabs on all the "conspirators" in Mexico. At one point he actually compiled a list of Americans who favored intervention, and who, presumably, would

never stop scheming to bring it about. If anything, his list was too
short, because it left off those in his own administration who scanned
the telegrams from Mexico City seeking an excuse to argue the case
for a move to the south. Had there been no Great War, the coalition
of "special interests" and aroused civil servants might have forced
Wilson's hand. Perhaps not, but it preyed upon the President's mind
that the war was only an interlude, as matters stood, to a new
outburst of both radicalism and reaction, of Mexican provocations,
and capitalist demands for order. Still, it was possible the war might
make American ideals healthy again.

Preoccupied with their own troubles, the Europeans could not
foment, better put, could not carry out interventionist plots. Carranza protected his own skin, moreover, by having the wisdom not to
make good on his worst threats to shut down the oil fields. Against
the background of the Mexican Revolution, the war began to take on
aspects—for the true Wilsonians—of a Miltonic struggle, at the end
of which, finally, Satanic imperialism would be thrust out of modern
capitalist civilization. All the powers of darkness would go tumbling
downward to a just and ignominious fate.

Of all places, however, the thought that the war would scourge
capitalism came to Wilson from Sir Edward Grey, the British Foreign
Secretary. Grey sent word to the President in round-about fashion
that he, too, knew things could never be as they had been, not in
Europe—not anywhere. Up to the outbreak of the war, Grey had told
an American diplomat, capital had ruled the world. "This war
showed that the capitalists had made a mess of it, and that capital
itself was being destroyed to such an extent that it had practically
disappeared and would have to be recreated before it could play its
former part in the economical sub-divisions of the state." After the
war, Grey predicted, labor would rule, would have to, in fact, in order
for the state to provide employment for men until industry recovered.

Wilson interrupted at this point to say that, while it had not
occurred to him before, it sounded like Europe was approaching
American ideas and forms, "where the people were the ruling power."
Wilson's understanding of British politics, or his understanding of
what Grey had said, one or the other, seems faulty at this juncture.
But he had not heard all the prophecy. Labor rule must be the
outcome in Germany, it had ended, because only a democratic form

of government there could ensure effective protection against a resurgence of the militarists with their dreams of glory.

Wilson's final decision for war in 1917 was taken, it is fair to say, in the expectation that Grey's prophecy would be fulfilled. Talking with French diplomats in early 1916, Wilson's closest adviser, Colonel Edward M. House, took up the same point when the discussion turned "to more general aspects of the war." The French recorded these words from House:

> Victory . . . would strengthen German militarism and reinforce the German feudal system. If, however, Germany was beaten and the Allies avoided all efforts to interfere with Germany's internal affairs, then it was impossible that the general discontent would not produce radical, even revolutionary, changes.

House and his French hosts also agreed that "this war was the last war between democracy and what remained of feudalism in the world." The world would be a much safer place, for example, for the Mexican Revolution, safer not only in the sense that the demise of German feudalism would weaken "rightist" forces in other countries, but, it must be supposed, in that the American ability to influence world affairs would increase accordingly.

Thus Wilson linked his advocacy of a military preparedness campaign in the United States, undertaken just as Colonel House was discussing the "more general aspects of the war" with European leaders, to events in Mexico and to the shape of the postwar world. Wilson traveled from New York to the large cities of the Midwest in January 1916 to explain why he had decided upon the need for military training and a larger navy. He was aware all the time that the charge was being made that the only result of such action by the federal government would be to install the worst features of European "militarism" (the most widely accepted cause of the war) in the United States. He was also aware that many liberals, as well as radicals, were arguing that the campaign was motivated by reactionary forces who had seized upon preparedness as a way of stopping progressivism in its tracks.

In New York, on January 27, 1916, Wilson made a skillful attempt to turn the argument. He asked his audience to consider what would happen if he decided to "go into Mexico." If he did that, he said, all the sympathies of the rest of Latin America would look across the water, and not northward "to the great republic which we profess to represent." By putting the issue this way, Wilson managed to suggest not only that he was anti-intervention, but that the preparedness campaign was a way of stressing the uniqueness of America. "We suppose that all armies are alike and that there cannot be an American system in this instance, but that it must be the European system, and that is what I, for one, am trying to divest my mind of."

In Pittsburgh he argued that his preparedness campaign was an effort, in fact, to rekindle "the old spirit of '76, which was not the spirit of aggression, but the spirit of love of country and pure and undefiled patriotism. . . ." Each speech he made was a call to arms, but a call to rally around liberalism as well. In Wilson's eyes, the preparedness campaign finally became a crusade in favor of divesting the "special interests" of their ability to influence national policy. This would be accomplished in two ways: first, in the postwar era, the League that was already taking shape in his mind would have at its disposal an international army, composed of elements from several nations; second, munitions and arms would become state monopolies.

The combined effect of these proposals, he believed, would be to take the profit out of war and reduce the level of militarism and its political counterpart, reaction, to a degree that no nation would be threatened from without—or (what was perhaps more important) from within. "It will be absolutely necessary," he would say in his January 1917 "Peace Without Victory" speech, "that a force be created as guarantor of the permanency of the settlement so much greater than the force of any nation now engaged or any alliance hitherto formed . . . [which] no probable combination of nations could face or withstand."

If properly implemented, this would constitute a safe covenant with power, a way for liberalism to expand, and to reassert its legitimacy against reaction or socialism. No better statement of the interconnections that fastened themselves in Wilson's mind exists than in his 1916 Jefferson Day speech, during which he turned again to Mexico. He had been talking with a gentleman, he began this speech, who once again asserted the position that the United States should assume a protectorate over that troubled neighbor. Wilson challenged the expounder to show him a single example in history in which liberty and prosperity had ever been handed down from above.

Yet he was also frank to admit the need for an active American policy "to serve the right."

When I see the crust even so much as slightly broken over the heads of a population, which has always been directed by a board of trustees, I make up my mind that I will thrust, not only my arm, but my heart, in the aperture, and that, only by crushing every ounce of power that I can, shall any man ever close that opening up again.

"Whenever we use our power," he concluded, "we must use it with this conception always in mind—that we are using it for the benefit of the persons who are chiefly interested, and not for our own benefit."

It was pointed out to Wilson that, while his image of what could be accomplished represented a benign interpretation of preparedness, state legislatures had already passed bills calling for compulsory military training. Criticism of his decision to send General John J. Pershing into northern Mexico to hunt down Pancho Villa, who had raided towns across the border, indicated that there were many "new" liberals who thought that the primary result of preparedness would be an increased willingness to intervene—not a world safe for democracy.

The President met with a group of anti-preparedness leaders on May 8, 1916. Their spokesperson, Lillian Wald, explained that the American Union against Militarism had been organized to combat the rising spirit of militarism and to challenge preparedness as antithetical to democracy. Wilson admitted that the danger was real. He was not sure, he said, that he could speak with any degree of confidence on the final outcome.

But a nation which, by the standards of other nations, however mistaken those standards may be, is regarded as helpless, is apt in general counsel to be regarded as negligible. And when you go into a conference to establish foundations for the peace of the world, you have got to go in on a basis intelligible to the people you are conferring with.

Go in with both the power and the will, he meant, to change the world. At one point, an "Unknown Person" in the Oval Office raised the fundamental question. Americans would have to recognize, began this speaker, that they were "just like everybody else," and not morally superior. "We are potentially more aggressive, because our economic organizations are more active, more powerful, in reaching out and grasping for the world's trade." Then this:

The organization of the international corporation is one of the great facts of modern history. And it seems to me that if you hitch up this

tremendously aggressive spirit of grabbing for the trade of the world
with a tendency to back up that trade, there is going to be produced an
aggressive nationalism in trade which would—

Wilson interrupted, probably aware that what had been said recast
his own fears of Theodore Roosevelt's "New Nationalism": "It might,
very easily, unless some check was placed upon it by some international arrangement which we hope for."

Wilson probably did not convince everyone who heard him that
day. The gamble was an obvious "leap of faith" even for the most
committed. But suppose Germany won, and German methods prevailed after the war? What was the outlook in that case? To imitate
Germany would mean a series of international confrontations, and
would place an intolerable stress upon liberal institutions that would
cause them to wither and die.

At least that was the way it appeared to committed "Wilsonians."
What could liberals offer, they asked, that would offset the claims of
reactionaries or radicals? A later generation of historians, the Cold
War "realists" of the 1950s, tended to blame Wilson for taking the
gamble. If America had stayed out of the war, had allowed the two
alliances to exhaust themselves on the battlefield, a compromise
peace would have resulted. By entering the war, it was argued, the
United States upset the balance of power that had preserved Europe
from would-be Napoleons for nearly a century. All Wilson accomplished was to make it possible for the Allies to crush Germany, and
thereby, it is further contended, to impose the Versailles settlement.
Versailles doomed liberalism, not the Kaiser's Germany.

Such assertions ignore the ideological component in reality.
Forced by political pressures to embrace the preparedness campaign,
Wilson schemed to make it serve his own purposes. He had a great
fear of what would happen if the nation went to war. A colleague
remembered his saying that, in the event of war, big business would
regain all the territory it had lost during the Progressive era—and
more. "We have almost ended their control of government," he said.
"But if we must go into war Big Business will come back and control
for twenty years."

By staying out of war, however, the same result might be expected.
If Germany forced the industrial nations into "defensive" measures,
liberals would have little room to maneuver against the overwhelming claims of patriotism. George Creel, the publicist Wilson would

place in charge of official ideology during the war, captured the essence of the challenge. By going to war, he would contend, Wilson gave Progressivism its only chance:

> A few years earlier would have found us still too absorbed in the problems of a frontier nation, too provincial to have responded unitedly to the world's cry of distress, too confident that the Atlantic was a barrier and not a home. A decade or two later might have found us unconsciously stratified in our own social organization and thinking, the prison walls of class consciousness shutting out the visions of our nation's youth. . . .

In such a cause, a covenant with power was justified. Shortly after the American decision for war in April 1917, Colonel House confided to British Foreign Secretary Arthur Balfour that Wilson would have found it difficult to go to Congress, except for the "famous German telegram to Mexico" and the startling events in Russia that saw the Tsar overthrown and a movement begun toward democracy in that great country.

The first reference was to an intercepted message, conveniently supplied to Washington by British intelligence sources, that indicated Berlin was trying to bribe Carranza should war between Germany and the United States become a reality. Details of the German offer were unimportant. Germany had thrown down the gauntlet before the Monroe Doctrine. An aroused American public would demand action. Or so it was hoped by those who supplied copies of the telegram. As House's confidence implied, Wilson was upset—but not for precisely the reasons contemporaries imagined. From his perspective, German meddling in Mexico had little chance of success; it was the dying gasp of the old diplomacy. It was laughable. But the success of the Mexican and Russian revolutions *was* in question. How the war ended might determine their future. Should Mexico and Russia continue to remain the scene of international rivalries, the revolutions would have little chance—little chance of remaining open to liberal influence.

Liberal impulses, if smothered in Mexico and Russia, might not survive elsewhere. Immediately prior to the German "telegram," Wilson's new Secretary of State, Robert Lansing, had sent Carranza yet another warning. When Bryan put the Constitutionalists on notice, no one imagined how far the revolution would go in just two years. Carranza's proposed new constitution for Mexico vested subsoil mineral rights in the nation, a radical departure fraught with overtones of "confiscation" and "expropriation." Lansing threatened Mexico with "grave consequences" if the constitution was interpreted so as to endanger the rights of foreign propertyholders.

Europeans thought it had taken Washington too long a time to come around to this point of view. Some months later, British diplomats hinted to Assistant Secretary of State Gordon Auchinloss that it would be an easy matter to depose Carranza, and thus remove the possibility of property confiscation. And then it would be possible to establish a real government composed of the "educated and respectable people." All it required, in fact, was a nod of approval— no, not even that, just a willingness to look the other way for a moment. When pressed, Auchinloss had to say that President Wilson's public utterances ruled out any intrigue.

Auchinloss's sympathies were no doubt divided, but Wilson's struggle with his conscience was a far more acute affair. If no new order emerged from the war, Garrison's old plea to march on Mexico City, and even more Lansing's warnings, would have to be accounted for. Indeed, one way that Wilson kept his virtue from being a cloistered talent, and his tempters at bay, was by issuing public statements that limited his own options. Thus in June 1918 Wilson promised a group of Mexican newspaper editors that capitalism would be transformed by the war. When the world came to its senses, he said, American principles would prevail: honor, fair dealing, and justice. Kept strictly within such bounds, capitalism could accomplish for liberals *their* true destiny, and improve the lot of all the world: "So soon as you can admit your own capital and the capital of the world to the free use of the resources of Mexico, it will be one of the most wonderfully rich and prosperous countries in the world."

A great leap of faith, true, but what were the alternatives? Wilson had to assume that the Constitution of 1917 contained restrictions on private property because of the abuses perpetrated by the "special interests," a situation not unlike the charges Americans had once placed against George III in the Declaration of Independence. Once these were removed—and that could only be done by a compact among the industrial nations—the radicalism of the Mexican Revolution would no longer threaten anyone.

Germany's resumption of unrestricted submarine warfare in early 1917 was the precipitating cause of America's entry into the war. But

Wilson was careful not to compromise his position, not to go to war *with* the Allies. He was encouraged to believe that America's role in the war was "special" by British Prime Minister David Lloyd George, who openly expressed his belief that only Wilson could save liberalism.

"We want him to come into the war not so much for help with the war as for help with the peace," Lloyd George wrote in a letter intended for the President's eyes: "I mean that he himself must be there in person. If he sits in the conference that makes peace he will exert the greatest influence that any man has ever exerted in expressing the moral value of free government." The belligerents were blind to their own best interests. The gore welling up behind their eyes was simply too great. "Those that win will want some concrete gains, old wrongs righted, or boundaries changed." Even Britain's spokesmen would have to yield to the "security demands" sure to be put forth by Dominion ministers. If Australia and South Africa, for example, had their way, Germany would be left without an acre of territory in Africa nor a single island in the Pacific. "Nobody therefore can have so commanding a voice as the President. Convey to him this deep conviction of mine."

Wilson liked to hear such things. Anyone would. But he also believed that the Allies, near exhaustion, could not stand out against a "liberal" program at the peace conference. They had made too many promises to their own people. The strategic position in 1917, in other words, could not exclude ideological factors. If by going to war we could "hasten and fix movements in Russia and Germany," he told the Cabinet of the growing liberal impetus brought on by the sheer horror of the struggle, "it would be a marked gain for the world and would tend to give additional justification for the whole struggle."

"Out of this immense horror," wrote a dedicated Wilsonian, Walter Lippmann, "ideas have arisen to possess men's souls." The old struggle was dissolving. In its place arose a stupendous world "revolution." Strategic frontiers, colonies, and all the rest had been forgotten. "Those were the stakes of a diplomat's war. . . . The whole perspective is changed today by the revolution in Russia and the intervention of America. The scale of values is transformed for the democracies are unloosed."

In a recent address, Wilson told the Mexican editors on that occasion in June 1918, he had mentioned to an audience of well-dressed New Yorkers that "we meant to stand by Russia just as firmly

as we would stand by France or England or any other of the Allies." It
was not a group of people, he went on, that one would suppose had
much intimate knowledge of the revolution, and certainly not much
concern about the ordinary Russian. "But that audience jumped into
the aisles, the whole audience rose to its feet, and nothing that I had
said on that occasion aroused anything like the enthusiasm that that
single sentence aroused." The President sent the Mexicans home with
his pledged word: "The whole family of nations will have to guarantee
to each nation that no nation shall violate its political independence
or its territorial integrity."

Exactly a month later at another White House conference, Wilson
and his political advisers agreed to send 7000 troops to take part in
the Allied intervention in Russia. The Provisional Government had
barely lasted out the summer of 1917. Those who ruled now in
Petrograd, the Bolsheviks, declared themselves obligated to no one
but the working masses of the world. When Russia left the war, the
Allies seethed. They had been betrayed; politically no less than on the
battlefield. At first no one believed—including Lenin himself—that
Bolshevik rule could last very long. When it did, two very different
arguments were made to persuade the President to intervene. It was
contended that the Eastern front could be restored if the Allies could
only provide rallying points for "loyal" Russians determined to fight
on. It was also argued that the only way the United States could
prevent the Allies from taking advantage of Russia's distress to carve
out new spheres of influence for themselves would be to take a full
part.

For six months Wilson wrestled with these arguments. He never
did believe that the military claims were anything but a dodge. The
second argument made sense. But probably more important was his
fear of seeming ineffectual, unable to make up his mind. Having
championed the right of revolution in Mexico for five years, where
was he now? Lenin mocked him, divided his followers, and strength-
ened his enemies. Liberalism had no future prospects, proclaimed
the Bolsheviks—because the concept of harmony between classes
was a delusion. Sure of their grip on history, if not on Russia,
the Bolsheviks announced that liberalism was part of the false consciousness of nationalism that kept the working class in bondage.

The Bolshevik triumph in November 1917 thus had an immediate
—and indelible—impact on the domestic politics of all nations. The
new liberal consensus Wilson hoped to forge simply fell apart. Liber-

als no longer even had a usable past. The pieces were blowing on the wind. Whether the Bolsheviks remained in power in Russia or not, the whole perspective had altered. To protect his revolution, moreover, Lenin had even absconded with the biggest piece of liberal theory: the principle of self-determination. Liberals were never able afterwards, as the politics of decolonization and the effort to portray the Chinese Revolution as an illegitimate offspring of the Kremlin would demonstrate, to reclaim nationalism for their own. Neither were they able, on the other hand, to counter effectively the conservative argument that "communists" always use nationalist slogans to take advantage of democratic freedom to destroy freedom.

Little wonder Wilson sweat blood over Russia. Lenin had departed from Marx to reach out and grab self-determination, and left Wilson nothing but his eloquence to ward off his opponents. It was not nearly enough. The impact was felt even in American politics. When Socialist Eugene Debs inveighed against the war as a capitalist enterprise, he was soon arrested and tried under sedition laws passed by Congress in the wake of the French Revolution. Debs's fate invited unhappy comparisons with the President's pledge of self-determination for the world's nations. What good was it if self-determination was denied at home? That Wilson had not wished to imprison Debs, and that the trial was held in a state court, did little to correct an impression that Bolshevism was an enemy to be defeated along with Germany, not a challenge to be met politically.

An effort was made to reconcile self-determination with "intervention" (inside Russia and inside America) by stressing "subversion" and the "agent" theory of revolution. If it could be established that the Bolsheviks were German "agents," were actually in the pay of the Kaiser, the dilemma resolved itself. To this end, Wilson, who was so skeptical of Allied arguments that intervention would enable the Eastern front to be reopened, accepted, and then published under a government imprimatur, a collection of documents that purported to prove the Bolsheviks nothing more than agents of Imperial Germany.

Wilson had good reason to feel aggrieved. The United States had been the first great power to recognize the Provisional Government in Russia in the first days after Nicholas II had been deposed. He had fully expected to work with "liberal" Russia at the peace table, in turn, to "depose" the ideas of the old diplomacy. Now all that was out the window. Lenin denounced liberalism; yet called upon liberals to respect the right of self-determination! Could things be worse?

Could things be worse, for example, so far as the President's ability to take a distinct liberal position vis-à-vis Germany? The Bolshevik Revolution cast a dark shadow over the "revolution" inside Germany that brought to power a civilian government in October 1918. The Allies took, with Wilson's approval, an ambiguous position toward the new government. In the armistice negotiations the Allies demanded that the Germans maintain their military positions in the East, and withhold the return of Russian gold. Yet they quibbled over the arms to be allowed to the Germans to maintain internal order.

In pre-Peace Conference conversations with Allied leaders, the President held that Germany could not be admitted to the proposed League of Nations until it had proved its worthiness. Attitudes toward Germany were shaped by a number of factors, revenge being the most important, but fear of a link-up between a "leftist" German republic and the Soviets had already made itself felt in the highest councils. Wilson was also caught between advisers who warned him that a hard peace would drive Germany to radicalism and the fears of Allied statesmen that a soft peace would undermine their governments.

From every direction, then, the Bolshevik Revolution narrowed options, raised the stakes, and undermined the President's peace program. How long Germany must remain outside the League, and what form Germany's probation period would take, mattered less than what had happened to the idea of the organized force of mankind Wilson had envisioned. The League of Nations now became instead an appendage to the peace treaty, an enforcement agency for a victors' peace. The Wilsonian thing to do, it soon occurred to many, was to remain outside the League in order to moderate Allied demands.

"For the time being at any rate," Wilson had told the Mexican editors, "and I hope it will not be for a short time—the influence of the United States is somewhat pervasive in the affairs of the world." This was so not because of America's military might alone, but because the less powerful had recognized a champion whose only desire was to do disinterested service. On his way over to Paris, the President had told members of the American peace delegation that he would be able to shape the treaty in a liberal mold because the Allies depended upon the United States for postwar economic aid.

The reality was quite different. American economic strength did not convert into equal parts of political leverage, another persistent difficulty that would continue to baffle policymakers down through the years of the Cold War. The longer negotiations took, moreover, the greater the danger that Central Europe would erupt, spewing forth a cascade of violence that would bury the Peace Conference itself under the molten lava of revolution. As between a deadlocked Conference, therefore, and acceptance of a "compromise" victors' peace, the choice was, unfortunately, painfully clear. Once Wilson yielded, he went all the way. The original foundation for postwar order was to be the absolute right of self-determination. He had excluded colonies, true, but the mandate system had not been intended as a fig-leaf of respectability for Europe's division of the spoils. And he had been firm once that American participation in the Russian intervention was to forestall any effort by the Germans, and their "agents" the Bolsheviks, or the Allies to deprive the Russian people of the right to determine their own future.

But by excluding Germany from the League, and, worse, accepting the proposed war guilt clause in the peace treaty, Wilson and the Allies not only violated the assurances given to the Germans at the time of the truce, but stored up for themselves a terrible and lasting fate. The ancient mariner's burden was light by comparison, and far less potentially destructive. The victors established a permanent competition with Germany to control Russia's future. Thus the Germans were to be punished, but they were also expected to keep the gate closed. Another element went into the making of this unhappy tale. Faced with the Leninist challenge, to exonerate Germany would mean, would it not, that the Bolsheviks were correct: the capitalist system was responsible for the war. If the Germans alone were guilty, that justified, did it not, the taking of German colonies and reparations. But this was a very different logic from what Wilson had pursued, originally, on the way to war.

It is unfortunate that Wilson wrote so many constitutions for organizations as a child and young man, unfortunate because historians too often treat the League of Nations as nothing more than the most grandiose of his schemes. Had he been more moderate in his demands, not expected so much of human nature, the argument goes, he might have had his League. But what the President had in mind had little to do with a personal idiosyncrasy, or with a supposed American obsession with moralistic legalism. It was put forward not merely as a substitute for the nineteenth-century concert of powers, but as an answer to the internal failures of liberalism and as a corrective to imperialism.

This League would realize its objectives, therefore, only if the work of the Council and Assembly, the effective bodies in the covenant, was informed by the findings of specialized agencies such as the mandate commission, the International Labor Organization, and similar fact-finding bodies. As the capabilities and capacities of the League grew, the demand for state intervention, whether in the direction of state capitalism or socialism, would diminish. By creating an international liberal environment, finally, the League would augment freedom's chances within the internal environment of nation-states.

Article III of Wilson's original draft pledged the contracting parties to guarantee to each other political independence and territorial integrity—but it modified this pledge to take into account territorial readjustments ". . . pursuant to the principle of self-determination," along with other reasons. It concluded with this sentence, "The Contracting Powers accept without reservation the principle that the peace of the world is superior in importance to every question of political jurisdiction or boundary."

In the wake of a lengthy debate over the future of Germany's colonies, and with reports coming in from Central Europe about deepening social chaos, Article III was shortened in Wilson's Fourth Draft of February 2, 1919. It now read that the contracting parties undertook "to respect and to protect as against external aggression the political independence and territorial integrity of all States members of the League." Germany and Russia were left in limbo, at least temporarily, by the phrase "members of the League." And the absence of the words "self-determination" made territorial integrity a more absolute and permanent feature. The League of Nations was now the equivalent, asserted critics, of the Congress of Vienna— nothing more, and (more ominous) nothing less.

Wilson's original draft of Article IV had stated that, "The Contracting Powers further agree that munitions and implements of war shall not be manufactured by private enterprise or for private profit, and that there shall be full and frank publicity as to all national armaments and military or naval programs." This article did not survive either. When Wilson first undertook the preparedness campaign back in 1916, he had promised doubters that his plan was designed (1) to ensure that the American voice would be heard at the peace conference, and (2) that it would diminish, or eliminate, the threat of militarism. Warned that his campaign, when hitched to an "aggressive nationalism in trade" would imperil the future peace, Wilson had said, "It might, very easily, unless some check was placed upon it by some international arrangement . . ."

Among the papers the President took to Paris was a much underlined memorandum from historian Frederick Jackson Turner, a scholar Wilson greatly admired and whose work he had incorporated in his own writings on American institutions. Turner was famous for the thesis that explained American democracy as a product of the leveling impact of the frontier, which had provided a safety valve, dispersing political power over a continent and inhibiting the growth of a rigid class system by providing easy access to new lands.

But what Turner now argued was even more intriguing and controversial. He thought that the once supposed unique genius of American liberal democracy might in fact be injected back into Europe. And, still more controversial, that the Allied handling of the Bolshevik challenge could be accomplished without doing violence to the Wilsonian covenant with power.

The gist of Turner's memorandum to the President, "International Political Parties in a Durable League of Nations," was that the American experiment was probably not unique after all. Perhaps the world had reached a stage where the American frontier experience might provide a model for Europe's future. There were plausible similarities between regional sections in the United States and the individual nations of Europe. The key problem, said the historian, was to find some mechanism for checking a resurgence of war-breeding nationalism without promoting radicalization. Political parties, after all, not vacant lands, were the essence of democracy. In the United States political parties had played a mediating role geographically as well as socially. They might work that way in a new Europe.

As matters stood, moreover, the "radical element" was already politically organized on an international basis. The League's most important assignment could well turn out to be the creation of a conservative counterpart, and thus a European party system that could balance off sectional and class differences. So long as the radical element was dominated by one or two countries, finally, it would be extended by intrigue with little regard to the welfare or the separate interests of other nations into which it was introduced. Instead of attempting to stamp out Bolshevism, the real solution was to spread it out. Or, as Turner put it:

> If one could keep the Bolsheviki serpent out of the American eden, he would hesitate to admit any international party organization. . . .

> But in the reconstruction and the ferment which will follow the return of peace, there will be doubts about the existence of edens anywhere, and the Bolsheviki serpent will creep in under whatever fence be attempted. May it not be safer to give him a job of international legislation rather than to leave him to strike from dark corners, and with no sense of responsibility?

Turner admitted that an international legislature might be used by an "ultraconservative majority" to check reform in a particular nation. But the plan was no more risky than the project of the American Founding Fathers. The memorandum went several steps beyond what Wilson had envisioned, at least initially, for the League. But there were clear similarities between this proposal and the President's developing conception of the League as a galaxy of large and small powers, each exerting a political and ideological pull on the other.

When Wilson traveled home during the Peace Conference to fulfill his constitutional duties as chief executive, both the similarities and the differences stood out. At a White House luncheon for the Democratic National Committee on February 28, 1919, the President delivered a brilliant extemporary answer, if one stated in a curious mixture of *Realpolitik* and pre-Peace Conference flexibility, to the charge that the Covenant was nothing more than a sop thrown to idealistic Americans, to keep them busy while the Allies fed on the spoils. The truth was, said the President, that the Conference had been concerned with some way to head off any renewal of German territorial ambitions. It had set up a barrier of new states as a fence "right in the path that German ambition expected to tread." Article 10 was the key, and the League was the "structural iron" needed to hold it all in place.

Shifting images, Wilson moved to the ideological. Germany would be overwhelmed by democracy. It would not fail, democracy, because of the strength of the League. Reaction could not grow in such a climate, inside or outside Germany. To the accusation that the League was only the Holy Alliance reborn, Wilson asserted that the men who sat with him around the peace table "had a great respect for the right of revolution." Yet there lurked contradictions beneath these assurances. The League would not guarantee any state "against what may happen inside itself . . ." If that were so, however, what was there to ensure the survival of a democratic climate on Germany's borders? Fear of revolution, explained Wilson, actually put a brake on overt anti-revolutionary behavior. "I read the Virginia Bill of Rights very literally but not very elegantly to mean that any people is entitled to any kind of government it damn pleases . . . Sometimes it will have a very riotous form of government, but that is none of our business. And I find that is accepted even with regard to Russia."

A brave statement, one that harked back to Wilson's Jackson Day Address in 1915, affirming Carranza's and Mexico's right to self-determination. At Paris, it was true, Wilson's "veto" had killed every project that arose for a frontal assault on revolutionary Russia. But when pressed for his alternative, whether an economic plan or a political approach, Wilson had none to offer. The only thing to do, he said of Russia at the White House luncheon, was to see "if we can help them" by "conference and suggestion" so that the "right elements" could get together and "not leave the country in a state of chaos."

Wilson went on tour to defend the League against his political opponents. The dichotomy of his views about Russia was perfectly reflected in the opposition, with some blaming him for bringing home a punitive treaty that forced Germany to accept sole guilt for the outbreak of the war, that stripped the country of its African colonies, and that saddled it with an unbearable reparations burden, while others described the treaty and the League as a betrayal of American independence and interests. Already weakened by the strains and stresses of a wartime Presidency, Wilson fell ill and could not complete his cross-country tour.

Prior to his collapse, however, Wilson had been incapacitated by the impossibility of reconciling "self-determination" with the felt need to establish a worldwide liberal order. Ill and embittered at the end of his life, Wilson turned over his private papers to a journalist friend, Ray Stannard Baker. Brought back from Paris in an old trunk, these documents had been set aside while the fight for the League and the peace treaty straggled on to the end of his term in office.

Baker's revelations shocked European statesmen by exposing the innermost secrets of the Peace Conference. He indicted the reactionary European statesmen for defeating Wilsonian liberalism. Theirs was a sordid quest for land and power—a purposeful effort as well to deny the peoples of all countries the victory that should have been theirs. Yet he left out of his three-volume *Woodrow Wilson and World Settlement* a section entitled "Bolshevism and Russia." "Wilson's mind was never quite clear on the question of dealing with Bolshevist Russia," mused Baker. "To his mind, fixed in the political mold of classical liberalism, the concept of government based primarily upon an economic theory was simply not to be grasped—was even abhorrent when that theory was one in which he could not believe."

Before the Bolshevik Revolution, the President's burgeoning "new" liberalism was flexible yet sturdy—the counterpart to the AEF —but as his options at Paris narrowed, so convictions faded that a liberal world order would emerge. The Russians had overthrown the Tsar and left behind the past. But what strange version of the present and future did they now wish to force upon the world? "It did not seem real; surely it could not last. It was the passing vagary of a little group of fanatics whose grip would soon be shaken off by the mass of liberty-loving Russian people anxious to get into the procession of the world's great democracies."

Perhaps Baker declined to publish this section of his manuscript for much the same reason that Wilson could not bring himself to pardon Eugene Debs, though the reason for his imprisonment had ended with the war. It muddled Baker's thesis about Allied responsibility for the failure at Paris to discuss Bolshevism, and for Wilson to pardon Debs might have suggested that the war had been fought in vain. It was terrible to imagine that Debs in prison was all that remained of the crusade to remake the world. Nevertheless, a few weeks before the national elections of 1920, Wilson told an old friend and political ally that if Warren Harding was elected, "we shall come very close to having a revolution in this country and the prospect that we shall have war with Mexico is very great."

Wilson's fears were not realized. The Harding administration desired no confrontation with revolution. When "I make up my mind that I will thrust," Wilson had said, "I will thrust not only my arm, but my heart, in the aperture," and only by crushing his strength would it ever be closed again. Liberals who followed Wilson took the same vow, but shuddered at the thought of going abroad again to redeem America.

Woodrow Wilson is the pivotal figure still for discussing the relationship of liberalism to power, the inherent dilemma policymakers have inherited. Wilson's legacy is thus a divided one, enabling Lyndon Johnson and Richard Nixon to call upon his example for support during "America's Longest War" in Vietnam and Jimmy Carter to ponder the liberal responsibility for national repentance. And the debate goes on. Professor Samuel Huntington decries the ascendancy of "moral" liberals, whose recent outbursts of "creedal passion" for egalitarianism caused Americans to embark upon a dangerous crusade against intelligence agencies, defense spending, the use of military force abroad, in an attempt to "expose, weaken, dismantle, or abolish the institutions that protected their liberal society against foreign threats."*

This deliberate crippling of American power, argues Huntington, only destroys what the "moral" liberals profess to want most: a worldwide expansion of democracy. The "moral" liberals, in other words, are naive, pre-Versailles Treaty Wilsonians. During the first great era of American expansion, 1898–1920, the Huntington thesis continues, the United States gave many Caribbean and Central American countries their first real chance at democracy; at the end of World War II, it literally forced Germany and Japan to change their spots, become democratic, and join the "Free World" community; and, before the advent of neo-isolationism in the 1960s, quite literally pushed the Latin American states toward decent standards of political conduct.

But American power was not merely altruistic. Indeed, that was not America's primary objective. America must have a favorable climate for its institutions to thrive, and perhaps even for them to survive. "[T]he world, like the United States in the nineteenth century or Western Europe in the twentieth century, will not be able to exist half-slave and half-free. Hence, the survival of democratic institutions and values at home will depend upon their adoption abroad." Wilson started at this same point—Huntington ends there. Between is the disputed territory of Wilson's legacy. If Huntington reveals no doubts about the covenant with power, Wilson never ceased to fear the outcome. "The nature of the United States has left it little or no

*"American Ideals versus Institutions," *Political Science Quarterly*, vol. 97:1 (Spring 1982): 1–37.

choice but to stand out among nations as the proponent of liberty and democracy," writes Huntington. Wilson would have agreed, but been more skeptical about the following. "Clearly," Huntington adds, "the impact of no other country in world affairs has been as heavily weighted in favor of liberty and democracy as has that of the United States."

Even if it were so, a problematical assertion, the great danger for Wilson was that, instead of removing the wedge, the impact of the kind of policy Huntington favors, would drive it home. Thus Henry Fairlie wrote in *The Kennedy Promise: The Politics of Expectation* (1973) that America's Cold War response to Russia and China erred grievously: by attempting to meet the challenge in terms of symmetry, subversion/counter-subversion, wars of national liberation/interventionism and counter-revolution. The only result has been to undermine the legitimacy of the liberal world order the United States has been defending.

From Wilson to Reagan, liberals and conservatives alike have had to concern themselves with the necessary conditions for the survival of American political institutions. The Russian-American confrontation has long since become a nuclear stalemate. The "test of wills" continues to escalate, however, with its demand that Americans load more and more missiles on board a ship ready to set sail on a quest to take back the missing limb from liberal theory that Lenin passed on to Mao, and he to Ho. The covenant with power has reached a point where it absorbs nearly all our intellectual resources, as well as our material possessions.

It is well worth our time to consider how we arrived at this place.

2

Franklin Roosevelt and the Crisis of Legitimacy

"Some people called our new policy 'Fascism'," Franklin Roosevelt wrote in a 1934 defense of the New Deal. "It is not Fascism because its inspiration springs from the mass of the people themselves rather than from a class or group or a marching army. Moreover, it is being achieved without a change in fundamental republican method. We have kept the faith with, and in, our traditional political institutions." Outside America the postwar order had collapsed; inside the nation a more immediate crisis, the Great Depression, had put in question almost every assumption held by political leaders and the citizenry alike. Economic recovery was the first essential; but there was a pervasive crisis in the 1930s, a crisis of legitimacy.

Roosevelt had asked Congress for emergency wartime powers to combat the depression. When it became apparent that the measures of the First Hundred Days of the New Deal would not be enough to do more than stave off disaster, and that permanent government intervention in the economy—if not outright state ownership of major industries—would follow, the New Deal itself was put on trial. The President titled his book, a collection of speeches, *On Our Way*. On our way to where? asked others. Roosevelt's jaunty manner, his buoyant rhetoric, calmed voters; and the barrage of legislative proposals laid down by the New Dealers repulsed the first wave of criticism. But would it be enough?

In the 1920s America had returned, as Warren Harding put it, to a state of "normalcy." Not isolationist, but insulated from Europe's political quarrels, or so they thought, Americans filled every nook and cranny they could find with loans and goods. The Red Tide that had lapped at the feet of the peacemakers of Versailles had receded, leaving behind only a few pools of dissent here and there. The tide had gone out. In fact, it had washed back over Russia so that the reality of the Soviet Union was covered under fathoms of official unconcern, as lost to the rest of the world as Atlantis. And the communist capital of Moscow seemed as fantastically remote as the Emerald City of Oz.

The Great Depression did not bring an immediate change in these attitudes. The first impact was to divide the capitalist countries. American exports fell, for example, by nearly two-thirds, from $7,034,000,000 in 1929 to $2,402,000,000 in 1933. Aside from the loss to the American economy, these figures represented a more significant loss of cohesion in the capitalist order. Lenin had absconded with a crucial piece of liberal theory, self-determination, but the loss was not felt so much in the 1920s, as America assumed leadership of the world economy, and resolved the reparations/war-debts tangle. But the depression undid all this effort. Everywhere things came unstuck.

Germany and Japan denounced the foundations of a liberal capitalist order, but Great Britain, too, departed, albeit without such a commotion, and with no intention of adopting totalitarian measures at home. British adoption of an Imperial Preference System at Ottawa in 1932 closed off the empire, or at least appeared to, which was equally bad from an American perspective. President Herbert Hoover spoke about economic cooperation among nations as the way out of the depression, but signed the Smoot-Hawley Tariff in 1930. He insisted upon the tenets of the Kellogg-Briand Peace Pact, but refused to try to employ coercion against Japan's aggression in Manchuria.

Roosevelt thus found himself facing a very difficult choice. Military action to restore the world order was out of the question, however, so the choice for democracy-in-one-country, the New Deal, was actually pre-determined even before FDR spelled out the details in his first messages to Congress in 1933. Presented to the legislators as America's unique response to the economic crisis, something quite different than Fascism or Socialism, the New Deal proposed to demonstrate that self-containment and liberalism were compatible.

British economic thinker John Maynard Keynes pronounced Roosevelt's "choice" the right one for America. He was less sanguine about the later progress of the New Deal. During the 1937 recession, a

major set-back for the New Dealers, Roosevelt made several queru-
lous public comments about "economic royalists," and told a close
associate of his fears that there existed a small group of men who
actually welcomed the continuing national malaise, hoping that way
to gain public approval for extreme measures, possibly even a coup
d'état. Less diplomatically than he should, perhaps, Keynes suggested that name-calling was not an economic program. Corporate
big-wigs were far more short-sighted than conspiratorial. Roosevelt's
denunciations only convinced them of government antipathy to capitalism, and the result had been a spiraling of mutual mistrust that
practically insured there would be no recovery.

Agriculture Secretary Henry A. Wallace, a Roosevelt loyalist to
the end, foresaw trouble in another direction. He had been badly
shaken after meeting with delegates to the Agricultural Labor Convention held in that gloomy summer of 1937—even before the new
economic downturn—who told him that they were all fed up with
old-line farm organizations and the Administration's landlord-
dominated farm program. They thought agricultural labor should
affiliate with the new Congress of Industrial Organization. If that
happened, Wallace warned the President, it could be fatal to American democracy: "This whole problem has in it so much dynamite,
political and otherwise, that we cannot neglect it much longer."

The specter of a new "Populism" stirred Wilsonian memories of
concern about old class-oriented uprisings, and Roosevelt's recent
rhetoric suggested he might be willing to play Bryan's role. At the
outset of the New Deal, FDR's request for emergency powers disturbed a few Wilsonian traditionalists, but most went along. It was
the permanent nature of Roosevelt's *intra*-nationalism that threatened the future of liberal democracy. If anticapitalist rhetoric was
now to be the mainstay of American politics, what end did that
foretell? The answer, to a growing number of critics (even within the
President's own party), was obvious. Roosevelt's blithe protests that
he was uninterested in philosophy, only in what worked, was no
longer calming. New Deal rhetoric, the court-packing bill and the
1938 attempt by Roosevelt to purge conservatives from the Democratic party, sharpened (and embittered) political debates. The President was crying "Fire!" in a crowded nation, stirring up fears that
would lead to a panicky rush against the normally safe exits of
political reform, overwhelming them with mob rule.

Roosevelt thus went into the critical years before Pearl Harbor at the head of a divided nation. While some critics accused him of maneuvering the country toward war to escape a day of retribution for a failed domestic policy—just to make things even more complicated—others believed a stronger reaction to Fascism was needed if democracy-in-one-country was not to become liberalism's last stand. As it happened, the Fascist states were forced outward first, not only by economic necessity, but by their dynamic. The two nations that had "chosen" isolation, the Soviet Union and the United States, were drawn into war. Stalin's socialism-in-one-country and Roosevelt's New Deal, both aberrant in terms of theory, joined together in a temporary alliance to defeat the Axis—and to set the stage for another confrontation in the manner of Wilson versus Lenin.

At the end of the decade Congress passed new neutrality legislation to prevent war. The Soviet Union had gone much farther. It had signed a treaty with Germany. Prospects for democracy-in-one-country never looked bleaker when the Nazi-Soviet Pact was announced, and within days World War II began. On May 27, 1941, Roosevelt declared the second state of national emergency during his administration:

> Tariff walls—Chinese walls of isolation would be futile. Freedom to trade is essential to our economic life. We do not eat all the food we can produce; we do not burn all the oil we can pump; we do not use all the goods we can manufacture. It would not be an American wall to keep Nazi goods out; it would be a Nazi wall to keep us in.

Roosevelt was not here retracting all he had said about the shortcomings of capitalism, seeking salvation in exports, or saying that the war made it necessary to turn the nation over to the "economic royalists." Quite the opposite, in fact. "Our Bunker Hill of tomorrow," he added, "may be several thousand miles from Boston." The issue was: what form would capitalism take in America if the world was to continue being dominated as it now was by totalitarian states for whom the economic marketplace was only a road to political hegemony within their spheres of influence?

Wilson had faced the same question. At the very least, he had concluded, the United States would have to undertake a "preparedness" campaign, which, if it became permanent, would threaten democracy. Roosevelt had very similar fears about how the New Deal would be reshaped under such conditions. Many years later a great admirer of Roosevelt's political skills would assert that it had been FDR's intention to dismantle the New Deal after the war, out of concern that it not be used as a foundation for a Fascist America. But the socialist-style "liberals" triumphed, said Ronald Reagan, and FDR's final instructions went unheeded. Reagan has it backwards. Roosevelt did fear what would happen if the New Deal fell into the wrong hands; but his increasing willingness to stand out against the Axis was because he wanted to make sure that did not happen.

On the emperor Hirohito's birthday in April 1931, Secretary of State Henry L. Stimson sent a special greeting to Japan. Reflecting on the successes of recent years, especially in the area of naval disarmament, the Secretary waxed eloquent about the atmosphere of mutual trust that now spanned the Pacific. "No clouds lie along the broad expanse of the Pacific to hide one of our countries from the other." In a few short months all that was changed. War clouds hung low over Asia. Japan had invaded, in September 1931, the Chinese province of Manchuria. Some Americans had once dreamed about developing Manchuria, but that was not on Stimson's mind in the third year of the Great Depression. Japan had overstepped the bounds, however sympathetic one might feel about its economic plight and the continuing disorder that made China's northernmost province such an irritant to Japan—and the world.

America "had no quarrel," Stimson would stress—even to the Chinese—with any of Japan's "rights" in Manchuria. The United States had no wish to line up with China. But something had to be done to demonstrate to Japan the danger of its undertaking. Assured by Japanese diplomats that what had happened was only a temporary aberration, Stimson viewed it as his obligation to come to the rescue of Japanese "liberals." He attempted to convince President Herbert Hoover to approve economic sanctions to that end, so that the Japanese military would be discredited. Hoover feared war over Manchuria, yet agreed that to do nothing would jeopardize the fragile "world order." What they decided upon was a diplomatic "sanction," the famous non-recognition doctrine that declared America's unwillingness to countenance any territorial changes brought about by military means.

A decent respect for the opinions of mankind, was that what America expected of Japan? Not quite, perhaps, but ideology ranked highest in this dispute, at least for Washington. Wilson had failed to get the League of Nations Covenant accepted by the United States Senate, but that did not lessen the dire implications for liberalism if Japan went unchecked. Tokyo's ambitions would swell, and, in the worst case, push out all other considerations. Progress toward further "liberalization" of Japanese politics would become impossible, and the distortions inside Japan would spread throughout Asia. When fighting broke out between Japanese and Chinese troops in and around Shanghai in late January 1932, Stimson and British Ambassador Sir Ronald Lindsay explored the long-range consequences of these untoward events. Sir Ronald feared that China's reliance upon an economic boycott, an old tactic used to bring pressure on foreigners, would produce a serious quarrel among the powers that might finally destroy the treaty structure, and produce chaos in its stead.

Stimson had a very different view. China's only real weapon was the boycott. Take it away, and the Chinese would be helpless. "She would probably have to do one of two things," he continued:

> either first, arm herself and become a military nation or she would be thrown into total subservience to a more military nation like Japan. Either of these results would be extremely injurious to the peace of the world and to the freedom of commerce which Britain and we had been striving for in the Far East. They would tend to destroy thus the work which we had been trying to do in the last thirty years in protecting the integrity of China and the Open Door.

Legalistic moralism, to be sure, but Stimson's argument was not that he (or any other American policymaker of the era) thought that Asian nations *ought* to understand Anglo-Saxon ways, but rather that world order required a determined effort be made to sustain such standards. America's chief concern, therefore, was not the Japanese forces running amok in Manchuria *per se*, but what greater evil might be set loose, politically, inside Japan, and then spread to China.

Stimson was gratified to learn that President-elect Roosevelt grasped the essential point. FDR's only question to Stimson was, why hadn't the non-recognition doctrine "been started sooner?" Stimson told his Hyde Park host at this pre-inaugural briefing that it had been hoped that the civilian government in Tokyo would regain control over the military. When it didn't, and when Japan seized all of Manchuria, there was no alternative. But the real meaning of Stimson's answer was another question: What would happen now that Japan had defied Washington and the League of Nations?

Like Hoover, Roosevelt had no intention of going to war. American interests in China were hardly enough to justify such a course in 1931, or in the foreseeable future for that matter. Nor had the domestic crisis in the United States gone on long enough to warrant concern that "totalitarianism" might gain an upper hand in the world's balance of ideological power. But the Stimson Doctrine, and Roosevelt's support, indicated that the issue was gnawing away at American leaders.

In April 1934 Japan announced its own doctrine—a more fateful step than the invasion of Manchuria. Henceforth, it was asserted, Japan stood guardian over China: "She will not find it necessary to interfere with any foreign country negotiating individually with China on questions of finance or trade, as long as such negotiations benefit China and are not detrimental to the maintenance of peace in East Asia." If the aim of the Stimson Doctrine had been to prevent the fragmentation of the world order, it was a failure. Stimson's successor, Cordell Hull, lodged a new verbal protest. The United States might not fight, he said, for China's integrity, or even for trade. "We would fight if Japan tried to tell us that we would not be allowed to trade with China; that would be a different thing and more abhorrent to the American nature."

Hull's meaning would become clear seven years later, when Roosevelt said that "Chinese walls of isolation" would be futile as a response to Nazism. "Japan has no design on our borders," Roosevelt confided to Arthur Hays Sulzberger of the New York *Times*, "at least not for this generation. She wishes to dominate the Far East and monopolize its trade. She wishes to direct the affairs of China without hindrance from other powers." To accomplish this Japan required a great navy. If Tokyo persisted, "we shall be obliged to build one as strong and keep it in the Pacific." At some point, in other words, if Japan continued down this path, its ability to disrupt plans for economic recovery and undermine liberalism would bring the two Pacific powers to a crossroads of decision.

One is struck by Roosevelt's tentative commitment to any *one* New Deal, and his confidence about the permanent features of world order. Roosevelt gave the impression that he believed Japan ruled out diplomatic adjustment in Asia. That was not quite the case. The subtleties of international diplomacy were lost or mixed-up in American minds with concern that any solution that imposed an unnatural order, a partitioned world economically and politically, had to be opposed. The conviction grew as the decade wore on. Tokyo had in fact offered to negotiate an "understanding" with both London and Washington. Evidence of these soundings only convinced the President that he must pay careful attention to British waverings, nothing else. And Cordell Hull would write in retrospect that any deal that involved China "would have made us a kind of silent partner in Japan's aggressions." Once again Roosevelt was positive that he understood foreign affairs, could gauge foreign leaders and their motives. "I am convinced," he told Sulzberger, "that the word of present rulers of Japan cannot be trusted."

American leaders had made up their minds that to negotiate bilaterally with Japan, or trilaterally with Japan and Great Britain, would imply that the only thing at stake in Asia was narrow self-interest. In the end, it was believed, such a posture would further discredit the West. Whether one liked or trusted the Japanese was always a secondary question. Signs of British "appeasement" caused great concern. American officials had discovered, to their chagrin, that "an important section" of British opinion was now ready to talk about the infamous 1934 Amō "Doctrine," naval equality, and possibly even diplomatic recognition of Manchukuo, the Japanese puppet state of Manchuria.

Roosevelt said he knew where the trouble was: it lurked within an old "Tory group" that remained obsessed with the notion that the Anglo-Japanese alliance of prewar years could be re-created—and ought to be! Such yearnings were dangerous. Roosevelt's diplomatic counselors thought nostalgia concealed something still more sinister, something that could not be spoken of openly—a desire by Britain and Japan "to exclude the United States from the Asian market."

Determined not to sacrifice *any* American interest to British efforts to save their drowning Empire, Roosevelt maintained that the first step must be to put down the notion, wherever it arose, that Japan's demands on the West for naval equality were legitimate. Tokyo was not to be let off the hook, even though the time when Japanese "liberals" could be rescued was long past. The onus for the destruction of the treaty system must fall on the Japanese. "If Great Britain is even suspected of preferring to play with Japan to playing with us," FDR informed his representatives, "I shall be compelled, in the interest of American security, to approach public sentiment in Canada, Australia, New Zealand and South Africa in a definite effort to make these Dominions understand clearly that their future security is linked with the United States."

These events of the mid-1930s, when American efforts to legislate "neutrality" in the hope of avoiding involvement in another war held public attention, along with the investigations of the munitions industry and its influence upon American entrance into World War I, are early indications of the concern Roosevelt felt to prevent the New Deal from having to face the crisis of what historian Walter Prescott Webb would call a "frontierless democracy." But why were the British so reluctant to follow an American lead in Asia? Surely, Japan's threat to destroy the postwar order was of importance to London as well.

British diplomats had long felt that the Americans were expecting too much of Japan. Instead of trying to "convert" Japan to liberalism, a missionary task of centuries, the United States should have tried to accommodate Japanese expansion in northern China—where the Japanese could also serve as a strong check on the spread of Bolshevism out of Russia. While claiming to uphold the broadest interests of Western civilization, the United States was in fact endangering them by courting a war with Japan. "There was a feeling in England," reported the American minister in China, "that the only solution for the dangerous world situation offered British industry by competition of Japanese-made products lay in giving Japan a free hand in China as a market."

Nor was it clear to them that the war Washington seemed so eager to fight would be against the right enemy. Neville Chamberlain, Chancellor of the Exchequer and later Prime Minister, argued that the United States would constantly push British statesmen into taking up advanced positions in Asia, thereby diverting resources from Europe, where the real peril was. This time, American aid might come too late to prevent a German victory.

Looked at from Chamberlain's perspective, therefore, "appeasement" of Japan was about the only way to maintain a social system based on private property and individual liberty. For Roosevelt, it would finally emerge, the world crisis defined the limits of the New Deal; for Chamberlain it defined the limits of what Britain could do in world affairs.

The mutual suspicions that plagued Anglo-American relations in the 1930s made it difficult for either country to pursue its chosen policy. Roosevelt constantly had to contend not only with his own doubts but with a general public impression that involvement in Europe meant pulling British chestnuts out of the fire. For his part, Chamberlain was convinced that the Americans would actually do nothing about Japanese expansionism until "Honolulu" was bombed, but meanwhile would spoil every effort at reaching an understanding with Tokyo.

After the failure of what he regarded as promising political talks with the Japanese in the fall of 1934, a failure he believed due to American intransigence on naval questions, Chamberlain took the lead, as Chancellor of the Exchequer, in designing a special economic mission to the Far East. Headed by the top financial expert in Whitehall, Sir Frederick Leith-Ross, the idea was to see if some over-all solution to the Japanese challenge was possible by circumventing the clogged channels of diplomatic or naval communications. The Americans had made sure those were closed off. The Leith-Ross mission aroused great anger in Japan. The Chinese were politer, but no more cordial to the idea of a British-sponsored settlement of the Manchurian question that would have them cede the province to Japan in exchange for an international loan.

Fearful that the Chinese might yield to British offers, American Treasury Secretary Henry Morgenthau warned the ambassador early in 1936 that Washington's help was far more important than "this constant pressure which you are being subjected to from all sides. Leith-Ross has done nothing and the Japanese are not going to help you." The episode was redolent of William Jennings Bryan's lecture aimed at Carranza. The world will not help Mexico, only America. Yet Washington's aid was hardly self-evident, so far as the Chinese were concerned in the 1930s. Morgenthau, for example, could only offer a modest program—actually a by-product of a New Deal domestic plan designed to spur inflation by increasing the world price of silver.

After almost destroying the Chinese economy because of its unilateral nature, the silver purchase program was redesigned by Morgenthau to stabilize Far Eastern markets. So far as it went, it worked well. But it did not go very far toward international co-operation, and reflected still the subservience of internationalism to New Deal intranationalism. Japan, meanwhile, marched on. On July 7, 1937, Japanese troops moved out of Manchuria into North China. If Tokyo managed to fulfill its ambition, to establish its hegemony in China, the autarchic powers, even without formal alliances, would soon be able to dictate terms in the world marketplace—with a crushing impact on the internal politics and policies of the remaining liberal-democratic states. They would also be able to insulate themselves from the power of outside forces, economic and ideological, that might be mustered to halt their advance.

Japan had walked out of the League of Nations when its forward policy in Manchuria had been challenged; Germany left over a dispute on disarmament. Those were symbolic acts, staged affairs. This was substance, an historical tide running against liberal democracy. "Henry," Roosevelt told Morgenthau, Hull's "trade treaties are just too goddamned slow. The world is marching too fast. They're just too slow." The President and his Treasury Secretary had much to ponder along these lines. A Morgenthau aide wrote of German-Japanese methods,

> Our international trade is being forced into ever-narrowing channels.
> . . . The sphere of our trade agreements is contracting as the area of
> political and economic domination of Germany and Japan expands. . . .
> The behavior of the aggressor nations may far more than offset the
> gains to our trade resulting from our trade agreements program.

Worse still, the "aggressor nations" were turning American trade to their own ends, distorting it to suit their needs. Morgenthau's weekly reports to the President began charting an ominous trend—a decline in cotton exports, an increase in war goods. Concerning the new trade with Manchuria and North China, said one,

> This area is, of course, under the control of Japan and, therefore, the
> fact that half of the . . . [week's trade] consisted of steel sheet and plates
> and practically all the remainder of copper and trucks suggests that our
> exports to those areas constitutes virtually exports for the use of
> Japanese military forces.

The world was closing in around the New Dealers. If the United States permitted exporters to continue on a business as usual basis, it would be aiding and abetting the would-be conquerors of China, and, at least theoretically, playing an accomplice's role in the destruction of the capitalist-oriented world economy. If the government put restrictions on foreign trade, on the other hand, it would extend the role of the state into the marketplace, imitating the methods of the aggressors and undermining the already weakened pillars of liberalism. The British had decided to shut up their Empire like an "oyster shell," complained Secretary of State Cordell Hull, and to compete on those terms. Would Roosevelt do the same?

As policymakers pondered these problems and the consequences of meeting the autarchic powers on their own terms, a serious economic recession undermined the Administration's political position at home. Roosevelt had never expected the domestic economic crisis to last this long, or to require a decision of this nature. American self-containment, he had imagined, was an emergency measure. The implications of state planning in a closed world were far different from those considered in 1933, when Roosevelt's optimism was as important to the nation in overcoming "fear itself" as any piece of legislation passed by Congress.

For the first time foreign policy questions were central to the New Deal. From Cordell Hull's vantage point this was a mixed blessing. Of all of Roosevelt's advisers, Hull was the most stalwart Wilsonian. Often excluded from the inner circle, he was quietly amused at the Brains Trusters' plight during the 1937 recession when bad news about the economy rained down on the administration like hailstones. They and all the rest of the original New Deal retinue—clustered about, seeking cover in the White House, and scattered throughout the alphabet agencies—were only now "catching up" to what he had always known: you can run a liberal capitalist system on national markets alone only so long.

Yet, strange to say, Hull had grown cautious about forcing an early showdown with the totalitarian states. If Roosevelt and he agreed that doing a deal with Japan or Germany created a secondary legitimacy problem, he feared that a sudden turn to "New Deal" internationalism would wreck what the State Department had been seeking to accomplish through patience and persuasion, both at home and abroad. As he saw it, his task was to prevent the New Dealers from turning Congress into a bedlam, parading their amateur enthusiasms and creedal passions about fascism's horror as sound foreign policy. What had to be avoided was an identification of left-leaning or socialist "do-goodism" with a responsible Wilsonian internationalism.

If Roosevelt now went out on an internationalist limb, an increasingly conservative Congress might not only saw off the branch, but then proceed to cut down the tree. Besides, what Hull needed at the moment was a quiet interval to complete negotiations for an Anglo-

American trade agreement. Trade treaties might be too slow to halt the advance of the totalitarians, though Hull was certainly loathe to concede the point, but if America had to go to war, an Anglo-American agreement could be used as a basis for postwar planning—and would forestall resurgent New Dealism. On Capitol Hill the conservative protectionists would be put in disarray; in the bureaucracy the state planners would be put to rout. Outside the United States the British imperial preference system would yield—and, with enough time, the bastions of autarchy crumble to dust.

Hull's old-time faith in the political virtues of free trade, his preachiness, had always struck Roosevelt as quaintly obsolescent. That world, Hull's world, was buried under tons of ash and mud, like Pompeii after Vesuvius. During the summer of 1937, FDR speculated about the possibility of an Anglo-American naval blockade against Japan. Then, in early October, he traveled to Chicago to dedicate a bridge, and delivered in an almost casual offhand manner a major proposal for a quarantine of aggressor states. Efforts to find out if Roosevelt was talking about a blockade or economic sanctions, or something else, failed. Roosevelt confessed to news reporters that he had no specific plan in mind. A few days later, however, the President delivered a radio address that set forth the rationale for a much more active foreign policy:

> As we plan today for the creation of ever higher standards of living for the people of the United States, we are aware that our plans may be most seriously affected by events in the world outside our borders.

This statement marked the end of the New Deal as originally conceived, a temporary intra-nationalist plan for democracy and prosperity in one country.

> By a series of trade agreements, we have been attempting to recreate the trade of the world which plays so important a part in our domestic prosperity; but we know that if the world outside our borders falls into the chaos of war, world trade will be completely disrupted.

> Nor can we view with indifference the destruction of civilized values throughout the world. We seek peace, not only for our generation but also for the generation of our children.

Roosevelt's foreign policy advisers offered him two choices for averting the chaos of war. Cordell Hull continued to insist that the correct path was a trade treaty with Great Britain, and, it was implied, some sort of "loose understanding." After the Germans had had time to assess this development, Hull argued, they could be offered substantial assistance on the condition that they would be good and behave themselves. The other option was put forward by Sumner Welles, the number two man in the State Department, but usually closer to Roosevelt personally and to his way of thinking. Welles suggested calling an international conference, at which both political and economic issues would be discussed. The plan had several supposed advantages. Aware that British Prime Minister Neville Chamberlain had sent Lord Halifax to see Hitler with the outline of an "appeasement" program, the Under Secretary (like Roosevelt) felt sure that there was not enough time for Hull's strategy to work.

What was brewing in Europe, argued Welles, was a new "Congress of Berlin," where, once again, the European powers would attempt to resolve their differences by reaching agreement on imperial boundaries in Africa. The Under Secretary's source of information was good, because a re-partition was precisely what Chamberlain had on his mind. An Anglo-German rapprochement based on such an arrangement would not only turn the clock back to the imperial era, it would almost certainly narrow the channels for world trade still more. If Roosevelt could capture the world's imagination with a dramatic gesture, he might be able to launch a new world economic conference. It would be easier to turn the clock back to 1933, in other words, than to 1875.

But even if the plan failed, it would have been put on the table—before the world—as an alternative to the sort of shameful "appeasement" that Chamberlain appeared to be seeking. It would wonderfully clarify the basic issues. Welles believed, also, that a Roosevelt initiative along these lines would force British leaders to reassess their own policies, and strengthen the hand of those inside England who wished to encourage stronger Anglo-American ties. Chamberlain was pursuing a phantom, argued Welles, if he expected Hitler to respond to an offer of African "colonies" in place of European hegemony. It was a dangerous phantom, as well, however, because once engaged in the diplomatic process, it would be very difficult to pull out short of giving Germany everything it wanted.

Should Germany and England reach agreement, finally, the potential left for an Anglo-American rapprochement would be meager indeed. Eventually the autarchic powers must collapse or conquer. If Great Britain was engaged in a web of diplomacy with Nazi Germany, it could hardly free itself in time to help America lead the world back to a reasonable world order. FDR liked the plan. He decided to approach London, however, before issuing general invitations to a world conference. Neville Chamberlain's advisers, with the exception of Anthony Eden, quickly noticed in the Welles plan that Roosevelt specifically excluded the possibility of American support for new territorial settlements in Europe. Instead, the basis of the plan was a re-examination of trade barriers and restrictions upon access to raw materials.

If Hitler wanted nothing to do with African colonies, why did Roosevelt imagine Germany wished to go back to a Wilsonian order that promised less? Of course it was always possible that the American President had something else on his mind. During World War I, for example, Wilson had appeared to ally himself with Germany at times in demanding "Freedom of the Seas." Could it be that Roosevelt would go so far just to destroy the Ottawa Preference System, and gain access to the markets of the empire? Roosevelt's plan would have had to end with a serious discussion of economic discrimination, and Germany would surely place before the world, under this aegis, its demands for relief from Versailles-imposed restrictions. The very act of calling such a conference implied—if indeed it did not mandate—a revision not only of territorial injustices, but of the postwar economic order.

If not sinister, then, the American plan was short-sighted, and a more perilous experiment than Chamberlain's "regional" concessions in Eastern Europe. On some fundamentals, in fact, Germany and the United States would have more in common than the English-speaking delegates. Indeed, the parallel with the "Freedom of the Seas" controversy was much too close. Absorbed by the struggle between liberal democracy and Fascism, both contemporaries and historians have missed the underlying significance of the Welles plan, and what it implied for the postwar world and the determination American policymakers felt then to avoid "appeasement," and block Soviet expansionism. The point is not that the British were correct in their fears in 1938, or that the United States alone wished to halt the German advance, but that the perspective of the observer ought not to be limited to foreground action.

What emerges from a closer look at the Welles plan is its consistency with other Roosevelt policies, some only half-formulated, in the 1930s designed to preserve what legitimacy remained, internationally and internally, to the world order, and keep the record clear for the future. The emphasis on intra-nationalism, or democracy-in-one-country, was, of course, an apparent contradiction. It was also true that foreign policy was a makeshift affair, often little more than a reaction to events so close to being out of control entirely. But down at the substratum level, the liberal conscience operated, even if its impulses were blocked by other priorities of the moment.

On February 20, 1938, the German dictator told the Reichstag that a new agreement had been reached with Austria. On March 11, 1938, the world saw what that agreement meant when his soldiers marched into Vienna. The Versailles system had been fatally breached. Almost immediately the crisis shifted to Czechoslovakia. In the British Prime Minister's mind there was only one thing left to do. His advisers had told him that, with Austria gone, there was no way to influence political events in Southeastern Europe. Hence Chamberlain called his proposal to visit Hitler, Plan "Z"—the last resort.

In the State Department a "death watch" was set up to track events in Central Europe. Joining State Department experts was an original Brain Truster, Adolf Berle, who was struck by the confluence of what was occurring in Europe with those forces pressing in on the New Deal as the economy simply refused to respond either to government stimulants or Roosevelt's appeals. As he saw it, there were three choices: a stepped-up anti-trust campaign, accompanied by strenuous rhetoric aimed at the malefactors of great wealth, a move towards full state capitalism, or a decision to make peace with business, and let matters run their course. What blocked a consensus around this last possibility, said Berle, was a disturbing insistence by most businessmen that "every social objective of the New Deal be called off."

Less dire than Berle imagined, the situation was, as he said, almost at an impasse: "Out of all this it is extremely difficult to make a government." Roosevelt never had to choose. Hitler tossed aside the Munich Agreement he had negotiated with Chamberlain in September 1938, declaring that Germany needed no British nanny to tell it what it might or might not do, and moved to occupy what had been left of Czechoslovakia after Munich. Neville Chamberlain responded by giving Poland, in March 1939, a unilateral guarantee of its frontiers.

Hitler then leap-frogged British diplomacy with a world-startling non-aggression pact with the Soviet Union. Secure against the danger of an immediate two-front war, Germany marched deeper into

Eastern Europe. War came to Europe for the second time in one generation. Roosevelt had new problems to face. Americans welcomed the return of prosperity, in large measure a result of Allied war orders and domestic rearmament. Deprived of the argument that the President had taken his New Deal beyond the point of no return for capitalism's natural recuperative powers, Roosevelt's opponents fixed on the next available issue: he was leading the nation to war. New domestic political alignments resulted. Some of the strongest believers in democracy-in-one-country were midwestern "isolationists," holdovers from the Wilson era. They now opposed him. But now, also, conservative Democrats and Republicans rallied to his side.

At Yale University a former Assistant Secretary of the Treasury, Dean G. Acheson, who had left the New Deal very early on, fulminating as he went about Roosevelt's betrayal of Western civilization by going off the gold standard, spoke out, confident he would attract favorable attention among Roosevelt's advisers. The last century, Acheson began, had seen an "amazing increase in the production of wealth and population." Far from perfect, pockmarked by injustices that demanded redress, the system now in decline had once furnished a healthy climate that made possible solutions to otherwise incurable social ills: "In terms of our own country, it made possible its material development and the evolution of a social order recognizing, however imperfectly, both the worth of the individual and the unity of society, the freedom of the human spirit and the interdependence of human life."

"I am not saying that morals are a matter of economics," he said, "but rather that there is high authority for the belief that if we are not led into temptation we may better be delivered from evil." Why had the system declined? Why did the very things it had produced now pose the danger of totalitarianism, as each nation strove to meet the demands of its enlarged citizenry for a standard of living at least approaching that of the recent past? The causes were many, more than he could trace, but at the center was Britain's faltering economic and military power. "We can see that British naval power no longer can establish security of life and investment in distant parts of the world, and a localization of conflict nearer at home."

The nineteenth century could not be brought to life again. Few would want that. But the world order that was vital to progress in human affairs, an order that depended upon a balance between the individual and society, was under "revolutionary" assault from the totalitarian powers. "The consequences of Russo-German and Japanese victories in terms of our own lives are too serious to permit indifference." If the totalitarian states won on the battlefields of Europe and Asia, they could isolate the United States in the Western Hemisphere:

> Here, surrounded by armed and hostile camps, we will have to conduct our economy as best we can and attempt to preserve the security and dignity of human life and freedom of the human spirit. This breakup of the world into exclusive areas of armed exploitation administered along oriental lines would have clear implications in terms of the defense of the great resources of our part of it.

National defense under those conditions would impose a severe regimen upon liberal theory, perhaps collapse it altogether. It would finish the job started, with the best intentions of course, by the New Deal. The United States Government would be forced to adopt a frankly imperialist policy toward Latin America, and to enforce state controls on a permanently mobilized domestic economy.

Invited to rejoin the Roosevelt administration some months later, Acheson immediately put his considerable legal skills to work devising a brief for the very expansion of Presidential power he had so feared in 1933, and then made a new career for himself during the war as the government's star witness before Congressional committees. He was especially concerned to testify on behalf of postwar economic and political planning, and against "isolationist" limitations on the same. The new foreign policy consensus inside the Administration was an alliance almost as complex and unlikely as the Grand Alliance that fought the Axis. Each of the participants had different goals in mind, or at least thought about different tactics.

Still, Acheson had successfully elaborated a dominant theme, even amongst the most dedicated of the committed New Dealers, none of whom had ever imagined that their experiment would have to be conducted in a closed world. Even better than Acheson's Yale speech, perhaps, were the observations of British Ambassador Lord Lothian, who supplied Prime Minister Churchill with an ideological appeal to justify requests for what eventually became Lend-Lease aid. Lothian's proposed draft stressed a Wilsonian interpretation of the covenant with power:

I can see no other prospect of lasting peace or of a reasonably liberal world after the war than that the United States and Great Britain, at any rate for a number of years, should between them possess unquestionable air and sea supremacy. Peace comes from power behind law and government, and not from disarmament and anarchy. Power in the hands of these two great liberal nations, with the free nations of the British Commonwealth and the American Republics associated in some way with them so as to ensure that that power is not abused, offers the only stable prospect of peace. It is clear that we shall be able to build nothing for many years out of the youth of Europe, which has been educated in Nazi and Communist doctrines. If we win victory we shall have to assume the major responsibility for a new world order.*

Churchill did not use Lothian's draft in his letter to FDR, but it remains a sophisticated analysis of the fears and desires of American liberalism.

In the debates between September 1, 1939, and December 7, 1941, many harsh words were exchanged. The President did not wish to prevent Congressional debate on Lend-Lease, the bitterest of the encounters the Administration fought on Capitol Hill, but he called upon members of his own party for support by reminding them that the liberal program was likely to go out the window if the nation went to war under a Republican administration. Congress was at a considerable disadvantage, already, as against the executive. In the first place it had granted FDR emergency powers to deal with the domestic crisis; it could hardly deny them in the face of a military danger. Senators and Congressmen were, for the most part, uninformed and uninterested in the details of foreign policy—a situation that remained constant down to the last days of the Vietnam War. Later Presidents would give Congress a good excuse not to exercise much scrutiny in foreign affairs matters by invoking "national security" considerations. Until the Vietnam War, moreover, many legislators appreciated the White House's concern to head off embarrassing inquiries before they became damaging all around.

That said, it must also be pointed out that the credibility gap begins here, in the final months before Pearl Harbor. FDR's reluctance to "level" with the American people has been explained as a conflict

---

*I should like to thank Professor Warren Kimball for calling Lothian's draft to my attention.

between what he thought right and necessary, and a dangerously uninformed public's refusal to wake-up and face the facts of the Axis menace. It was that. But it was something more. The domestic agenda of the 1930s, the New Deal program, had been, itself, an aberration on liberal theory. Roosevelt had never fully leveled on that account; and now, by stressing in the 1940 election that American boys were not going to be sent into any "foreign wars," he could not yet bring himself to embrace publicly the Wilsonian faith in a covenant with power.

There is a striking difference between Wilson's confidence that his course was right (at least until after the peace treaty was signed) and FDR's cautious, and at times frankly duplicitous approach to going to war. Yet the credibility gap was not simply a Presidential exercise; it was a national project. Everyone helped out. The best-informed people in America were the admirals and the generals, occupants, ironically, of the New Deal's most elaborate public structure, the Pentagon. They were aware, for example, of the joint military planning with the British chiefs, and of the President's increasingly provocative naval actions in the Atlantic. Roosevelt even dropped hints from time to time of the likelihood of an "incident" leading to war, as when, for example, he told reporters in January 1941 that Lend-Lease would be useless unless the products could be gotten safely across the sub-infested Atlantic; and when there was convoying there was "apt to be some shooting—and shooting comes awfully close to war, doesn't it?"

But Congress was never told officially of all that was being done, and in some cases specific denials were issued. Indeed, months later, the Administration was still insisting that convoying was not being done, or even under consideration. The most famous "incident" during Roosevelt's undeclared war against Germany was the attack upon the destroyer *Greer*. Roosevelt's "Fireside Chat" of September 11, 1941, proclaimed the incident a wanton attack by a German submarine against an American vessel engaged in a perfectly legitimate mission:

> In spite of what Hitler's propaganda bureau has invented, and in spite of what any American obstructionist organization may prefer to believe, I tell you the blunt fact that the German submarine fired first upon this American destroyer without warning, and with deliberate design to sink her.

Ship logs would reveal that the *Greer* was operating in close co-operation with British aircraft, and that it broke its course to pursue the submarine, and, finally, that the German commander fired two torpedoes only at the end of an hour during which the *Greer* had continued to track the submarine for the benefit of British aircraft. The *Greer* then began its own attack on the U-boat, dropping a total of eight depth charges in an unsuccessful effort to sink the undersea marauder. What made the *Greer* episode so important, however, was not Roosevelt's misleading description of the events in the Fireside Chat—but his use of the speech to develop public opinion in favor of a "shoot on sight" policy against German warships, a move that positively courted war with Hitler.

Dean Acheson, who played an important role in searching out the proper legal examples to justify Roosevelt's "trade" of fifty destroyers for bases in the British Caribbean, had far fewer compunctions about stretching the constitutional authority of the Presidency in such a cause than he had displayed about the expanded domestic authority Roosevelt had asked for in 1933. Secretary of War Henry L. Stimson was less than happy, however, with Roosevelt's "disingenuous" means of supporting the British convoys: "I wanted him to be honest with himself. To me it seems a clearly hostile act to the Germans and I am prepared to take the responsibility of it."

The Secretary kept these thoughts to himself, confiding only to his diary his fears, fears that had more to do with the future than going to war. Yet the two were inseparable, for the way America got into the war was as important as winning it. Stimson was worried about Roosevelt's decision to "hide" the Atlantic patrols under the notion of a purely reconnaissance action. "However, as he fully realizes that he will probably get into a clash with the Germans by what he does, it doesn't make much difference what he calls it." Stimson knew better, but went along.

War came in the Pacific, however. Up until the signing of the Axis Pact in September 1940 it had been in the back of policymakers' minds that at some point Japan would call it off. Finally realizing that American opposition to their plans was immutable, cool heads in Tokyo would prevail. To that end American policy was to constrict, gradually, Japan's options by applying economic pressure. After the invasion of China, for example, loans from the Export-Import Bank to facilitate purchases of cotton were curtailed. The pace of this approach was too gradual for many, including the newly appointed Stimson, who joined Roosevelt's "War Cabinet" in the summer of 1940.

Stimson might be a worrier so far as the undeclared war in the Atlantic was concerned, but inside the Cabinet he was a staunch advocate of firm action in the Pacific. He told his colleagues that when Woodrow Wilson had had difficulties with Tokyo, he embargoed silk—and the Japs literally crawled out of Siberia. The War Secretary also used Theodore Roosevelt's example, declaring that all he needed was time to get the "Big Stick" ready, then let 'em come! This was a reference to the placing of B-17 bombers in the Philippine Islands, America's most up-to-date "deterrent" force in being.

In a way, of course, Stimson had not given up on the idea that Western "rationality" had penetrated the deepest recesses of the "Oriental mind." When diplomatic discussions did, in fact, take place over the summer of 1941, Western rationality offered the Japanese little except a better tomorrow. To get there they would have to admit defeat in China, and repudiate the Tripartite Pact. The Japanese attempted to go over Hull's head to Roosevelt, suggesting a "summit" meeting between FDR and Prime Minister Konoye. Tempted, Roosevelt was dissuaded by Hull and Stimson, who used the argument that such a meeting would have to have an agenda. What points was Roosevelt ready to compromise?

By 1940, observed George Frost Kennan in 1974, Roosevelt had come to a point where he actually wished to see the United States in "both of these wars." His approach was oblique, designed, whether consciously or not, to force the adversaries to move against the United States in such a way as to make it possible to contend that there was no choice. Hence the steadily increasing naval role in the Atlantic, and hence, also, the policy pursued toward Japan in the last months and weeks before the December 7, 1941, attack on Pearl Harbor:

> Opinions will differ, of course, about this; but surely it cannot be denied that had FDR been determined to avoid war with the Japanese, he would have conducted American policy quite differently, particularly in the final period, than he actually did. He would not, for example, have made an issue over Japanese policies in China, where the Japanese were preparing anyway to undertake a partial withdrawal for reasons of their own, and where this sort of American pressure was not really essential.

He would not have tried to starve the Japanese navy for oil. And he would have settled down to some hard and realistic dealings with the Japanese, instead of letting them be deluged and frustrated by the cloudy and unintelligible moralisms of Cordell Hull.

Roosevelt's mind is usually admired, or despaired of, as a layered complexity, fully capable of holding two or more contradictory notions simultaneously. The so-called "Oriental mind," sometimes blamed for the war, would have little to teach such a master. No doubt he used Hull, and in the way Kennan suggests, but not just to get into the war. "I rather think," Hull would begin one of his musings on the future during Japanese-American discussions

> that in postwar economic reconstruction, probably the principle of non-discrimination will be an all-encompassing one. What I would like to see is Japan and the United States working together for the principle of non-discrimination. Now all along I've fought against the preferential system of the British Empire . . ., and now we are talking it over with England. I don't want you to tell anybody about this, but don't you know, only lately Great Britain is coming around to my point of view.

Secretary Hull's happy dreams of a New Deal-less world, the secret that had sustained his vision of Wilsonian internationalism, blended into newer versions of Atlanticism espoused by his assistants, Adolf Berle, Dean Acheson, Will Clayton, and even by the former social worker who became FDR's special messenger and informal foreign secretary, Harry L. Hopkins. At last out from under the lowering clouds over domestic politics, Roosevelt became once more the "happy warrior" on behalf of liberalism's "second chance."

A permanently mobilized American economy, a nation constantly prepared for war, Dwight D. Eisenhower would write his Secretary of State, John Foster Dulles, only a few months after Dulles took office in September 1953, "would either drive us to war—or into some form of dictatorial government. In such circumstances, we would be forced to consider whether or not our duty to future generations did not require us to *initiate* war at the most propitious moment that we could designate." What Eisenhower was willing to talk about, FDR had never admitted, even to himself. The differences can be measured in decades, and the similarities in a common conviction that self-containment was no way out of the crisis of legitimacy.

3

The Battle over Eastern Europe

At 8:00 a.m. on Sunday morning, June 22, 1941, Prime Minister Winston Churchill's aides brought him the news he had been expecting. Germany had invaded the Soviet Union. Throughout the day Churchill worked on a speech he would deliver to the nation. A private secretary noted the irony of this sudden turnabout, not Germany's betrayal of a sometime ally, but that Winston Churchill, of all people, should be preparing to welcome the Soviets as allies. "If Hitler invaded Hell," retorted the Prime Minister, "I would make at least a favorable reference to the Devil in the House of Commons."

Still, Churchill did feel compelled to explain himself and the circumstances that required him to speak out at once. "No one has been a more consistent opponent of Communism than I have for the last twenty-five years," he explained. "I will unsay no word that I have spoken about it. But all this fades away before the spectacle which is now unfolding. The past with its crimes, its follies and its tragedies, flashes away." What remained, striped of ideological coating, was the most basic survival instinct of humankind. "I see the Russian soldiers standing on the threshold of their native land, guarding the fields which their fathers have tilled from time immemorial." There had been widespread speculation inside the British Government (and elsewhere) that Hitler would seek to capitalize on political divisions within the liberal democracies by portraying his war in the East as a crusade against Bolshevism. Having had experience with this temptation within his own party, the Prime Minister decided he must confront the issue:

This is no class war, but a war in which the whole British Empire and Commonwealth of Nations is engaged without distinction of race, creed or party. It is not for me to speak of the action of the United States, but this I will say: if Hitler imagines that his attack on Soviet Russia will cause the slightest division of aims or slackening of effort in the great Democracies who are resolved upon his doom, he is woefully mistaken.

The speech is worth examining closely. It had been constructed by Churchill almost in seclusion, at the end of a long weekend at Chequers, the country home of British Prime Ministers. The references to the United States, in this paragraph and others, attempted to associate the two nations in a military cause that had been made critical by the invasion of Russia. It was his strongest statement thus far that the "security" of the Americans and their "system" had been put in jeopardy by the clanking "hideous onslaught of the Nazi war machine." From this initial reaction to the war in Eastern Europe down to the battle for Stalingrad, Churchill's primary concern was the prevention of Nazi hegemony. After that turning point, his problem took on a different shape.

Post-Stalingrad Soviet expansionism threatened in two ways. It posed a danger to British interests in areas near the Empire's lifeline through the Mediterranean, an external balance of power issue, and it threatened political stability in Western Europe, an internal balance of power issue. Yet to invite America in to redress these balances also presented risks. Like his predecessor, Neville Chamberlain, Churchill was never completely sure that the United States would not want to redesign Europe and European diplomacy to suit its own interests.

Roosevelt had other concerns. Early in the war he could not risk the possibility that Stalin might see an advantage to negotiating a separate peace. All logic ruled out an accord between Berlin and Moscow, but it had happened before in the Treaty of Brest-Litovsk, at Rapallo, and in the Nazi-Soviet Pact. Later in the war, FDR was concerned to make it possible for Stalin and his heirs to take part in the "structure of peace," as later policy-makers would call their efforts to channel revolution into an interlocking world order. Strategy and tactics both required a careful handling of the Eastern European situation so as to get the most out of the Russo-German war, politically as well as militarily.

Churchill had seized the initiative with Russia at the outset, long before Roosevelt was free to do so. On October 1, 1939, just a month after war began, the newly appointed First Lord of the Admiralty reviewed events in Eastern Europe. Poland's destruction was the obvious place to begin, but this was not to be an ordinary speech once he turned to "the assertion of the power of Russia."

> I cannot forecast to you the action of Russia. It is a riddle wrapped in a mystery inside an enigma. . . ."

Cold War studies too often stop there, with the word "enigma," thereby claiming Churchill's authority for a contention that rational dealings with the Soviets were impossible. But that was not the First Lord's purpose that evening.

> . . . enigma; but perhaps there is a key. That key is Russian national interest. It cannot be in accordance with the interest or the safety of Russia that Germany should plant herself upon the shores of the Black Sea, or that she should overrun the Balkan States and subjugate the Slavonic peoples of Southeastern Europe. That would be contrary to the historic life-interests of Russia.

Churchill published both portions cited above in his *Memoirs*, but omitted even stronger references to Russia as a bulwark against German expansion into the Baltic States, as well as an unmistakable invitation to Stalin that he could switch alliances without forfeiting his territorial gains from the Nazi-Soviet Pact of August 22, 1939.

> Through the fog of confusion and uncertainty we may discern quite plainly the community of interests which exists between England, France and Russia—a community of interests to prevent the Nazis' carrying the flames of war into the Balkans and Turkey.

Under the terms of the pact, Russia had been able to reabsorb Estonia, Latvia, and Lithuania into the Russian "Empire," occupy Bessarabia to the south, and take up military positions in the center: eastern Poland. Churchill was full of the same indignation his colleagues felt at Russian perfidy and moral callousness, he wrote, but not surprised at the Nazi-Soviet accord: "They owed us nothing." He also offered an assessment that he thought put things in their proper perspective: "Russia has occupied the same line and positions as the enemy of Poland, which possibly she might have occupied as a very doubtful and suspected friend. The difference in fact is not so great as might seem."

In this paper, in the speech he gave on October 1, and in practically every other speech he gave during this period, Churchill spoke of

Russian actions as if they created an "Eastern Front" against Germany.

Roosevelt, breaking the Wilson boycott against diplomatic dealings, had recognized the Soviet Union in 1933. Closer relations had not developed, however, and the President's advisers hued closely to Wilsonian views. Dean Acheson's description at Yale University of the impact of a "Russo-German" victory set the tone for the "Atlanticist" interpretation of the dangers threatening America. But the Nazi-Soviet Pact had jolted the entire liberal community, especially when it was followed by a Russian military attack on Finland in early 1940.

That assault had also brought out Churchill's ever-present zealousness in defense of "Western" civilization, but he was concerned even more to prevent Finnish nickel ore from falling into German hands. As soon as the Russo-Finnish War ended, moreover, London resumed efforts to negotiate a trade agreement with Moscow that would divert at least some of Russia's trade to the Allies, and, symbolically at least, keep open channels of political communication. Churchill was very careful with the Americans about Russia. He warned Roosevelt on June 15, 1941, that he expected a German attack:

> Should this new war break out, we shall, of course, give all encouragement and any help we can spare to the Russians, following the principle that Hitler is the foe we have to beat. I do not expect any class political reactions here, and trust a German-Russian conflict will not cause you any embarrassment.

Roosevelt quickly replied that he would second any statement that the Prime Minister made "welcoming Russia as an ally." This did not extend to economic or political "deals" about the future. Roosevelt sent this caveat by cable, and in the person of Harry Hopkins. In the following weeks Roosevelt dispatched Hopkins to Moscow to talk about military aid for Russia, and invited the Prime Minister to a shipboard conference for the first discussion of postwar matters. The joint declaration, known as the Atlantic Charter and "signed" on August 12, 1941, committed them to "certain common principles" for the future.

Point Two of the eight-point declaration spoke directly to the danger of a new "appeasement." "They desire to see no territorial changes that do not accord with the freely expressed wishes of the peoples concerned." That same day Roosevelt and Churchill also sent a message to Stalin outlining conditions for a "long-term policy." "Our resources, though immense, are limited, and it must become a question as to where and when those resources can best be used to further to the greatest extent our common effort." American and British military experts had expressed grave doubts about Russia's ability to withstand the German blitzkrieg. Such caution about dispensing Anglo-American resources was, therefore, only prudent. But the message also made it clear that (a) Russia would have to deal with the nation in a position to make aid available in large quantities needed for victory; and (b) military aid was not free of strings. President Truman made the same points—in much blunter fashion— a few days after Roosevelt's death in April 1945.

In between, however, the political undercurrents of East-West relations were often hidden from sight. Eastern Europe was a third priority, if not lower, in the calculations of both British and American planners. Churchill and Roosevelt gave first consideration to fighting a "parsimonious" war, "stingy" about spending human life while extravagant in all other ways. After that, Anglo-American interests diverged. Imperial factors weighed heavily with the Prime Minister; while Roosevelt set about the tasks of creating a new global order. Where Eastern Europe touched on Empire lines of communication, as in the Mediterranean, Churchill felt the greatest pressure; whenever "spheres of influence" talk surfaced, the President winced.

Leaders in both English-speaking nations worried about—indeed, according to the British Chief of the Imperial General Staff, Lord Alanbrooke, were haunted by—the prospect of a separate peace. Alanbrooke thought it nonsense to make military plans, or political plans either, for that matter, on such a basis. Stalin could not disengage. Roosevelt and Churchill believed, on the other hand, that the Russian leader could not be allowed to brood alone, even at the cost of certain concessions—hoped to be temporary in nature, but realistically, probably not. The duration and extent of such concessions were a matter that required serious thought.

Crisscrossing Anglo-American reactions to the threat of Soviet expansion "west of Vienna" was the resentment, expressed most strongly in the State Department and the Foreign Office, that the West had been doubly compromised at Munich. First, it had been compromised by leaving Russia in the lurch, for appearing, in fact, to point the way for Germany to expand in the east. Second, and more deeply felt, was the concern that the West had been damaged ideologically. Munich implied that the liberal democracies simply lacked a conscience and would deal with anyone who promised "peace in our time."

Roosevelt arrived at no safe conclusion from all these considerations, but it does help to explain the President's seemingly contradictory attitudes to keep in mind that he was constantly juggling many factors. At any given moment, therefore, one priority might appear more important than all the others, and the difficult thing was not to forget the rest. Listing the various concerns also provides a clue to Roosevelt's desire to keep the decision process, and the final decisions, in his own hands. He simply did not believe that the State Department was equipped with the right "skills" to handle the ambiguities and uncertainties that permeated the Grand Alliance.

Perhaps the closest Roosevelt ever did come to elaborating on his diplomatic problem, and his faith in personal solutions, was in a 1942 message to Churchill. "I know you will not mind my being brutally frank," he wrote the Prime Minister, "when I tell you that I think I can personally handle Stalin better than either your Foreign Office or my State Department. Stalin hates the guts of all your top people. He thinks he likes me better and I hope he will continue to do so. . . ." Churchill was also given to understand on several occasions that the American approach was sound because, when the war came to an end Russia would desperately need economic aid for reconstruction. Though FDR never was able to work out the details of such an "offer" to Stalin, he did succeed, certainly, in stiffening for a time British resolve against granting Russia's demands for a treaty guaranteeing its 1939 Nazi-Soviet Pact frontiers.

Wending a strange path through this tangled thicket of Anglo-American diplomacy was Churchill's close friend and quondam Minister of Production, Max Beaverbrook. His visit to Washington in March 1942 set in motion the first round of true East-West negotiations about the postwar world. On the day before he left for the United States, Churchill's friend wrote to Stalin that he was going to see the President for the express purpose of discussing Russia's prewar frontiers. In the House of Commons the Prime Minister indicated, obliquely, that Beaverbrook did indeed carry with him such a commission.

For reasons best known to himself, Beaverbrook prefaced his

statements to American officials with a dismal assessment of British diplomatic failures. "Stalin says that Britain treats the Russians like natives or negroes," he explained to Harry Hopkins. If they wanted to save their own skins in this war, he went on, British and Americans alike had better wake up. They would have to yield to Russian demands for strategic security—that is, the prewar frontiers—grant Moscow an equal voice in the conduct of the war, pool war supplies on a basis of equity, and admit Stalin to a full share in determining the peace settlement in Europe. "Delay in taking decisions, and procrastination in all our proceedings have almost destroyed the hope of effective collaboration with Russia."

Roosevelt responded by insisting that he was ready to take decisions but not in a panicky rush to buy off Stalin with Eastern Europe. No, not that, but he was willing to make a decision to launch a second front. Beaverbrook left Washington an ally of Roosevelt, but he found Churchill in a dark mood. The Prime Minister was disturbed by Roosevelt's game. Anglo-Russian negotiations over a treaty that would have included recognition of Stalin's territorial claims had stalled, in part because of American objections. Russian Foreign Minister V. M. Molotov reluctantly accepted a substitute that ignored territorial questions but extended the alliance for a twenty-year period. Molotov then traveled to Washington, in Beaverbrook's wake, while Churchill wrote to Stalin to express his appreciation for "meeting our difficulties" over the treaty: "I am sure the reward in the United States will be solid, and our three great Powers will now be able to march together united through whatever has to come."

But Churchill could not march united with what came out of the Roosevelt-Molotov discussions, a promise that a second front in Europe would be "formed" before the end of the year. As he explained to Roosevelt, with the crisis in the Middle East, he did not have the troops. And neither did the Americans for that matter. A new emissary was sent, Lord Louis Mountbatten, to explain all this to the President. This time Churchill was satisfied on all counts. Admiral Mountbatten concentrated solely on military questions and succeeded in dissuading Roosevelt from attempting a premature assault on Europe. Instead, plans were laid for a North African campaign.

Why did Roosevelt yield? Were the British reverses in the Middle East sufficient evidence that an Anglo-American offensive in Europe was indeed impossible, a foolhardy scheme that promised only disaster? Roosevelt's own military chiefs had argued long and hard that nothing should be allowed to get in the way of the ultimate strategic goal: the early defeat of Germany. They had even persuaded Roosevelt to forsake opportunities in the Pacific to this end. If British strategists could conceive of no plan for a successful landing in France, that was one thing; but it was quite another to accept the North African venture as a substitute.

Roosevelt's decision was essentially a political one. He had vowed that American forces would go into operation against German armies in 1942. He would keep that promise. But there was more to it than that. Where his military advisers feared being drawn into a defense of British "imperial" interests, at a cost of a tragic delay in opening a true second front, FDR saw an opportunity. During Anglo-American military consultations in June 1942, word was brought to Churchill that Tobruk had fallen, with the loss of 33,000 men. A crucial turning point had been reached.

"It was a staggering blow," recalled Lord Alanbrooke. "I cannot remember what the actual words were that the President used to convey his sympathy, but I remember being vividly impressed by the tact and the real heartfelt sympathy which lay behind these words." Roosevelt offered immediate aid for the Middle East. It was proposed that the First Armored Division be sent at once. Alanbrooke wondered if that was wise: "This division was only partially trained, and it would have entailed forming an American front in the Middle East." For the moment, the offer of troops was put aside, but in the final agreement on a North African campaign the extension of an "American front" reappeared as a key issue. On July 24, 1942, the American Chiefs of Staff finally agreed to give up their insistence upon planning for an "immediate" attack on the Continent in favor of the North African campaign—under the command of General Dwight D. Eisenhower. "In order to obtain this we were prepared to accept an American armored division in Persia and to stand certain cuts in proposed air allotments."

It was indeed a turning point. The United States now took charge of the over-all military effort in the West. Added to control of the Pacific campaigns under General Douglas MacArthur, the decisions concerning the launching of the TORCH operation (the North African campaign) placed American forces in operation around the world. Stalin would be disappointed. But there were tremendous compensations. An assault on Europe in 1942 would have left the

British in command in the Middle East. At least this way Roosevelt could stand aloof from any responsibility for having disappointed Stalin, could inject American forces into a new vital area politically, and then, when the invasion of Europe did come, be in a position to take complete charge.

The delay in opening the second front fortuitously put the United States in a position to prevent a repetition of what had happened (with dreadful political consequences for the League of Nations and the Wilsonian world order) during World War I, when, thought Americans, General John J. Pershing's "doughboys" had held off the Germans on the Western front while the Allies completed the carving up of the Ottoman Empire. "I cannot help feeling," FDR wrote Churchill on the TORCH decision, "that the past week represented a turning point in the whole war and that now we are on our way shoulder to shoulder."

Churchill readily accepted the assignment to tell Stalin that the second front would have to be delayed. It gave him the opportunity to reassert his personal authority in Big Three deliberations, an authority undermined by the steadily eroding command he could exercise over military affairs. "TORCH" was the last British "victory" in World War II. At their Moscow meeting in the summer of 1942, Stalin alternated between sympathy for TORCH and angry insults about Western failings. Churchill almost walked out, but thought better of it. He had not come this far (since 1939) to allow the war to be lost because of pride; neither was he sure that the future political battle over Eastern Europe would be a simple East-West affair. There were matters, perhaps, that only Russia and Great Britain should decide.

The North African campaign led quickly to a military victory, and a showpiece conference at which Roosevelt made an even more successful grab for the newspaper headlines with his famous demand for Unconditional Surrender. He had urged Stalin to come to Casablanca, so that genuine three-power talks might take place. The Russian preferred to stay at home. But FDR still saw a way to "talk" person-to-person. The Unconditional Surrender statement was an effort to reassure the Soviets that America was not fighting the war to restore the colonial empires, but would settle for nothing less than the eradication of Nazism.

Very little is known about Stalin's reaction to the Unconditional Surrender proclamation. He may have thought it an unnecessary complication. The Soviet leader had said, on the other hand, that he preferred arithmetic to algebra, an immediate agreement on postwar frontiers to FDR's talk about the Big Four policemen, or, even more abstractly, a new League of Nations. For him, the truly important event at the moment was the surrender of the Germans at Stalingrad. On January 31, 1943, after five months of desperate struggle, with a million soldiers engaged on each side, the decisive battle of World War II had come to an end.

By contrast, the victory celebration at Casablanca meant little to the Russians—and no immediate help against the Germans! It ended with yet another postponement of the second front, the result of a decision to clear the Mediterranean and land instead in Sicily. American generals were disappointed. Harry Hopkins was dumbfounded at how it had happened. "I told him," Roosevelt's most trusted adviser reported of a conversation with Churchill, that "it seemed to me like a pretty feeble effort for our two countries in 1943."

In truth, the pace of American mobilization was as much responsible as British reluctance for the delay. But it galled Americans that the place where Allied armies would finally meet on the Continent was being settled at conferences with the British, while the Red Army's momentum carried it into Central Europe.

After discussing the situation with former Ambassador to Russia Joseph Davies, who had since become a "contact" man with the Russian Embassy in Washington, Roosevelt asked him to convey to Stalin in person his keen desire for a face-to-face meeting. Davies liked the idea. But, he warned, that would mean a discussion of Poland's western border. Well, if it finally came down to "spheres of influence," it was better to have the decision made in Washington, not in London. And maybe when Stalin saw that Roosevelt really had no "designs" on Eastern Europe, he would relent. Maybe.

Without explicitly authorizing agreement to the so-called Curzon line, drawn in 1919 by a British Foreign Minister, and which approximated Russia's desired settlement of the Russo-Polish frontier, the President allowed Davies to sweeten the American invitation to a Big Two meeting with this sentence: "We think you are entitled to the Curzon line, but think it unwise to insist upon it now." Davies's report on his mission confirmed Roosevelt's fear that his Unconditional Surrender manifesto had not erased Soviet suspicions. The Russians would carry the war into Germany, said Davies, only as part of a concerted plan "carried on simultaneously by the Allies." They were determined to "take back what they considered was wrongfully taken from them," but were not disposed to intervene in the internal affairs of other governments.

Learning of Roosevelt's desire to have a tête-à-tête with Stalin, Churchill started raising all sorts of objections. "He would be more frank in regard to [the] Balkan States, Finland and Poland," Roosevelt explained. "I want to explore his thinking as fully as possible concerning Russia's postwar hopes and ambitions." Churchill was not mollified. Stalin only wanted a second front, he grumbled to Averell Harriman, so as to keep the West out of the Balkans. Harriman thought the Prime Minister overlooked the key point. Stalin needed a firm understanding with Roosevelt—he needed it "more than anything else." Russia's postwar security and economic reconstruction depended upon it.

Harriman was one of a handful of Americans whose families had had business dealings with Russia since Tsarist days. In 1941 he had urged Roosevelt to take a chance by extending Lend-Lease aid to the Soviet Union. If the gamble paid off—which it did—the return on this investment would be immense. German hopes of conquering Eastern Europe would be smashed, and American-Russian relations would be put on the right course for the postwar era. Harriman accepted the post of Ambassador to Russia under the expectation that he would be charged with the responsibility of carrying out Roosevelt's plan to entice the Soviets into a Western-devised security system.

At the Moscow Foreign Ministers' Conference in November 1943, Harriman sensed a new atmosphere. The Russians no longer believed that there was a Western bloc operating against their interests. They are "genuinely satisfied" with the way things are going, he reported, "and are ready to make important concessions to further the new intimacy." Russia demanded a "friendly" Poland on its borders, but Davies had been right: they were ready to promise the Poles could determine their own political and social system. The Ambassador admitted to some skepticism about Soviet assurances that they had no desire to extend the communist system. If that was the only way that they could obtain satisfactory relationships with states on their borders, then they would send out the commissars—regardless of anything or anybody else.

Yet Harriman saw nothing at Moscow that made him feel unduly pessimistic. Molotov had, he said, been quite forthcoming about Russia's desire for good relations after the war: "In the conference, however, it was indicated that although they would keep us informed they would take unilateral action in respect to these [border] countries in the establishment of relations satisfactory to themselves." Could anything have been plainer? Whatever the Western powers thought at the outset of the Cold War, it was surely hard to complain that they had been deceived—except by their own illusions.

Roosevelt himself struck a note of realism amidst the growing euphoria about the postwar world that emerged in the wake of the Moscow Conference. Congratulated on the achievement of a sound statement on Big Three unity by Walter Lippmann, the President wrote back on November 8, 1943, "Moscow was a real success. Sometimes, however, I feel that the world will be mighty lucky if it gets 50% of what it seeks out of the war as a permanent success. That might be a high average."

On January 11, 1944, moreover, Hull and Stimson talked over newspaper reports that reprinted a Russian statement about Poland. "We discussed the various areas which would be left to Poland," Stimson recorded:

> Hull thought that the main thing to do was to establish the rule that there could be no acquisition by force. I answered that I thought we had to consider other things more realistic than that, such as the feelings which would actuate Russia: (a) that she had saved us from losing the war; (b) that she prior to 1914 had owned the whole of Poland including Warsaw and running as far as Germany and that she was not asking for restitution of that, etc. etc."

Roosevelt did not achieve a private meeting with Stalin, except as a preliminary to a Big Three conference with Churchill at Teheran, at the end of November 1943. During this brief conversation the President put certain propositions on the table, much in the manner of a knight's move in chess, two squares in one direction and over one. He hinted at a Polish settlement according to Russian terms, and a willingness not to inquire closely into what happened to the Baltic States. But he could not make any firm commitments, he said, until after the 1944 elections—a year away, and, presumably, when American forces would be advancing across Europe from the west.

Harriman had hoped for some solid decisions about postwar economic policy toward the Soviets. There were none. All Roosevelt did at Teheran was to suggest that some ships from the captured German fleet might be made available. For his part, Stalin received the "offer" with a comment that the ships might prove useful in expanding

Russo-American trade along the lines of industrial goods for raw materials. And that was that.

The only written decisions at Teheran concerned the second front. Roosevelt went out of his way during military discussions to demonstrate disagreements with Churchillian geopolitics, and his determination to stay out of the Balkans. But he did not speak as one simply eager to please his new friend at any cost. Rather, FDR wanted to make sure that Stalin understood basic fundamentals: the United States, not Great Britain, had the power and the resources to say when and where about the invasion; and the United States, not Great Britain, defined the political commitments the West would make (and uphold); and, finally, the United States, not Great Britain, had the wherewithal to help with Russia's immense task of reconstruction.

It is probably more correct to speak of Teheran as the high point of Allied unity, if there was a high point at all, rather than to look for it at the Yalta Conference. After D-Day, the Allied troop landings in France of June 6, 1944, there was a steadily decreasing area for maneuver. As the anti-German armies approached the center of Europe from east and west, they left in their wake areas devastated both physically and politically. The reorganization of European society had to begin even as the war continued; temporary decisions imposed by local military commanders had but one objective: to establish order. It was hardly to be expected that Russian commanders would tolerate "pro-Fascist" parties any more than Western generals would call upon left-wing leaders to head up provisional governments. Spheres of influence were hardening behind the closing circle around Berlin. There was simply no way that Russia could be kept from establishing "friendly" regimes in Eastern Europe short of an out and out confrontation with the Red Army.

Waiting in the wings, ready to take over once the shooting stopped, were rival "exile" governments which had, even in the Soviet Union, made known their displeasure with the hegemonic diplomacy of the Great Powers. For a time in the summer of 1944 these rivalries focused on Poland, where the Russians refused Anglo-American pleas to allow an airlift to resupply the valiant fighters during the Warsaw uprising. In their frustration, exile leaders blamed Roosevelt as well as Churchill. And as it happened New York's Archbishop Francis Spellman was in London. What he heard left him badly shaken. The President was more pro-Russian than pro-British, the exiles told him. Spellman repeated this to the American Ambassador, and the warning quickly found its way to Harry Hopkins in Washington.

Spellman should not lend himself to being used this way, Hopkins complained in reply, "by the former ruling classes of Poland." No softie about Stalin or Soviet Russia, Hopkins had the social democrat's skepticism of leftist dogmas—but he also had a keen insight into conservative folly: "I have always felt that both immediately before and during the war the Vatican was more interested in the defeat of Russia than of Germany." Hopkins's alarm at the activities of the Archbishop, as presaging the possible formation of a Catholic-led anti-Communist "international," was not unjustified. Roosevelt faced a tough election in 1944. He was now a wartime leader asking for support to finish off the enemy, not the New Deal prophet summoning working men and farmers to a national town meeting to resolve a common problem. Patriotism is a conservative's issue. The patriotism aroused in Polish-Americans and other Eastern European hyphenates by the war was likely to become a powerful anti-Russian force, especially when joined to the Church's rising voice of protest. Such considerations made Roosevelt cautious, more determined than ever not to go ahead with definite political or economic proposals to the Russians.

Seen from the State Department, and related war agencies, the Russian "issue" had a different complexion, and a deeper complexity. Not present at any Big Three meeting, the "bureaucrats" had been charged with fleshing out the plans Roosevelt approved for the postwar world. It was to their hands that such abstractions as the "Four Big Policemen" and the Final Declaration of the Moscow Conference had been commended; it was their task to resolve any and all contradictions. Sooner or later, therefore, their concerns had to be met. They dare not fail. Two world wars and the Great Depression had undermined the foundations of liberal capitalism, and discredited many (probably most) of its prewar European political leaders.

America was unscathed physically, but there were deep wounds of the spirit that had barely had time to heal. It was dangerous to contemplate a postwar United States populated by men standing in soup lines or selling apples, by farmers burning crops too costly to transport or dumping milk in ditches. Already the Democratic coalition was breaking down over how much of the New Deal (or *how much more of* a New Deal) would be necessary to ensure domestic tranquility after the war. The evidence was there for all to see at the

1944 Democratic National Convention, when the "Progressive" Henry A. Wallace was replaced by a relative unknown, Harry S Truman, for the second spot on the ticket.

Roosevelt stayed aloof, and that sealed Wallace's fate. Another, related, issue was the growing problem of the President's increasing reliance upon "Dollar-a-Year" men, businessmen on loan to the Government by their companies at no government expense, for "expert" advice on postwar economic policy. During the New Deal years, 1933–38, Roosevelt's good friend and Secretary of the Treasury, Henry Morgenthau, Jr., had vowed to move the financial capital of America from New York to Washington—a much greater distance philosophically than two hundred miles.

A Democratic party policy that encouraged (or even appeared to) a Russian advance into Western border states, that promised economic aid for the communization of those areas, and that allowed a Soviet state-trading "bloc" to participate in the proposed international agencies, the International Monetary Fund and the International Bank for Reconstruction and Development, was a tough proposition. State Department professionals who might have their differences with Secretary Hull could, nevertheless, find a Wilsonian common ground with the "Dollar-a-Year" men on two counter-propositions: first, that some of the President's New Deal advisers had a penchant for over-admiration of the Soviet experiment; and, second, that the road to socialism was often paved with the best liberal intentions. With Will Clayton and Dean Acheson (both famous anti-New Dealers) operating as most trusted assistants of the new Secretary of State, former U.S. Steel head Edward R. Stettinius, Eleanor Roosevelt wrote her husband after his re-election, "I can hardly see that the set-up will be very much different from what it might have been under Dewey."

Eleanor was her husband's conscience. But what were the choices? In the last year of the war, the President became a mediator. He mediated between domestic counselors across the spectrum from those determined to hold the New Dealers in check to those concerned with preventing a return to Hoover Republicanism; he mediated between Russian security demands and Western post-war political plans; and he mediated between his own divided impulses. Only a few days after D-Day, Roosevelt signed Hull's complaint to Churchill that he had had to learn from the Russians of pending discussions about "matters in the Balkans." Reluctantly, and with many hedges, the President agreed to another Churchill mission to Moscow for the purpose of establishing temporary boundary lines in Southeastern Europe. Even this concession he tried to keep secret from all but a few trusted aides.

It was a particularly touchy subject, especially at the very moment that the United States was hosting a preliminary conference on postwar world organization. The major issue that emerged at the Dumbarton Oaks meeting was over Russian insistence that the Big Four veto power in the proposed Security Council not be limited. Thus if the question before the Security Council involved an accusation against one of the Big Four, that nation could block any and all action.

Despite Roosevelt's personal intervention the Russian delegation would not yield. The delicate balance that the President had hoped to maintain between the Grand Alliance and plans for the new international security organization was put in jeopardy. If he met Russian wishes, he opened himself to criticism from Wilsonian purists; if he held firm, he risked dividing the Grand Alliance. The obvious thing to do was delay, until the war was over. But the issue was not that simple. Permutations of the veto question and spheres of influence penetrated into almost every daily discussion of policymakers, and into the press.

If American opinion shifted against the United Nations because of the veto demands of the Russians, an "isolationist" mood prevailed, and the world was again fragmented, what prospects were there for the future? Roosevelt needed some formula for reassuring contradictory claimants, opposing constituencies. He most certainly was not planning a Cold War. What good would it do to place the onus on the Russians, if the only result was a division of Europe? He needed their cooperation.

Much that is confusing about FDR's attitude toward Russia in the final months of the war can be understood in these terms, not in excuses that he was ill, or that he put his trust in Stalin. Walter Lippmann, who had long since shed his Wilsonian enthusiasms, saw exactly what was going on. Any organization committed to the suppression of aggression, he wrote privately, "directed against everybody in general and nobody in particular, would quickly develop a pro and anti-Russian alignment," since the first area of contention was sure to be the former German satellites—states bordering Russia's frontiers. Disagreements over the veto were inextricable from the debate over spheres of influence.

Roosevelt's October 4, 1944, message to Stalin and Churchill, about to meet in Moscow to discuss Eastern Europe, reached for some middle ground. He did not say they should cease and desist talking about spheres of influence, but he placed a hedge. "There is in this global war," it read, "literally no question, either military or political, in which the United States is not interested." According to his later account in *Triumph and Tragedy*, written at the height of the Cold War, the Prime Minister proposed a trade-off, Russian predominance in Rumania for a free hand in Greece, Russian control in Bulgaria, and a fifty-fifty split in Yugoslavia and Hungary.

It was quickly done, Churchill recalled, perhaps implying that like Roosevelt, he, too, saw it as a temporary arrangement pending genuine Atlantic Charter-style free elections. But contemporary records show the negotiations were difficult, and touched upon questions far removed from Southeastern Europe. These included, at Churchill's initiative, Russian willingness to restrain Communist politicians in Italy, the Polish question, and the veto. In regard to this last, the Prime Minister gave Stalin an oblique hint that he agreed with his stand. Churchill instanced a possible Chinese demand that Hong Kong be returned. If the Soviets would not oppose his efforts to recover the Empire, Churchill implied, he would not stand out against Russian efforts to surround the Soviet Union with friendly states. This was the kind of arithmetic Stalin understood.

The British had long feared that the sentimental Americans would wind up doing something foolish about China. Roosevelt was as much a romantic about China as the ancestors he often talked about, pioneers in the old "China trade." But that was not where trouble came for an Anglo-Russian understanding. Instead, it surfaced in press attacks on British policy in liberated Greece. In December 1944, Churchill had ordered British troops to fire upon leftist-led forces that were seeking to prevent King George II from reclaiming his throne. Roosevelt, who had wanted to avoid precisely this kind of predicament, proposed to the Prime Minister the idea of a tripartite commission to investigate matters. It was no better received in London than Roosevelt's prewar suggestion to Neville Chamberlain outlining an alternative to appeasement.

As they had promised in Moscow, the Russians kept their distance.

The British were grateful for that. Roosevelt's blundering diplomacy once again, as in 1938, appeared to make it possible for a power, this time Russia, to up its demands, and cause no end of trouble. Could Moscow resist the temptation to stir up a civil war in Greece should Roosevelt's plan be adopted, particularly if it would divert attention from difficulties it was encountering in restoring "order" in Poland? Could Moscow suffer the embarrassment of turning its back on the left with the Greek situation spread across the front pages? Either way, ironically, it was the Americans who would incur the blame for disrupting the admittedly difficult process of restoring order.

Greece was not a British "colony," but for Churchill it was just as essential to the Empire. And he did not intend to give up the Empire without a fight. On January 8, 1945, Foreign Secretary Anthony Eden wrote the Prime Minister what he thought about handling the Americans: "We are anxious to persuade the Americans not to go in for half-baked international regimes in any ex-enemy colonies they may take over, nor to advocate them for others, but to accept colonial responsibilities on the same terms as ourselves." If Eden had written "ex-enemy countries" he would have given an equally apt description of British policy toward Europe.

Ten days later Churchill faced another challenge. Restless members of the House of Commons had requested a debate on foreign policy before the next meeting of the Big Three. The debate lasted two days, January 18 and 19, and some very remarkable things were said by the Prime Minister. Calling Anglo-American understanding essential, Churchill defended himself vigorously against the "melancholy exhibition" by journalists on both sides of the Atlantic. Reviewing the action of British troops, he said:

> For three or four days, or more, it was a struggle to prevent a hideous massacre in the center of Athens, in which all forms of government would have been swept away and naked, triumphant Trotskyism [!] installed. I think "Trotskyists" is a better definition of these people and of certain other sects, than the normal word, and it has the advantage of being hated in Russia.

Those sentences must rank with the best diplomatic double-entendre ever uttered. Did Churchill know how brilliant they were? Stalinist lexicons listed "Trotskyist" as traitor, a collaborator with the Nazis. The Prime Minister no doubt had that definition in mind. But Trotskyist had another meaning in Marxist debates. It meant a believer in world revolution as opposed to socialism in one country. Stalin was the formulator of socialism-in-one-country. Churchill's ambivalence, even if unintended, was exquisite praise of socialism in one bloc.

Hardly less inspired was his response to the Labor accusation that Britain was playing "power politics" over the former German satellites. " 'What are power politics?,' " he began, explaining that he knew "some of our friends across the water so well" that he could speak frankly without causing offense:

> Is having a Navy twice as big as any other Navy in the world power politics? Is having the largest Air Force in the world, with bases in every part of the world, power politics? Is having all the gold in the world power politics? If so, we are certainly not guilty of these offences, I am sorry to say. They are luxuries that have passed away from us.

With the war's end now only a few months away, Churchill was at bay. German and Japanese defeat a certainty, postwar questions were at the top of the agenda. The Prime Minister and his aides fretted that Roosevelt—like Wilson before him—had found no way to deal with Soviet Russia. It was not even clear that whatever policy the President wished to follow in that regard would win approval from the public. Two options appeared to offer some chance of success. The first, followed at TOLSTOY and in the Commons debate, concentrated on securing "good fences" in the hope of making the Russians good neighbors. The second, pursued with much greater vigor after Yalta, stressed rousing the Americans to their duties.

For his part, Roosevelt had stayed clear from the first, while trying to encourage Stalin to believe the United States sought nothing in Eastern Europe, except that he be able to present the situation as consistent with stated war aims; and, as for the second, Roosevelt never let down his guard against being taken in. The public impression, however, was, increasingly, that foreign policy-planners had lost their moorings. Reports from liberated areas, Italy and Greece in the west, and what could be gleaned from happenings in the east, portrayed a Europe on the verge of a great partition.

That could not, must not, be allowed. Roosevelt's plan, if he had a plan, was known only to himself, a situation that the men who had been in charge of the details of postwar planning found intolerable. It was also intolerable that press criticism indicted the "administration," not just FDR. Roosevelt's death in April forestalled an inevitable showdown, not with Russia, but between Roosevelt "loyalists" and the burgeoning bureaucracy under the leadership of dollar-a-year men, and a broad sweep of strong-minded "internationalist-Atlanticists" such as Dean Acheson at the assistant secretary level.

That struggle would have made Wilson's fight for the League of Nations seem a tame affair. Roosevelt did not differ with the objectives of his critics, most of them, but he was most certainly concerned about a premature leap into the postwar era, without even a transition period so that the victors had an opportunity to sort out what was essential and where they could compromise. Few New Dealers, by 1945, would dispute that self-containment was not the way to preserve the economy from a postwar depression, or society from anti-liberal trends. It had been a damn close thing in the depression decade. Unless Russia was somehow restrained from expanding into Europe, the future was dark. Churchill's TOLSTOY attempt to define spheres of influence would simply repeat earlier mistakes, and, at the very least, disintegrate into a situation best labeled permanent crisis.

Such an environment, Wilson had recognized, was congenial only to reactionary or socialist thought and politics. America had mobilized too late to prevent Pearl Harbor. Now it was making the same mistake by its slowness in facing up to crucial postwar issues. Hamilton Fish Armstrong, editor of *Foreign Affairs*, the publication of the Council on Foreign Relations, wrote to Secretary Stettinius that the British had already put their plans into operation. Look at Greece and Italy. Convinced that the Russians would pursue their security interests quite apart from Big Three considerations, and afraid that the Americans would once again withdraw from active participation in Europe's affairs, Churchill was seeing to the Empire's needs.

Restive stirrings in Congress finally prompted Roosevelt to meet with key Democratic and Republican Senators on January 11, 1945. He did not offer them a prospect that the creation of the United Nations would provide the answer, or even that America could use its new power to effect a change in Soviet behavior:

> The president took the situation in the Balkans as an illustration. He reviewed the discussions at Teheran regarding the Western Front and stated that he and Marshal Stalin had strongly taken the view that the concentration of power should be in France and that he had refused to employ American troops in Greece or the Balkans.
>
> In brief, the president stated that although spheres of influence had been

mulled over at Teheran the idea kept coming up because the occupying forces had the power in the areas where their arms were present and each knew that the others could not force things to an issue. He stated that the Russians had the power in Eastern Europe, that it was obviously impossible to have a break with them and that, therefore, the only practicable course was to use what influence we had to ameliorate the situation. In reply to a question from Senator Vandenberg, he stated that our economic position did not constitute a bargaining weapon of any strength because its only present impact was on Lend-Lease, which to cut down would hurt us as much as it would hurt the Russians.

Roosevelt's candor with the Senate leaders was part of a "plan" emerging in his mind to limit discussions at the forthcoming Big Three conference at Yalta in the expectation (better said hope) that the best thing to do for the postwar world would be to give the Russians time to "acquire confidence" in the machinery of peacemaking. Hence he decided not to pursue either pending, or more recent, projects for postwar "credits" or "loans" to Russia. Neither would he discourage the idea of their availability. Hence also he would approve a State Department-drafted Declaration on Liberated Europe that called for self-determination in the former German satellites, but without the Emergency High Commission to see that the Declaration was carried out.

Because the President died within two months of the Yalta Conference, a major historical debate has arisen over what he would have done once it became clear that Russia could not be cajoled or coerced out of Eastern Europe. It is a particularly intriguing question because it cuts across more general interpretations of the origins of the Cold War, with both "orthodox" and "revisionist" accounts contending that Roosevelt would have acted in a consistent manner with what did take place when Truman succeeded to the Presidency—or, conversely, with both agreeing that there was a sharp break.

One recent account suggests the answer is really fairly obvious: "had he lived, Roosevelt would probably have moved more quickly than Truman to confront the Russians. His greater prestige and reputation as an advocate of Soviet-American friendship would have made it easier for him than for Truman to muster public support for a hard line."* Perhaps that is so. Yet Roosevelt also had initiated a policy course that, while it left considerable room for maneuver,

---

* Robert Dallek, *Franklin D. Roosevelt and American Foreign Policy, 1932–1945* (New York, 1979), p. 534.

minimized, as he would say, day-to-day arguments over transition-period difficulties.

Roosevelt's death shortened the transition period. But that does not mean, it has been pointed out, that Truman did more than pound the table about Soviet behavior in Eastern Europe. He did not go chasing after Stalin with the atomic bomb, or set a lure for him with economic loans. He wavered for almost two years, in fact. What was different about Truman's policy was that it originated in a different epoch, even though he and FDR were almost the same age. Roosevelt's constant reference point was Wilson's failure in 1919, Truman's was Munich. Stalin and Churchill were similarly required to make up for areas of uncertainty, to improvise on the basis of what could be expected out of Washington now that the all-dominating figure Roosevelt had become during the war was removed from the scene. But while FDR's death focused attention on all unfinished business, the sharpest reminders were contained in Averell Harriman's strident telegrams from Moscow.

Appointed Ambassador in 1943, Harriman had been among the most optimistic of American policymakers about a "new beginning" in Russo-American relations. He had been one of the earliest advocates of Lend-Lease, had reassured Churchill of the soundness of American policy, and had awaited instructions to present a concrete economic proposal to the Soviets. Alarmed over evidence that the Soviets were determined to establish a sphere of influence in the Balkans, Harriman now reported to Washington that the real cause for concern was not what happened in that area so much as that when such methods were used "under the guise of security it is difficult to see how a line can be drawn." Summoned home for a discussion of policy, Harriman arrived in time to brief Truman on the situation, and his growing fear that a great opportunity was about to slip by—never to reappear. "As you know," he prefaced comments in Early April, "I am a most earnest advocate of the closest possible understanding with the Soviet Union so that what I am saying only relates to how such understanding may best be attained."

Harriman was still seeking, in other words, a concrete proposal, something to hold out to the Russians as a *quid pro quo* for co-operation. The ultimate weapon, he believed, was economic aid. Russia depended upon American Lend-Lease. Without it the Red Army was "a disorganized mass of human beings," and without assurances of future aid the Soviets would have little hope of reconstructing their country or of fulfilling Lenin's dream of what could be accomplished through electricity and Soviets.

Wilson had shied away from every plan for economic "intervention" his advisers produced in 1919; Roosevelt, too, had delayed making up his mind about how to use the economic cudgel. Harriman believed with all his heart that Washington would have to convince Moscow that it meant business. At some point in the future, he simply assumed, the Soviets would come to understand that their own security would be better protected by this method than if the world was re-partitioned into spheres of influence.

At Yalta, the illusion of Big Three unity continued to be played out with bravura performances. Yet Churchill was sincerely grateful to Stalin for displaying restraint over Greece, in contrast to Roosevelt's recent suggestions and the State Department's eagerness to set the world right. "The Russian attitude could not have been more satisfactory," he would report to the Cabinet. "There was no suggestion on Premier Stalin's part of criticism of our policy." When the Russians made a bargain, he concluded, "they desired to keep it."

The Americans, however, had trotted out another of their "documents" that, like the July 4, 1776, manifesto, stressed as its highest priority a decent respect for the opinions of mankind. Or so it appeared to Churchill, who, while he probably agreed with the sentiments in the proposed Declaration on Liberated Europe, resented the notion of everyone signing on the dotted line, and was particularly vexed that it was discussed at the same Big Three session on February 9, 1945, at which the Americans presented a new version of a colonial trusteeship system.

Recovered from a Victorian spasm, Churchill had assented to the Declaration, "as long as it was clearly understood that the reference to the Atlantic Charter did not apply to the British Empire." He reminded his fellow members of the wartime triumvirate that this was not the first time he had entered such a caveat. He had done so at the outset of the Grand Alliance, when he returned from the first "summit" meeting off the coast of Newfoundland. Churchill's perception of American policy, and the connections he saw between defense of the Empire and recognized spheres of influence, never entirely disappeared from British policy (especially under the Conservatives) and it appeared again, to the keen observer, in the famous Iron Curtain speech in 1946.

By speaking out in this fashion, the Prime Minister called attention, implicitly at least, to persistent Soviet caveats about Eastern Europe dating back also to the signing of the Atlantic Charter. At Yalta, Stalin kept silent and allowed Roosevelt and Churchill to carry on their spotty dialogue. Perhaps he anticipated that the Prime Minister's resistance to American wishes would have to give way before reality. He probably did not anticipate the dramatic change, however, or the agility with which the Prime Minister could bring it off. "Premier Stalin was a person of great power," Churchill told the War Cabinet on February 19, 1945, "in whom he had every confidence." Less than three weeks later, on March 8, 1945, the Prime Minister sent the first of a series of urgent cables to Roosevelt expressing concern about Russian disregard for the Yalta agreements on Poland. Soviet behavior was indeed crude and cruel. Had the Prime Minister ignored its impact, moreover, he would have risked giving the Labour party an issue in the upcoming general elections. The January 18 debate had really signaled the end of the wartime political truce, and it would be absurd for Conservatives to attempt to defend Communist actions in an election.

Beyond that consideration were other, more subtle, forces at work below the surface. In *Triumph and Tragedy*, Churchill noted the danger of getting involved in a direct argument with Stalin because of the continuing difficulty in Greece. He could call attention to Soviet actions in Rumania, but that would only lead to comparisons "between his aims and ours." Churchill feared that kind of thing more than any other, in part because it endangered his relations with the United States. On the other hand, by directing American attention to the Russian behavior in Poland, he gained breathing space in Greece, and perhaps (though this is mostly speculation) disrupted any nascent Soviet-American alliance on Far Eastern questions. Roosevelt's private talks with Stalin concerning the Soviet entry into the war against Japan, from which the Prime Minister was pointedly excluded, had at times touched not only on China's postwar role but even on "colonial" questions such as the future of French Indochina.

These were, however, undercurrents. On the surface the unfolding events demonstrated that war, instead of speeding the processes of history, often held them in suspension. On April 12, 1945, Roosevelt died. Harry Truman inherited his ambiguous legacy. The change was not from Roosevelt the coalition leader to Truman the cold warrior, but from wartime strategy (a personal diplomacy) to peacetime requirements (an institutional subject). At San Francisco the United

Nations organizing conference was in progress. Delegates were buzzing with the Polish "crisis," while less than a thousand miles away the atomic age was about to begin at Alamagordo, New Mexico. Germany had not yet surrendered when on April 29, 1945, British Foreign Secretary Anthony Eden told news reporters at the UN Conference that his government thought Truman's threat to withhold economic aid unless Russia agreed to accept Western interpretations of the Yalta agreements on Poland was exactly the right way to produce the desired changes in Soviet behavior.

As it turned out, American policymakers had correctly predicted that the effort by Russia and Great Britain to define spheres of influence would lead not to harmonious East-West relations but to interminable squabbles. Yet, having disavowed any lingering Roosevelt acquiescence in spheres of influence, Truman's advisers were much less certain of exactly what it was that they expected the Soviets to change in their behavior. For a time, indeed, Secretary of State James F. Byrnes went out of his way to solve the problem by suggesting that the Soviets emulate America's Good Neighbor Policy toward Latin America.

Byrnes was anxious, as his special assistant on Russian affairs put it, to persuade the Soviets that the policies they were pursuing would divide the world into armed camps. "On the other hand," said Charles Bohlen, "we should not in any sense attempt to deny to the Soviet Union the legitimate prerogatives of a great power in regard to smaller countries resulting from geographic proximity." Squaring the circle would have been easier to accomplish than this formula. Algebra had, in the end, tripped up everyone. When Washington tried to do it with economic equations—as Harriman had always wished—the quotient for "x" never appeared, not then, and not in the détente era.

American ingenuity simply failed to find a space, somewhere between Churchill's simple bargain at the TOLSTOY conference in 1944 and the complicated motives behind the Declaration on Liberated Europe, that would allow for each side's "security" interests, Russia's desire for a buffer zone and America's ideological frontiers. Bohlen's colleagues, rebuffed by an early Russian rejection of "Dollar Diplomacy," sought to establish "a healthy American influence" in Eastern Europe by a more direct route, economic relief to the satellites and Poland. "We should strive to obtain from the New Polish Government of National Unity a promise that it will follow a policy of equal opportunity for American interests in trade, investments and access to information." Were the Russians supposed, then, to be welcome in Latin America with Marxist propaganda offices and other accoutrements of their system?

During his first days in office Truman had often talked about the difficulties of world economic reconstruction if political barriers were placed athwart the natural connecting routes between Western European industrial centers and the raw materials of Eastern Europe. What he eventually found, however, was that this deprivation could be turned to advantage, as it forced the Western countries to forsake age-old rivalries (at least temporarily) for the common good. The example of Soviet "police states" in the East rehabilitated the reputation of liberal democracy, thus eliminating a psychological barrier even more important than those erected across Central Europe's roads and waterways by the Russians.

The Cold War thus became, inevitably, the perfect climate for the dark and shadowy enterprises of the KGB and the CIA, as each side vowed to wage covert warfare against the other in endless John LeCarré plots. Outside Europe these became very dangerous indeed; but inside Europe they reflected an acknowledgment of a mutual interest in keeping things under control. By the end of 1947, George Frost Kennan, the "author" of the containment policy and head of the State Department's new Policy Planning Staff, already felt he had to warn his superiors against continuing a serious rollback effort in Eastern Europe. Despite the likelihood that Czechoslovakia would soon disappear behind the "Iron Curtain," he said, the Soviet advance had been halted. Russia was on the defensive.

Soon, he continued, the Kremlin would have to tighten up; but no matter what it did, the Russian empire would start to crumble: "The Kremlin may then feel itself seriously threatened internally and may resort to desperate measures." Did this desire to avoid rousing Soviet fears stretch far enough to suggest an obligation to sustain the Russian empire? Not in Kennan's original corollary to the containment doctrine, perhaps, but down the road it did. Two decades later another State Department theoretician, Helmut Sonnenfeldt, would spell it out: to preserve world peace the West must encourage "organic" unity to develop between Russia and Eastern Europe.

How, then, was détente different from spheres of influence? From Churchill's first reaction to the Soviet-Nazi pact down to the détente era, everyone recognized that a Russian advance into Eastern Europe was a bad situation. It had to be handled carefully. British efforts to contain it, limit its damage to the Empire (above all else), seemed *un*-careful, as ill-considered as Munich, and even frenzied. They convinced Americans that British diplomatic efforts were a positive danger in and of themselves.

Churchill's approach seemed to be: if Stalin wanted more room for socialism-in-one-country, that was fine if, in turn, he agreed to cease meddling outside his sphere. Spheres of influence was associated, therefore, with "appeasement," and the declining fortunes, ideologically, of prewar liberal democracy. It was also thought to be a precursor of a disastrous postwar economic policy that would reconstrict the world rather than reconstruct it. Besides, it wouldn't work. The turmoil inside Greece, for example, already demonstrated that drawing boundary lines like those Churchill approved was useless as a barrier against political unrest. What Americans eventually discovered, however, was that it was enough, and safer, to isolate the Soviets in Eastern Europe—just so long as the grip of "old world" diplomacy had been broken, and "Western unity" had been assured in the Marshall Plan and NATO.

Even as Roosevelt was dying, Gore Vidal would write of him, the elegant, ravaged old President would pursue,

> the high business of reassembling the fragments of broken empires into a new pattern with himself at the center, proud creator of the new imperium. . . . The United States was master of the earth. No England, no France, no Germany, no Japan . . . left to dispute the Republic's will; only the mysterious Soviet . . .

4

The New Anti-Comintern Pact: Western Europe and the NATO Protectorate

In August 1949 the Chairman of the Joint Chiefs of Staff, General Omar N. Bradley, testified in executive session before a combined Senate Foreign Relations and Armed Services Committee meeting. In his prepared statement, the General assured the Senators everything was well: "The tide of communism is being stemmed in Europe. We are not impelled by a crisis of desperation or fear of impending war. If we were I should recommend—and I am sure you would insist upon—a greater effort than is called for in this program."

Under consideration at that moment was the Administration's request for $1.3 billion to inaugurate a military assistance program, primarily for North Atlantic Treaty Organization (NATO) members, but with smaller sums designated for Greece and Turkey, the "general" China area, Iran, Korea, and the Philippines. For those who had been predicting since the announcement of the Truman Doctrine in 1947 that "containment" would prove a costly enterprise—whether they favored the policy or not—here was solid evidence.

The Senators had other concerns. They were worried about endowing the President with authority to send military equipment and advisers wherever he willed. They worried also about diverting European energies from recovery to rearmament. And they had begun to wonder if critics might be right: the military aid would provoke the Russians to undertake an arms race, yet not offer recipients what was needed to defend themselves if war came.

If, as Bradley said, there was no impending crisis, then what lay behind the Administration proposal? The General dealt with these questions in terms of a farm analogy. Everyone knew that North America enjoyed natural fences, the oceans, and up to 1939 there had existed a good second line of defense in Western Europe, a barrier which had helped to keep "the stock out of our pasture." Well, the Military Assistance Program (MAP) would put in European hands the materials necessary to rebuild that wall.

Senator Elbert Thomas—no enemy of the Administration—still had doubts, not just about the pending bill, but concerning the dangerously narrow focus of American policy. Since FDR's death, he said, Washington had concentrated almost exclusively on checking "Russia" and "Communism." Turning Bradley's phrase around, Thomas called American policy keeping a mad dog locked in a corral, "and we limit the corral for him." That attitude was bound to produce an overemphasis on the military. Draw a line, said the Senator, and every time, for sure, some people would think you had to fight to keep the dog locked up.

War was unlikely said Bradley. The Russians could not count on overrunning Europe. "We do not think her industrial capacity is such as to support her in a long drawn-out war which she would undoubtedly face, and she probably knows it." This answer reinforced Bradley's prepared statement that there was no pending crisis, but it did not speak to the central issue: what was the military assistance program designed to accomplish?

Bradley's response produced the following exchange, which, almost by accident, defined also the covenant with power:

> *General Bradley.* The more you build up the security of those countries, the more you encourage those people to fall away from communism. . . . I believe a lot of people are communists only because they want to be on the right side if something goes wrong.

> *Senator Bourke Hickenlooper.* That would seem to me to go entirely to the morale of the people, rather than to their actual military strength to resist.

> *General Bradley.* That, as I see it, is the big purpose of this aid. Nobody has an idea that this will stop anybody. It is a morale builder. . . .

Bradley's skill in answering the Senators' questions suggests that the newly unified armed services were more than up to their Cold War tasks, where the dividing line between military assignments and political responsibility was no longer so clear. The military assistance program was a morale builder, and so, too, were the Marshall Plan and NATO. Each formed part of a whole. Together they were designed to "mold the military character" of the Atlantic nations, prevent the balkanization of European defense systems, create an internal market large enough to sustain capitalism in Western Europe, and lock in Germany on the Western side of the Iron Curtain.

Averell Harriman had said in 1944 that the difficulty with permitting the Soviets a "sphere of influence" was where to draw the line. Critics of "containment" replied that the Truman Doctrine now made it impossible to draw the line between defense and the entanglements of an interventionist-protectorate policy. Walter Lippmann was perhaps the most prophetic about where it would all lead:

> It would require, however much the real name for it were disavowed, continual and complicated intervention by the United States in the affairs of all the members of the coalition which we were proposing to organize, to protect, to lead and to use. Our diplomatic agents abroad would have to have an almost unerring capacity to judge correctly and quickly which men and which parties were reliable containers. Here at home Congress and the people would have to stand ready to back their judgments as to who should be nominated, who should be subsidized, who should be whitewashed, who should be seen through rose-colored spectacles, who should be made our clients and our allies.

Skeptics among the Senators who heard Bradley also included Walter F. George, who had been the floor leader of the fight for Lend-Lease back in 1941. He always recalled that assignment with considerable pride. But now he was troubled. A deep foreboding colored his statements to fellow committee members:

> Now, I do not myself think there is any war possible in Europe in the immediate future, if we do not bring it on; if we do not emphasize this armament race to a point where it will not be any deterrent. . . .

> Actually, I cannot see any war in Europe, but I can see a vast reason for this program. I can visualize it as a mammoth pump-priming program, if you want to put it plainly, and I know what all international financiers and all manufacturers in this country want to do about it.

Senator George also delivered a more traditional conservative warning that one day, perhaps in the not-too-distant future, Americans would wake up to find their vast reserves depleted, their economic system—the only real barrier to Communism—on the skids.

But proponents of the military assistance program easily carried the day. Cold War inertia was already a powerful force. Having given approval to the Truman Doctrine only two years earlier for military aid to Greece and Turkey, would Congress now "pull the rug out"just as American policies were beginning to show returns?

General Bradley had presented the Senators with another grim possibility. The very success of the Marshall Plan and other economic remedies posed a great danger to the Soviets, he said; and rather than see the world Communist movement fail, they might lash out in frustration. That made the circle complete. If European nations were to succeed in the immediate future against "Fifth Column" forces operating from within, they needed the morale booster of American military aid; after they succeeded, they would need American military aid to turn back the desperate lurchings of a Communist leadership backed into a tight Kremlin corner.

Devastated almost beyond imagination by Hitler's armies, Russia had repulsed the invader and now stood, torn and bleeding, in the center of Europe. American generals who had a first-hand look at the Red Army stared in awe at the Soviet achievement, all the more so because of its battered and ragged appearance. Behind the Red Army the Stalinist political system had survived intact, perhaps the more remarkable feat, undoubtedly the greater cause for future concern. Whether admired or feared, the triumph of Stalinism (meaning in these days before the full revelation of the "costs" of the Five-Year plans and collectivization, one-party rule) was in stark contrast to the prewar failures of the fractured political systems of Western Europe.

But if Russia was a credible threat, on military or political terms, it was a necessary evil as well. It was hard to see how the Cold War could be won, a cynic might mutter, unless Russia played its role "straight," issuing menacing utterances, and, even more important, imposing Stalinism in Eastern Europe. Only in this way could Congress be inspired to pursue "bi-partisan" foreign policy; only thus could weak spots in Administration logic be swept aside or overlooked entirely. And without the Russian frightfulness, Europeans would have resisted co-operation, and nothing would ever get done.

It could be argued that, once the shock wore off, the postwar division of Europe was a godsend. The State Department's Atlanticist, free-trade, multilateralist—call it what you will—vision of the postwar world, its Open Door "empire," was always more than a little utopian. Given the nature of the American political-economy, to start with, it is hard to see how Congress could ever have been persuaded, especially with the Republicans back in control after 1946, that the Administration's foreign policy was not a New Deal for the world. Russia saved the day. Congress was won over by a hard-headed, mercantilistic vision, one that, because of its strong military content, made distasteful economic decisions palatable. So while Bradley encountered criticism, he was still in friendly territory with MAP.

Political economists David P. Calleo and Benjamin M. Rowland put it this way:

> While American business had traditionally ventured far into the outside world, the United States had never been thought to nurse grand schemes for world military empire. Hull's free-trade imperialism might have been expected, but not a new Roman Empire with an Atlantic *Mare Nostrum. It was almost as if the United States, spurning Europe's colonies, had decided to annex the mother countries instead.**

Annex is probably not the right word for the NATO "protectorate," since American leaders were certainly aware that one motive, para-doxically, for their Cold War policies was to keep Europe at a distance. From the end of the First World War forward (and espe-cially again in the 1980s), it had become apparent to government officials and economic leaders that the United States faced an uncom-fortable set of choices. If it opened its domestic market to foreign producers and behaved as a great creditor nation should, vital inter-ests at home would be placed in jeopardy. Unable to repeal *all* of its "Corn Laws" in the manner of Cobdenite England, Americans, if they were going to sustain an international capitalist system, would have to find some other way of supplying customers with dollars.

The war loans in World War I served this purpose, as did the famous Dawes and Young plans of the succeeding decade. But that jerry-built structure collapsed with the crash heard round the world in 1929. The emerging NATO protectorate offered, it was supposed, a much more reliable solution. It would protect and expand the inter-nal European market, substituting a common goal for prewar rivalry; and it would assure American business great new opportunities for investment. Here was, indeed, a vastly superior balance of power compared to nineteenth-century models, a balance that would keep

* *America and the World Political Economy: Atlantic Dreams and National Realities* (Bloomington, Ind., 1973), p. 46. Emphasis addded.

the Americans involved, yet not subject domestic producers to too much competition.

Something of this was already clear to Senator George when he deplored military assistance as a system of outdoor relief for American industrialists and financiers. It was even clearer to France's wartime leader, General Charles de Gaulle. De Gaulle's obsessive fear of Americanization crowded out many other legitimate concerns affecting the well-being of his country; but it was as well a precursor to German *Ostpolitik* in a later era, because resistance to Americanization was also part of a whole.

In November 1944, de Gaulle and Prime Minister Winston Churchill spoke together about a possible Anglo-French alliance, based in large part upon a supposed common interest in protecting colonial empires against Russian and American "disinterestedness." But de Gaulle also wanted to know more about Churchill's thoughts on postwar Europe. Did the Prime Minister now see himself, at long last, now see himself and his countrymen as Europeans or (however reluctantly) as junior partners in an Anglo-Saxon bid to "buy out" the old owners? Did Churchill content himself, in other words, with a jackal's role, while the bourgeois Americans and proletarian Russians haggled over the spoils?

If an Anglo-French pact meant a mutual resolve not to allow the giants to settle things between them, he said, he was for it. Otherwise not. Together they could, Britain and France, create a peace that would preserve Europe—and a political conception that offered hope against the "progressive mechanization of societies." "If you are willing to do so, I am ready." One had to admire de Gaulle's verve, if not his sense of the attainable.

Since the Atlantic Conference in 1941, Churchill explained in reply, down through TOLSTOY in October 1944, he had been trying to "channel" America's vast resources in the cause of Europe's regeneration. The Americans did not always use their immense power to best advantage, he went on, but through his close relationship with Roosevelt, a chance existed that things would turn out as they both would wish. At present Russia could not be channeled. It was a "great beast" which had been starved for a long time. "It is not possible to prevent her from eating, especially since she is now in the middle of the herd of her victims. But she must be kept from devouring everything." Stalin had a large appetite, but he was not devoid of common sense. "Meanwhile, I am present everywhere, yield nothing for nothing, and manage to secure a few dividends."

General de Gaulle, always in danger of being swept away with notions of European "grandeur," was a sure-footed realist about the concessions Churchill would have to make, the self-deceptions involved in Britain's hope to maneuver between Moscow and Washington. He was also fully aware of what those would mean in terms of French interests. No matter how "Americanized" Europe became, no matter how much France wanted and welcomed dollar investments, suspicions always remained that Great Britain was a stalking-horse for American hegemonists.

Over the next several months Anglo-French relations deteriorated, with serious quarrels developing over the Franco-Italian boundary, the future of the Levant, and the postwar treatment of Germany. De Gaulle, meanwhile, had himself journeyed to Moscow (much to Anglo-Saxon consternation), where he promised support for Russian demands that Poland's future western boundary be pushed to the Oder-Neisse line in compensation for territory the Poles would lose to the east, a solution he knew was designed to prevent a future German-Polish rapprochement, and which, he hoped, would make Stalin receptive to his ideas for amputations in the West.

Stalin welcomed French support, and perhaps the opportunity of a treaty relationship that would allow him to meddle in French internal politics. But he promised nothing. Yet de Gaulle departed with a signed document, a treaty that certified, by virtue of Stalin's imprimatur, that France must be treated as a great power. The Franco-Russian treaty of December 10, 1944, passed over as inconsequential in the early years of the Cold War, was in reality the original "charter" for de Gaulle's later diplomacy, and a forerunner of German *Ostpolitik* still later. But it did not give de Gaulle the leverage to prevent the American NATO protectorate.

The central fact of European life for twenty years was the Cold War. Churchill had begun, soon after Yalta, trying to draw Roosevelt into disputes with Stalin. Given other factors discussed earlier, and his conversations with de Gaulle, the Cold War, by design or not, had already developed a very complex personality, something much more elusive than the *vin ordinaire* of big power conflict. If American attention was to be diverted from the Greek situation (where de Gaulle, incidentally, predicted British policy would remain active to compensate for losses elsewhere to the Americans—and in hopes of gain at French expense), Churchill needed to focus concern on Poland. Second, Churchill was disturbed at the precedent set by Roosevelt's private talks with Stalin concerning China and the Far East. His vision of the future had room for only one special relationship, and it was not a Roosevelt-Stalin combine he had in mind.

At Potsdam in the summer of 1945, Roosevelt's successor, Harry S. Truman, did not welcome the Prime Minister's continuing efforts to "channel" American resources and policy "in the right direction." Truman had few thoughts of his own about foreign policy when he came into office. Neither was he a born and bred "Atlanticist," like many of those who occupied key advisory positions during the war. Yet he was perfect for the job. A "man from Missouri," as the saying went, he had to be shown. That meant, in a foreign policy context, that Truman stuck with the tried and true, in this case what he imagined FDR would have done.

One of Roosevelt's great skills, however, was his ability to put off deciding exactly what it was his policies meant. Those who knew him well were often frustrated (or incensed) by the President's nonchalant expectation that something would turn up to make it all come out. Others, like Truman, had Roosevelt's rhetoric to guide them. After Yalta, the President (the only President many had known in their adult years) assured Congress that he had brought back "a unanimous settlement" of the liberated areas question. He did caution that complications and compromises were part of international life, but he was sure the agreements reached there promised a more stable Europe than ever before. Yalta "ought" to spell the end, he finished, of unilateral action, of exclusive alliances, of spheres of influence, of balances of power, and all the other expedients that had been tried for centuries—"and have failed."

Even those nascent Cold Warriors who saw Russia looming as the ultimate problem had few doubts about the importance of "reforming" Europe, in both senses, so as to prevent a new outbreak of "imperialist" diplomacy, whose symptoms Roosevelt had described in his Yalta message. Wilson's experience was very much on everyone's mind. "One of the tragic aftermaths of a world war," Truman would write later, "is the harvest of little Caesars and their acts of aggression." The only person he named was General de Gaulle, who, he asserted, illustrated the "difficulties we faced," and "the need we had for firm and orderly procedure."

Certain of Roosevelt's old advisers (already a fast declining number) had assumed that Yalta also meant that Russia and the United States could now go to work to guarantee that "old world" politics did not wreck the peace. Ardent "New Dealers" and "Atlanticist" liberals could agree, for example, that Germany and Japan had to be rebuilt so that what emerged from the rubble had a solid structural foundation, strong enough this time to support world order. The former put great emphasis on internal social change, however, while the latter sought to construct along more "classical" lines.

In the shift from Roosevelt to Truman, and (more important) the transition from war to peace, a not surprising tendency developed toward the right side of this spectrum. The New Deal became part of American history, while the near-unanimous desire to "bring the boys home" and demobilize the economy added a subtle impetus to forces and individuals wishing to move the nation in that direction. Indeed, it began to be accepted that big government itself *produced* fascism (or socialism) without reference to antecedent social or economic conditions.

Truman told the nation after his encounter with Stalin at Potsdam that the Eastern European countries were not going to be recognized as anyone's sphere of influence. The decisions on reparations at that conference did much, however, to ensure that very division. It would be impossible to repudiate Yalta, either by taking back what Stalin had gained there, or, ironically, by backing off from Roosevelt's "domestic" foreign policy assurances that the Conference spelled the end of spheres of influence and all the rest of the old diplomacy.

In practice, this would mean what the Cold War term suggested: a policy based upon a commonly accepted contradiction. Living with Cold War confusions meant that even greater efforts would have to be made to enforce a "firm and orderly procedure" in both domestic and foreign policy. A New Deal supporter throughout his career in the Senate, Truman had always felt uneasy about the free-wheeling nature of the Roosevelt administration. His own Fair Deal program was designed to rein in "theorists" by various methods. He asked Herbert Hoover to study the federal government to reduce the administrative chaos of the New Deal/wartime years, proposed both a medical care program and universal military training, and unified the military services.

The same spirit dominated foreign policy thinking. Above all,

Truman, like Roosevelt, did not want "little Caesars" running around, staking out private claims, and in general making recovery problems still more vexing. Neither President much liked de Gaulle, but their personal reactions to the General cannot really be separated from a strong distaste for what he symbolized. To American policy-makers, the General represented the worst tendencies in Europe, all the more so now that Nazism had been eliminated: narrow nationalism, economic exclusivity, and unrepentant colonialism.

These were the very sins Roosevelt had listed in his Yalta message; the very attitudes, also, that had, it was now being argued, disrupted the world economy, brought on the Great Depression, and all that followed. Against the Russian threat Truman had two weapons to use—at least in theory. He could deny the Soviets economic aid for reconstruction, had in fact already stated his intention to do so in the first Cold War encounter over Poland's future government; and, after Hiroshima, he possessed what many believed to be the ultimate weapon. Neither was effective in getting the Russians out of Eastern Europe; but both were essential, in a different way, to establishing the NATO protectorate.

Within a month of succeeding to the Oval Office, Truman had become aware that he faced serious problems in "containing" tendencies to redefine American policies and objectives according to "European" interests. In mid-May, for example, Truman had tried to make it clear to General de Gaulle's spokesman, Georges Bidault, that the only way French troops could participate in the "liberation" of Indochina would be under conditions set by the American commander in the Pacific, General Douglas MacArthur. De Gaulle himself came to Washington in August determined to demonstrate that France must be treated as a great power, an equal at the council table. He brandished his treaty with Russia, but to no avail.

The President simply turned aside the General's references to alliances with a remark that he thought France would do well to seek its security in an effective world organization. "The United States possessed a new weapon," he went on, "the atomic bomb, which would defeat any aggressor. What the whole world needed most was economic re-establishment. At present, all the powers, including England and Russia, were asking for assistance from the United States." The President also raised some "questions" about the Communist ministers in the French Government, and the obstructions

American businessmen had found in their attempts to co-operate with French industrialists.

De Gaulle countered that these were internal policy matters, and raised his own queries. How long, he asked, would Americans continue to occupy military bases on French territory in the Pacific? It was not a good meeting. The General departed fully convinced that his ideas would receive even less attention in Washington than they had in Moscow. Over the next several months the situation inside France worsened, while the Cold War developed so rapidly that there was little room left to the old Free French leader for maneuver.

After de Gaulle's resignation, Franco-American loan negotiations moved speedily to a conclusion, providing Paris with a $1 billion credit. The formal announcement came on the eve of a crucial election to determine the new government. The first "internal" challenge to the Cold War consensus had been overcome. In the United States, a similar tightening process was under way, as the last ideological New Dealer, Henry Wallace, was "fired" from the Cabinet for questioning the "tough line" Secretary of State James F. Byrnes had taken over Eastern Europe. An unlikely pair, de Gaulle and Wallace were united in a belief that the division of Europe was not inevitable.

Without Wallace, however, the Fair Deal was a safer sequel to the New Deal, and without de Gaulle, France would be able to contribute to a liberal reconstruction policy that concentrated on results rather than notions of "grandeur." "On commercial policy," concluded Ambassador Jefferson Caffery in Paris, "we have secured France's articulate support to our views as well as the removal of certain practices adverse to our business interests."

Throughout these early travails, Truman had received strong support from Prime Minister Churchill. Exasperated at one point by de Gaulle's military actions in northern Italy and the Levant, the President had prepared a strong statement for the press. Churchill regretted it had not been used. It would have caused the General's downfall, he wrote Truman. France was a vital ally, but de Gaulle posed a great danger. "De Gaulle's present program of defiance and scorn to Britain and the US . . . leads only to unimaginable misery and misfortune."

Gratefully accepting the Prime Minister's support, Truman ignored the implied "special relationship" Churchill always wrote into these messages. The atmosphere was very different, of course, in early 1946, when Churchill, now the West's leading "elder statesman," delivered the "Iron Curtain" speech at Westminster College in Fulton, Missouri. With Truman sitting behind him, the former Prime Minister offered thanks to the deity that the "dread agencies" of atomic energy had been entrusted to "the United States, Great Britain, and Canada," rather than to some neo-fascist or communist state.

Yet try as he might, Churchill could not convince Truman or his advisers, the audience he most wanted to reach, of the advantages of a close Anglo-American military partnership. The Iron Curtain speech, useful as it was in alerting the public to Soviet intransigence, really did not mark an advance over well-known positions. Churchill described the dramatic division imposed by Moscow between the "ancient states of central and eastern Europe" and the remainder of the Continent, but he did not recommend using force to undo that unhappy result of the war, let alone to intervene in the "internal affairs" of the newest hegemonic power.

Churchill's remarks, it ought to be pointed out, were hardly different from what he had been saying throughout the war in defense of spheres of influence! The tone was sharper, but the speech positively reeked of the old diplomacy. What had he said, for example, that would help educate Americans to European recovery problems? How was one to read this sentence: "Except in the British Commonwealth, and in the United States, where communism is in its infancy, the Communist Parties or fifth columns constitute a growing challenge and peril to Christian civilization. . . ." Did one hear a call here to take the lead in eliminating the basic conditions that caused the peril? Or was it really only an argument, *sauve qui peut*, that the highest duty of the English-speaking peoples was to secure their homelands against the pestilence set loose where sanitary conditions had never been too good? These were not necessarily contradictory aspirations, but surely the emphasis was different—very different. Consider the one specific problem Churchill discussed: Greece. No doubt he was looking for vindication in the at last opened eyes of the American press. But Churchill was thinking less of modern-day Greece and its troubles than of mythical ancient Athens "with its immortal glories"—and its role in imperial planning.

Stalin did not hesitate to compare Churchill's "race theory" to

Hitler's odious theories, and to denounce the Iron Curtain speech as "a call for war on the U.S.S.R.," though even he was puzzled by the former Prime Minister's statement that the term of the 1942 Anglo-Soviet Treaty might quite well be extended to fifty years. When American policymakers took up the burden in Greece, thirteen months later, they deliberately sought to "universalize" the issue so as to free themselves from such ambiguity, and to make clear that the mission they were embarking upon was not the rescue of some latter-day General Gordon stranded in the far-off Sudan, or any other hero from the dusty annals of Queen Victoria's reign, but upon a modern enterprise fully worthy of the signers of the Declaration of Independence.

Original drafts of the message Truman would deliver to Congress on March 12, 1947, had included this version of that mission:

> Two great wars and an intervening world depression have weakened this [capitalist] system almost everywhere except in the United States. Continued chaos in other countries, and pressure exerted on them from without, will almost certainly mean the end of free enterprise and democracy in those countries. If, by default, we permit free enterprise to disappear in other nations of the world, the very existence of our own democracy will be gravely threatened.

Fearing that his speech writers and State Department experts were giving him an investment prospectus instead of a state paper, the President deleted this general statement and one or two more pointed references to Middle Eastern oil. Why risk making the issue a choice between capitalism and socialism? Stalin would be the only beneficiary of such a presentation. It would sorely offend the Labour Government in Great Britain, and open a crevice as wide and deep as any in recent years within European politics.

At home as well, the Truman Doctrine speech was designed not to provoke the conscience-isolationist liberals who had turned the interwar period into a referendum in retrospect on the "merchants of death" causes of American entry into World War I. Future Presidents, also, must be able to hold up the Truman Doctrine to the light without embarrassment. More now even than the commitment to the United Nations, the Truman Doctrine was to sustain the image of America as a defender of liberal world order.

How truly fortunate it was, therefore, to be associated with a

British Labour Government in the fight to save Greece for democracy. For some American policymakers helping socialism out of trouble, even in this fashion, was hard to swallow. But the idea went down easier whenever one began to add up the advantages. Imagine what it would have meant, for starters, to be associated with a Churchill-dominated Conservative Government trying any way it could to hold on in Greece? From the time of the attempted bargain with Stalin in 1944 down to the Iron Curtain speech in Fulton, Missouri, Churchill stood four square for a bygone era.

Bearing no deep imprint of imperialism and class rule at home, nor carrying the albatross of appeasement around its neck, the Attlee-Bevin Government was in many ways a perfect counterpoint to fill out the main themes of American policy. Bankrupt financially, and fast declining as a military power, a postwar Tory Government would only have added ideological difficulties to American concerns in the early Cold War. In later years the situation might change, though not entirely even then, but British Labour was invaluable as an ally.

"How many divisions has the Pope?," Stalin once quipped at a wartime Big Three meeting to demonstrate his disdain for nontangible factors in international relations. But British Labour was worth more than a score of divisions, ensuring back-up support for American policies throughout Europe, and showing Washington how to work with "moderate" socialists.

During the British election campaign of 1945, which brought Clement Attlee to power, the future Foreign Secretary, Ernest Bevin, had assured voters that "Left will be able to speak to left." That was taken to mean that the Labour Party better understood how to deal with Soviet Russia. Bevin spoke all right. He dressed down his Russian counterpart, V. M. Molotov, as if the latter was a rival labor leader who had to be put straight about a few things. As Foreign Secretary, "Ernie" proved as tenacious as Lord Curzon about the "Eastern Question." If he used fewer syllables than had the noble Lord, his words displayed no tint of appeasement.

Better still, from an American point of view, Bevin represented a Government that, while weaker in traditional power terms, projected an internationalist image as opposed to the spheres of influence outlook that characterized Conservative foreign policy. Evidence of close Anglo-American co-operation also "proved" that liberalism was not hostile to rapid social change. It reinforced American insistence that "modern capitalism" did not need imperialism, and worked better without it. So much then, for the thundering "Old Testament" jeremiads and prophecies still being uttered in Marx's name from the Soviet capital.

When Truman appeared before Congress on March 12, 1947, all the elements were in place. He told the legislators that the Administration must have $400 million to spend on military aid "if Greece is to survive as a free nation." The "absent-minded" agglomeration of power was over; from here on out the talk would be about "commitment" and "obligations." Not only did Truman declare that it "must" (changed by him from the State Department's "should") be the policy of the United States to support "free peoples" resisting attempts at subjugation "by armed minorities or by outside pressures," he added another sentence pledging the nation to resist "changes in the *status quo* in violation of the Charter of the United Nations by such methods as coercion, or by such subterfuges as political infiltration."

Who was to judge of these matters? Quite obviously, as the "reborn" internationalist, Senator Arthur Vandenberg, chairman of the Senate Foreign Relations Committee, admitted to his colleagues in executive session, there was no use in pretending that $400 million would buy peace. "It is merely a down payment. . . ." Haphazard as it was, especially in the "First Hundred Days," nothing in the New Deal was as open-ended as the Truman Doctrine. Congress would have to take it on faith that the Administration not only knew, but would have the ability to define, the limits of American responsibility.

Truman's speech did not make that task any easier. By excising all references to protecting capitalism—and carefully avoiding specific mention of the Soviet Union—the President achieved an ideological focus at the cost of distorting other realities. Part of the requested $400 million was earmarked for modernization of Turkey's armed forces. That was fine if the Truman Doctrine was sold as a defense measure, a plan whereby Greece and Turkey were assigned to bar Russia from gaining access to the Mediterranean. But Truman's primary thrust had been to portray the world in mortal combat between the forces of good and evil, democracy and totalitarianism.

Members of the Senate Foreign Relations Committee felt somewhat uneasy about the ambiguity. Turkey might be good, but it was not a democracy. Henry Cabot Lodge, Jr., suggested that his colleagues ought to go *beyond* the Truman Doctrine, and resolve their concerns by tacking on an amendment that read like the Bill of Rights.

> No assistance shall be furnished under this act which shall have the object (a) of promoting the continuance or expansion of any totalitarian purpose or goal, whether communistic or fascistic; or (b) of rejecting the proposition that individuals have inalienable rights and must be both free and the masters of their government.

"The idea is quite all right," Acting Secretary of State Dean Acheson assured the Committee; but Lodge's proposed exegesis of the Truman Doctrine dropped out of sight for thirty years, not to reappear until Jimmy Carter's human-rights campaign in the wake of Vietnam. Already, however, Senator George had a chilling premonition of what awaited the nation on that journey. "I do not know that we will have to go anywhere else in this world," he began,

> and I do not say that at the moment. I do not see how we are going to escape going into Manchuria, North China, and Korea and doing things in that area of the world. . . . [W]e have got the right to exercise commonsense. But I know that when we make a policy of this kind we are irrevocably committing ourselves to a course of action, and there is no way to get out of it next week or next year. You go down to the end of the road.

No one was prepared to say George was exaggerating. "There they are," said his colleague, Alexander Wiley, of the alternatives. "My America is stepping out into a new field, reaching out and, yes, without mincing words, assuming the function of the British Empire, which she so gallantly handled in the century that is past." Wiley admitted his uncertainty. "I may seem to be impractical, but God, the thing appeals to me so that for the first time in a long time I have been in doubt as to which way to go." Wiley voted yes; so did George; so did all thirteen.

A few weeks after Congress passed the Truman Doctrine appropriation—the down payment—Secretary of State George C. Marshall announced to the world that the United States was prepared to respond to a European-initiated recovery plan:

> Our policy is directed not against any country or doctrine but against hunger, poverty, desperation, and chaos. Its purpose should be the

revival of a working economy in the world so as to permit the emergence of political and social conditions in which free institutions can exist.

The only condition Marshall established was that the Europeans first agree upon an over-all proposal. The United States would not take part in a half-dozen or ten different "Marshall Plans." Aside from the basic inefficiency that sort of approach promoted, American policymakers had two other concerns. They did not want to re-create the prewar situation where each European state vainly sought shelter from the political crisis by individual methods; and they did not want Europe to undermine world recovery by an over-concentration upon "austerity."

Emerging from World War II as from a long nightmare, European governments were obliged, morally and practically, to move toward "social democracy" regardless of what party dominated within each state. Austerity was a key word, symbolizing not merely actual conditions but commitment and intent. In the United States, however, where the demands upon the state resulted in the "G.I. Bill" and the "Full Employment Act of 1946," the war had *created* prosperity far beyond the dreams of the most hopeful New Dealer.

Now, much more so than in the 1930s, American wealth was such that Congress could guarantee every veteran decent medical care, an education, and a low mortgage home, without touching upon the "social question." Public spending was safe—just so long as it was not undertaken to provide a platform for democracy-in-one-country. In Europe, the situation looked to be quite different. The election of the Labour Government in England, for example, reflected a popular feeling that the "socialists" were better equipped, and far more willing, to make the difficult decisions dictated by a semi-permanent condition of austerity. At the very least, Labour would get the priorities right. The "social costs" of peace would have to be borne by the capitalists, the ones who had always made the most out of war. Labour would not be put off any longer.

Under Secretary of State Robert Lovett spoke for many in the policymaking community who feared this trend of thought. It was a "disease" spreading across Europe, he said, that might eventually lay waste to "American efforts for international free trade." Should this happen, Congress might conclude that the United States should just "Let Europe go." Defense Secretary James Forrestal agreed, noting that the old isolationist prophets would rise up from their deathbeds to pronounce a final curse. Their bony fingers pointing to Europe they would say "we were wrong to have fought Germany and exterminated Hitler, thus finding ourselves in a much worse position—that of the Russians swarming over Europe and no balance of power available to check them." If it were in fact possible, as the isolationists insisted, to separate America and Europe, ideologically as well as economically and politically, that would make it easier on everyone. But it was simply not possible to believe that the American system could function successfully for very long under the combined pressures of political radicalism abroad (austerity carried to an extreme) and isolationism (self-containment) at home.

Thus confronted by the need to work with the Labour Government in England, and with similar regimes elsewhere, and, as already noted, perceiving certain very great advantages to doing so, American policymakers devised a sophisticated strategy for adapting to "austerity" demands. What this came down to was maintaining a balance of sympathy for social democracy within an international framework that ensured continued access to, and promoted the expansion of, the capitalist sector. For their part, moreover, European statesmen were aiming at much the same thing: a balance between encouraging the investment of needed dollars and preventing "Americanization" from going too far.

Washington would not seek to prevent the nationalization of various industries within states, but work instead for an international capitalist-oriented economy. Later on, Americans would become concerned about what happened to individual industries in the "developing nations," but that was not an immediate factor in policy planning. Finally, in postwar Europe Washington could count on— over the long-run—the re-emergence of a well-established and powerful capitalist class, as well as the normal antipathy social democratic parties had for Moscow-run Communists in their midst. After all, these posed a much greater danger in the reconstruction period than did American capitalism.

The upshot of all this was that Americans found it surprisingly easy to work with de Gaulle's successors and the Attlee-Bevin regime, despite fears that that might not be the case. In the wake of a failed Foreign Ministers' Conference at the end of 1947—at which the Big Four could not even engage in a meaningful dialogue about the German peace treaty—Bevin sought out Secretary Marshall. The former was already proving to be a staunch ally, and a most remarkable person. Added to these qualities, he now showed himself an inventive statesman as well. America's problems, he had declared, brought to mind the "plight" of Great Britain after the Napoleonic Wars. America now held more of the world's wealth than had Britain at the outset of its golden age. For approximately twenty years after Waterloo, Britain "practically gave away her exports." But she was repaid with a hundred years of peace.

It is hard to say what actually weighed more in Bevin's mind in late 1947, a concern for room for British socialism to maneuver without fear of a Soviet-inspired threat or a different version (more palatable to Americans) of Churchill's "special relationship." Either way, Bevin was no utopian. And he had no intention of leaving Europe to the dreamers who saw some way around, over, or through the developing Cold War. The disagreement between East and West over Germany, he told Secretary Marshall as the Conference broke up, was more than a "mere quarrel." The fundamental issue was where power was going to rest. A few weeks later, in early 1948, he elaborated on what he had called vaguely a "spiritual federation of the west."

Calling Great Britain and the United States the "chief protagonists" of the ethical and spiritual forces within Western civilization, Bevin proposed a "union" of democracies in Europe to construct a "counter attraction to the baleful tenets of communism within their borders and in recreating a healthy society. . . ." He did not use the term "military alliance," or the word "patriotism"—Tory concepts that jarred Labour sensibilities. But no one doubted what he meant. Twice in the months that followed, at the time of the Czech "coup" and the Berlin blockade, alarms were raised that the Russians actually were preparing to march. These crises made a military alliance not merely plausible but apparently necessary, if only as a tripwire mechanism to activate the American atomic force. By establishing credible military boundaries, what would become the North Atlantic Treaty Organization could serve as a genuine deterrent to Soviet attack.

Yet policymakers had a hard time even convincing themselves that the Russians would be foolish enough to launch a military invasion. Years later George Kennan would write,

Merciless as he could be, and little as his purposes may have coincided with ours, Stalin was entirely rational in his external policies; war, for him, was not just a glorified sporting event, with no aim other than military victory; he had no interest in slaughtering people indiscriminately, just for the sake of slaughtering them; he pursued well-conceived, finite purposes related to his own security and ambitions.*

Kennan also suggests that he was perplexed back then that the Europeans, who were actually doing very well in terms of economic recovery, should have initiated the discussions leading to NATO. "From that moment on, things moved with great rapidity. Gone, now, was all serious thought of a negotiated political solution to the problems of the continent. We now had, to the relief of many people, a new military opponent." "The Soviet Union," Dean Acheson would explain to Congress had been "drawn" into the troubled postwar situation, "and that made quiet relations within the rest of the world impossible." Acheson's subtlety and Bevin's straightforwardness made a solid team, as the former later recalled:

> There was also a very strong belief that economic recovery was closely connected with some sort of progress in the security field. It was felt that economic recovery had progressed through what might be called the primitive economic stages: agriculture had been brought up to a tolerable level, what had been done in industry was what could be done without the investment of any considerable capital. But to go beyond the point where the European countries were in mid-1948 required a greater degree, a greater sense of security before there could be the additional economic development which required their confidence, the return of capital which had taken flight from these countries, new investment in plant through the capital of the countries concerned.

NATO would have the immediate effect of altering the balance within member countries from a preoccupation with "socialism" and internal concerns to the defense of civilization and the re-creation of prosperity. Budgets would reflect the change, attitudes even more.

A small group within the policy-making elite became concerned, in fact, that over-militarization of the Cold War might produce negative economic results as priorities were shifted. Unable to understand completely why his colleagues did not share this perspective, Kennan, author of the famous "X" article that had set forth the basics of the "containment" worldview, wondered if American domestic politics accounted for the "deeply subjective" reactions he deplored, rather than any "theoretical considerations of our international position." Over-militarization, he feared, would delay Europe's economic re-

* *The Nuclear Delusion: Soviet-American Relations in the Atomic Age* (New York, 1982), p. 32.

covery. At most what needed to be done was to supply military assistance to a small inner group of nations—"whatever was necessary to bolster their internal morale (which was, after all, the heart of the matter). . . ."

Put off by Kennan's dissent, Acheson labeled the Soviet expert a mystic. Acheson was always in favor of simplifying things: for Congress, for Truman, and for the Russians. Of course internal morale was the key, but ordinary people seldom made distinctions along such lines. Acheson's formidable gifts for simplifying were put to a test by Republican Senator Alexander Wiley, which began when the lawmaker asked for an interpretation of the words "armed attack" in the proposed treaty. They were taken from the United Nations Charter, responded Acheson, where they were also not defined—and for a very sound reason. Any attempt to pin down specifics would only prompt an ingenious mind to develop a method that did not fit.

Wiley was ready for that answer, however, and moved the dialogue up a notch or two, making Acheson reach a bit. "We know about France and Italy," said the Senator, referring to fears about elections in those countries, and how they had wavered back and forth, buffeted by competing ideologies. It was not beyond peradventure to say that perhaps one of those countries, after it accepted membership in NATO, "will become Communist through the application of, let us call it, ideas. That would not be covered."

> *Secretary Acheson.* A purely ideological offensive would not be covered. If you would have a combination of the use of force with an internal fifth column, of course it would.

> *Senator Wiley.* Now we are getting down to where I was going to lead you. [!] An internal fifth column would be force if it were connected with the so-called mother country, Russia.

> *Secretary Acheson.* Well, what I was trying to point out is that what you are likely to get is both the use of external force and the use of internal revolution, as you have in Greece. That is the pattern which you are likely to see. That would clearly be an armed attack. Whether you would reach the same conclusion if the thing were entirely generated from inside, with external political stimulation, is another question.

Wiley and Acheson went on for several more minutes attempting to refine this last point, the internal limits of the NATO protectorate. The Greek "example" was already a standard for judging the "close calls." If Moscow had the kind of influence that the founding fathers of NATO supposed it had with foreign Communists, the alliance would have a political deterrent effect of vastly greater potential than the tripwire on military response. Even if it did not, the increase in internal security made possible by changed attitudes would frustrate a "Leftist" challenge to order and stability. Nor would its usefulness end there. NATO would permit the United States to harness the vast economic power of German industrial strength on behalf of European recovery without stirring fears that the Frankenstein "monster" had been unloosed again to rampage through the countryside, a creature without a conscience, the mistake of a marriage between Prussian nationalism and capitalism.

A month after the NATO treaty was signed, Secretary Acheson was in a jubilant mood. News had just come that the Russians had lifted the Berlin blockade, or had agreed to, and it was clear the West had triumphed in the most dramatic encounter yet in the Cold War. Buoyed by these twin successes, Acheson was ready to answer all questions. "The Atlantic Treaty has given these Western European nations," queried the old New Dealer and early Cold War critic, Senator Claude Pepper, "some confidence against a resurgent Germany as well as Russia?" "Yes," was his reply. "Yes. It works in all directions."

If that were so in Europe, however, it most certainly did not appear to be the case in Asia. Conditions out there mocked policymakers' claims that the epidemic of Communist expansion had been contained. Out there a process of slow strangulation seemed to be underway.

5

Stopping the Slow Process of Strangulation: The Korean War, Europe, and America

Judged by normal military standards, American accomplishments in the Korean War might be accounted meager. Washington could claim nothing more at the time than that it had avoided defeat. No peace treaty resulted. And when the truce negotiations at Panmunjom finally ended, after months of seemingly pointless haggling, Korea appeared no more important strategically than it had on June 25, 1950, the date of the initial North Korean attack.

The Joint Chiefs had never accorded Korea a high place on any master list of places to be defended. It was just about the least "cost effective" spot imaginable to engage an enemy. From his vantage point in Tokyo, moreover, General Douglas MacArthur had grown impatient waiting for the last American forces to be evacuated from the peninsula, lest they be drawn into what both he and Pentagon planners feared was coming: a civil war. Should that happen, America might face a distasteful choice between humiliation and disaster.

Yet within hours of the June 25 attack, MacArthur did an about face. "Here in Asia," he intoned, "is where the communist conspirators have elected to make their play for global conquest.... Here we fight Europe's war with arms while the diplomats there still fight it with words." MacArthur fared worst of all those about to become involved in Korea, ending his career in a welter of confusion and controversy, and leaving behind a tortuous stalemate where men fought and died for one hill indistinguishable from any other against a bleak horizon.

Over the years a leveling-out process has relieved MacArthur of sole responsibility for certain blunders, many of which, it now becomes apparent, were the result of questionable political decisions. That process is far from complete. The General's reputation will rise and fall as military experts and biographers replay his triumphant sweep across the Pacific in World War II and the ill-fated march north to the Yalu five years later. But what of the assertion, "Here we fight Europe's war with arms while the diplomats still fight it there with words."

That sentence can be read, as critics usually do, as a desperate attempt to redeem error by expanding the war to China. An "Asia First" strategy would have given MacArthur his chance to retire in triumph, the nation beholden to its far-seeing and courageous military genius. But there is another way to read that sentence—that is, as an accurate description of America's first attempt to apply limited power for diverse political ends.

For forty years Korea had been a part of the Japanese empire. Before that, however, the "Hermit Kingdom" had led a perilous existence on the periphery of world politics. As World War II came to an end, Japan's expulsion from the peninsula posed a tricky problem. Clearly, Korea could not be left to its own devices, however much policymakers might wish it so. How did the peninsula fit into Russian plans, for example? The Soviets had shown themselves no less anxious to acquire warm-water ports in the Far East than the Tsar's ministers had been. When they entered the war against Japan, the Russians already had Roosevelt's word that they could secure "leaseholds" over Dairen and Port Arthur. What else did they want?

A perennial longing for warm-water ports could be satisfied, but what if this were combined with an ideological stimulus—perhaps originating in Asia even, rather than in Russia itself? That could produce conflict on a different level. "It is believed," read a 1943 State Department memorandum, "that Korean guerrillas operating in Manchuria have close Soviet connections." In all likelihood Moscow would seek to use a "free" Korean movement for its own ends, just as it sponsored "free" German and Polish movements in Europe in the anti-Hitler struggle. But once victory was achieved, these "free" movements were not so easy to put back in the bottle.

In China the United States was trying to prevent an outbreak of civil war once the Japanese were defeated. To that end Roosevelt had sought to play the role of mediator between Russia and China, trading "concessions" (e.g. Dairen and Port Arthur) for Stalin's pledge to support Chiang Kai-shek's regime. To that end as well, the best solution to the Korean problem appeared to be an international "trusteeship," leading eventually to independence. Alas, the Cold War overtook the best-laid hopes and plans. All that was ever agreed to was that Russia should occupy Korea north of the 38th parallel, while American forces took charge below that line. Two "Koreas" resulted, each professing the social and political objectives of its mentor, both suffering from the disruption of internal economic ties, and both denied the right of self-determination.

Korean instability was largely hidden from view, however, by the mountainous problems towering above it over Asia—to say nothing of Europe. China was the most intractable. As feared, the Japanese withdrawal set the Chinese to fighting amongst themselves once again. Not only did the Kuomintang-Communist struggle frustrate postwar hopes for China, it threatened to upset plans for Japan and increase the difficulties of the decolonization process already beginning to worry Washington officials.

For a brief time Roosevelt had flirted with the notion of working with the Chinese Communists. The idea appealed to those who had despaired of the Kuomintang's ability to purge itself of corrupt elements. Hence in 1944 the President had authorized a secret "Dixie Mission" to Yenan, the seat of Mao Zedong's government. It was a unique undertaking, of uncertain duration and unclear purpose. The Dixie Mission constituted blatant interference in China's internal affairs; that was the only certain thing about it. Did it not presume, for example, that the United States formally recognized Mao's status as a "belligerent"? Was it possible to suppose that the Chinese Communists would obligingly disband their army at war's end, content to savor a reputation as defenders of the land, happy to return to peacetime pursuits? No, of course not, the implication of the Dixie Mission, as Republican critics would point out, was that either the President knew what he was doing and welcomed Chiang Kai-shek's downfall or he was duped by traitors allowed into the inner councils by New Deal zealots.

American policy toward China rushed along toward nowhere, little more than old slogans bobbing up and down on a flood-swollen river that would surge over the banks in the coming civil war. In March 1945 Roosevelt confided a little secret to the pro-Mao journalist Edgar Snow. He had it in mind to send supplies and liaison officers to the Eighth Route (Communist) Army as American forces drew near to the North China coast and Japan. Snow was puzzled. How could the United States support two governments in China? " 'Well, I've been working with two governments there.' The President threw his head back decisively. 'I intend to go on doing so until we can get them together.' "*

Roosevelt sounded as if he expected a race to Yenan. Not as important to him, surely, as the race to Berlin was to Churchill and Stalin, an American presence at the Communist "capital" still might have an impact on the shape of things to come in Asia. It might, but it didn't. Despite his confidence to Edgar Snow, FDR had neither the stamina nor the time left to convince himself to make such a dramatic gesture. The military supplies were not sent. His successors were not so imaginative, but to be fair, the options looked quite different with Russia already in Manchuria. The all important consideration was how to contain Soviet influence before it further destabilized a vast area already teetering as a result of the Japanese collapse, a wave of anti-colonial nationalism, events in China—and the atomic bomb. As the date approached for Russian entry into the Far Eastern war, agreed upon at Yalta, Americans worked feverishly to ready the bomb. The first thermonuclear weapon was dropped on Hiroshima on August 6, 1945; a second destroyed Nagasaki on August 9, 1945.

It had been expected that the Russians would declare war on August 8, and within a short time questions arose as to whether or not the bomb had been hurried into action to forestall that occurrence. Memoirs and archival records are replete with policymakers' speculations on the diplomatic significance of the bomb. On August 9, 1945, Russia did declare war on Japan, a move that, Truman records, "did not surprise us. Our dropping of the atomic bomb on Japan had forced Russia to reconsider her position in the Far East."

Later observers who have added their speculations to those of the participants have suggested several possible variations on the general theme of "atomic diplomacy." Not all of these are inconsistent with Truman's insistence that he only regarded the bomb as a military weapon. As the circle enclosed around Japan, Washington was anxious not to see the war end with headlines describing the defeat of the huge Japanese Kwantung army in Manchuria—by the Russians. (After all, it will be remembered that Stalin was obsessed about the

*Edgar Snow, *Journey to the Beginning* (New York, 1958), pp. 347–48.

possibility of a Western dash across Europe after the Red Army had suffered—all Russia had suffered—at the hands of the Germans.)

Matters of pride and prestige, then, as well as desire to demonstrate that Americans enjoyed a "Mandate from Heaven," have to be accounted for in any evaluation of "atomic diplomacy." Yet the bomb created two new problems for each one it appeared to resolve. Japan's empire disintegrated not soon enough to keep the Russians out of Manchuria, but elsewhere there was nothing to take its place. This situation produced a number of makeshift administrative decisions, including the use of Japanese troops as "policemen" (in South Korea), the ferrying of Chinese troops (to North China and Formosa), and the turning over of areas to former colonial powers (as in French Indochina). Each was fraught with specific consequences; together they threatened to undo the results of the Pacific war.

"It appears that if Manchuria and perhaps North China are not to pass to Chinese control," Secretary of State James F. Byrnes was warned of another peril at the end of November 1945 by his colleagues at War and Navy, "but rather to pass to Soviet control or separate states under its domination . . . then Russia will have achieved in the Far East approximately the objectives Japan initially set out to accomplish." Which was, in fact, the greater risk, the service heads asked, to allow that to happen or to get behind Chiang? They preferred the latter, a policy that looked a good deal more complicated and elusive from Byrnes' perspective.

American aid to the Chinese Nationalists (in any amount) would be ineffective without a change in Kuomintang attitudes. But the elements surrounding Chiang offered little hope of a transformation, on either the political or military front. Washington, indeed, estimated Mao's chances as greater than the odds then being offered in Moscow. When the Chinese Communist leader visited the Russian capital, Stalin advised him to disburse his People's Army and retreat to "pre-revolutionary" political tactics to ensure the best chance for survival while the American dynasty lasted.

The "highest-ranking" viceroy of that dynasty was General George C. Marshall, whose famous mission occupied only a span of months, a length, however, that seemed like an eternity to men pressed to find immediate solutions to a myriad of postwar problems. Marshall's proposals for a "coalition" government came to naught. His "successor," General Albert C. Wedemeyer, tried to convince Chiang of the wisdom of placing Manchuria under some form of international trusteeship. He, too, was unsuccessful.

Questioned by business magazine editors about China in mid-1946, President Truman admitted that the difficulties in China were "still very, very bad." That did not mean a pullback. "Our future, I think, lies in the Pacific, from a foreign trade standpoint, if we can get peace in the Pacific—and I think we will eventually get it." But perhaps not with Chiang. Consciously or unconsciously, the view began to insinuate its way into policy papers that Chiang was not worth saving—at least not at a price, morally as well as financially, that America could afford to pay. "While a collapse of the National Government would be deplorable," the head of the State Department's Policy Planning Staff, George F. Kennan, advised the new Secretary in early November of 1947, "it probably would not be a catastrophe for American interests in China."

The assumption here that "American interests" would survive, and, more important, were independent of Chiang, was akin to FDR's fleeting notion of establishing a "beachhead" on the North China coast close to the Chinese Communists under the cover of "military expediency." It was also a forerunner of the more serious notion that Mao would become an Asian "Tito." "No convincing evidence has been seen," Kennan said, "that, even should the Chinese National Government collapse, the communists could in the foreseeable future assume effective authority over all China and at the same time remain seriously susceptible to Soviet guidance or control in international affairs."

Kennan usually deplored Roosevelt's gestures in foreign affairs, but here was a statement that verged, albeit surrounded with diplomatic hedges, upon a suggestion that the sooner Chiang was gotten out of the way—the better. The major task in the days ahead, he said, was to keep the so-called China "lobby," a conglomerate of Chiang supporters with powerful friends in Congress, distracted while nature or fate took its course:

> While it is highly doubtful that any foreign intervention in China can produce the results desired, there exist strong traditional ties of sentiment between the U.S. and China and a highly vocal body of opinion in this country advocating U.S. aid to the National Government in the current Chinese civil conflict. For practical reasons these voices cannot be ignored. Furthermore, a certain amount of aid to China at this time

is justified as moral support to the Central Government, the rapid collapse of which would be contrary to our interests.

It follows, therefore, that the United States should extend the minimum aid necessary to satisfy American public opinion and, if possible, to prevent any sudden and total collapse of the Chinese Government.

The longer the civil war went on, and ironically perhaps especially if the Chinese Nationalists appeared to have a chance of actually winning, the greater the danger of an American involvement near Manchuria—"an area of vital military and political concern to the U.S.S.R." Russian mentality was such, added Kennan, that the Kremlin had probably interpreted the Yalta agreements as indicating American acceptance of pre-eminent Soviet interest there. "Should the U.S., however, aid the Nationalists to such an extent as would threaten a reversal of this process, the U.S.S.R. would probably take compensatory measures."

To the extent that the race to Yenan now became "Waiting for Mao!," Republican critics could build a strong case for a deliberate "sell out" of Chiang Kai-shek. The difficulty of pursuing a European policy along lines of the Truman Doctrine, while simultaneously adopting such a studied approach to Asia, was never resolved, not until the Korean War. In fact, policymakers themselves could not make up their minds. The race to Yenan was an event that never came off, and "Waiting for Mao!" never played well, not even before Democratic audiences.

Out of this frustration arose a redefinition of "containment" in Asia, known as the "defensive perimeter" concept. Far from precise itself, the perimeter concept placed Japan at the center of America's Asian policy. Chiang's obstinacy in refusing to consent, let alone aid, in the rebuilding of Japan as the "workshop of Asia," was quickly put down as another black mark beside his name in Washington. Certainly, also, it hardened Chiang's opponents of old and made new enemies for him in the corridors of power.

But China's grip on the American imagination had always been a powerful one. It could not be wrenched free without risking disenchantment generally, especially in the postwar "uncertain years" until Japan had been rehabilitated. One of the few fixed points in Asia was Korea. Logically enough, therefore, Under Secretary of State Dean Acheson made his most serious attempt to reconcile the Truman

Doctrine with policy in Asia, by policy toward *Korea*. Testifying in executive session on behalf of the President's request for funds to aid Greece and Turkey, Acheson made the great leap of faith.

Asked by Senator H. Alexander Smith to comment on criticisms that the United States might be spreading itself too thin already, Acheson agreed that there were parts of the world where "It would be silly to believe that we can do anything effective . . . That is within the Russian area of physical force. We are excluded from that." Then came this spontaneous affirmation: "There are other places where we can be effective. One of them is Korea, and I think that is another place where the line has been clearly drawn between the Russians and ourselves."

Before it was entirely settled, then, that Japan should once again become Asia's primary industrial power, Korea had *already* assumed an ideological importance far beyond its size, or even its utility as a cork-stopper to prevent an actual outflow of Communist influence. "It is here," Truman's personal representative to Korea, Edwin W. Pauley, wrote him, "where a test will be made of whether a democratic competitive system can be adapted to meet the challenge of a defeated feudalism, or whether some other system, i.e. Communism will become stronger." Our success throughout Asia, he asserted, may depend upon the outcome.

Republican critics and others were suspicious of this growing commitment to Korea. They suspected, not without some reason, that it stemmed from a guilty conscience about China. Doubts of another sort arose in the Pentagon. On April 4, 1948, Truman approved a recommendation of the Joint Chiefs of Staff that read: "The United States should not become so irrevocably involved in the Korean situation that an action taken by any faction in Korea or by any other power in Korea could be considered a 'casus belli' for the United States."

Was Korea inside or outside the defense perimeter? While the military position was unequivocal on paper, the pull of political forces was growing stronger every day. Japan's political recovery, for instance, was out of phase with its sluggish economic progress. Democracy would not have a long life in the Land of the Rising Sun, it was widely feared, without something more than MacArthur's efforts at artificial respiration. Those who cared little for Chiang's fate were given pause by this thought; for, without China where was Japan to find markets?

In short, Japan must return to the mainland, if not to China, then elsewhere. At Senate hearings in July 1949 the room was filled with words of praise for the benefits Japan had once bestowed upon Korea. "If you are going to restore the economy," insisted Elbert Thomas of Utah, "you have to restore the economy in connection with the type of trade and the type of thing that has been going on for the last 40 or 50 years."

Senator Vandenberg. Where does that lead you, Senator? . . .

Senator Thomas. Build up Japan; make her strong. . . . [W]hen the Japanese went into Korea, Korea was the nation in the world that was deliberately committing suicide. They were burning everything that grew to try to keep warm; they had no economy that was sustaining itself. They were overcome with money lenders, and even to this day, with all of the decent teaching about money lenders which the Japanese tried to do, you can not bribe a Korean to borrow money at under 12 or 13 percent. Those are old habits that last forever. So that whatever you have of the type of thinking in a people we like to think is like ourselves has been given to them by Japan.

Thus prompted, Administration witness Edgar Johnson, director of the Korea Division of the Economic Cooperation Administration (which administered the Marshall Plan in Europe), detailed the "complementarity" of the two economies. From Korea, Japan could count on supplies of food, marine products, and low-value minerals. In return, it could be expected that Japan would again invest in hydroelectric projects, textile mills, shipbuilding, and railways.

Johnson's "boss," Paul G. Hoffman, head of the Economic Cooperation Administration, summed up: "I do think—this is just a guess—we will have a chance to demonstrate in South Korea the democratic way of life can be successful on the economic front. In other words, that people can have liberty and they can have bread." Although Hoffman insisted that Korea was "infinitely simpler as compared with China," the Administration's request for $150 million to aid Korea ran into trouble in the House of Representatives.

Truth was, Korea was smaller, but it was not simpler. Having failed to persuade the Soviets to cooperate in all-Korean elections, or, before that, to allow the problem to be resolved in the United Nations, the United States went ahead with elections in South Korea. As expected, the winner was the old nationalist leader, Syngman Rhee, whose domestic policy encompassed one objective: reunification. The election, and Rhee's methods of governing, produced a new worry in Washington. Was he really going the way of Chiang Kaishek? At the end of 1948, Truman's newly appointed Ambassador, John J. Muccio, reported to Washington that Rhee's government was "incompetent" and "without strong public support."

In North Korea, by contrast, a government had emerged, that, while certainly more authoritarian, was also far more stable than its southern counterpart. Both "Koreas" made feints at one another, and actual raids across the 38th parallel occurred upon occasion. Americans in Seoul, Tokyo, and Washington, all took seriously Rhee's vows to reunite the peninsula. And they were all determined that he should not be given an opportunity to involve American forces in such a wild endeavor. As a result the North Koreans had at their disposal, by the time of the June 1950 attack, modern weapons including heavy artillery, tanks, and aircraft, while south of the parallel, recalled General Matthew Ridgway, "we left a rather sorry force that we did not even dare call an army." Washington imposed this severe restriction on the military, claimed Ridgway, because it was obsessed with disengagement, so much so "that our people in South Korea were not permitted to use the word 'army' in referring to the police force we were endeavoring to build to keep order after our withdrawal." Korea was written off.

How strange, then, that Administration spokesmen continued to promote Korea and ask for money to complete the experiment in nation-building. Thus Paul Hoffman's assertion that South Korea, far from following China's path to perdition, had set forth on the high road to liberal democracy:

> [T]his Government of Korea today does represent the people. In other words I should say today an overwhelming percentage of the people voted for this form of government and the Government is their government. In addition to that you have something of the crusading spirit among the Government people that you had in the early days of the Chinese Republic.

That testimony can be read several ways. But certainly Korea represents for Hoffman the China that should have been, and could be, if the Pentagon director of intelligence was correct in his estimate that the military forces in Korea were about equal numerically, and in other ways as well. "They do have good equipment," General W. E. Todd said. "Fifty thousand of their forces have standard United

States Army equipment." Besides that, he went on, the Russians had little to gain in Korea. "We feel that if the Soviets attach any priority to areas in which they would like to move by means of armed aggression, Korea would be at the bottom in that list of priorities."

"You get a real feeling out there," Hoffman soared to the heights,

of evangelism on the part of this group. Syngman Rhee considers himself the George Washington of Korea, and I think that on the whole that kind of atmosphere pervades in high official circles. . . . After all, I think one way we could perhaps learn to appreciate liberty more is to have it taken away from us for 40 years or more. They have been under Japanese domination and they are determined to make a success of this Korean Republic.

In this context, John Foster Dulles's later comments on Korea as a "moral salient in the otherwise solid Communist despotism" in North Asia, and his praise of Rhee as a worthy successor to the ancient church fathers out on the periphery of the Christian world, seem restrained and even circumspect. As each witness sat down, the stakes rose higher, to imaginative peaks, finally, that rivaled the Himalayas. "If we fail," testified Under Secretary of State James Webb, "we will provide a rallying cry by which the Communist leaders in all countries from Japan to India will attract more and more people to their cause."

Unfortunately, and despite these glowing accounts of Rhee's government, there were many ways to fail. How could the United States hope to maintain its influence in Japan or Southeast Asia if, following the now imminent collapse of Nationalist China, yet another country where American prestige was so deeply committed failed to make effective use of U.S. aid but instead followed a blundering domestic policy that neither offered citizens democratic rights, nor, what was even worse, safety from their enemies? Suppose, on the other hand, that Rhee initiated a rollback policy. What a fine example that would be! If he won, criticism throughout Asia would weaken the ideological front. If he lost, America would be humiliated.

On June 28, 1949, at the same time the Administration witnesses were testifying on behalf of economic aid to Korea, George F. Kennan acknowledged the strength of the adverse reaction to its general Far Eastern policy. The Policy Planning Staff, he wrote Secretary Acheson, felt that the "Executive should aggressively assume the offensive in what is rapidly developing into a major issue between it and the Legislature." The first step should be the publication of a "White Paper," followed by an anonymous interpretative article based on that collection of documents, and a speech by President Truman affirming the correctness of the China policy.

> Finally, and perhaps most importantly, the foregoing train of events should be immediately followed by a series of carefully and closely timed actions by this Government designed to demonstrate a positive and affirmative policy in the Far East. These acts will, of course, speak louder than any words and will serve to take the eye of both the public and Congress off the dreary record of the past.

Among the steps taken to pursue the policy outlined by Kennan was the summoning of a group of "consultants," Asian experts and others, to the State Department for discussions on the future direction a positive and affirmative approach might take. The "terrific problem" the United States faced, Kennan told the consultants, was how the Japanese were going to survive "unless they reopen some sort of empire toward the south." Korea was not enough. After all the discussants had had their say, a general thesis was proposed: "We should seek to insure that the general revolutionary movement in this area, through which the indigenous peoples are endeavoring to attain national independence and improve conditions of life, is not captured by Moscow. In areas in which the movement has already been captured by Moscow, we should seek to free it."

A much modified version of this paper prepared for Acheson and Truman was sent to the Secretary on November 16, 1949. Gone from the consultants' reworked thesis was any mention of what could only be termed a rollback policy. "The situation in areas already firmly controlled by Communist regimes must be met by a recognition of realities rather than by a fruitless attempt to reverse or ignore the tide of events." Also diluted was the stronger statement in the consultants' report warning that the South Korean Government should not be allowed to fail.

In any event, the principal result of these discussions was to tie South Korea, identified as a "demonstration project," into a post-China Southeast Asian policy. Policymakers themselves may not have realized how tightly they were binding the threads that would make it impossible to perceive events in Korea except in relation to a larger scheme of things.

The consultants had also recommended against early diplomatic recognition of the new regime in China. That would amount to a passive acceptance that the United States could do nothing to influence the Asian revolutionary movement. If recognition was given, it should be as part of a reformulated Asian policy, and not until that policy had demonstrated an active determination to take the lead in resisting Communist efforts to capture the revolutionary movement. A paradox was in the making. The United States could not recognize Mao's government until it had shown the world Communism was not the wave of the future; once it did that by its reaction to the North Korean attack, it could not recognize Peking because China was an aggressor nation.

Meanwhile, Truman was very much pleased by the work of the consultants. He had found himself, he told Acheson, thinking about the Asian situation "in a quite new way." The Secretary responded by elaborating on what he thought the consultants had meant in their discussion of China policy. One approach that could be adopted would be to oppose the Communist regime, harass it, needle it, "and if an opportunity appeared to attempt to overthrow it." The other would be to seek to detach it from Moscow, "and over a period of time encourage those vigorous influences which might modify it." The consultants were unanimous in favor of the second course.

With Republican criticism mounting, soon to be led by Senator Joseph McCarthy's slashing attack on Communist conspirators in government, Truman had to approach the Chinese puzzle with great caution. He was strongly inclined to agree with Acheson's recommendation, he said, but would reserve final judgment. What he was waiting for, apparently, was some way of getting a handle on the paradox, some way of creating a "situation of strength" that would permit him to recognize the new government in China and to exploit the assumed Sino-Soviet tensions.

On January 12, 1950, Acheson appeared before the National Press Club. Remembered ever after as the defense perimeter speech, and criticized accordingly for placing South Korea in a twilight zone outside that line, the main thrust of his remarks was actually directed toward the need to understand Asian nationalism. Nationalism was the predominant revolutionary force at work, he asserted, and it was an amalgam of revulsion against poverty and determination to resist foreign domination. The first, he went on, played the major role in Chiang's defeat, but the second would produce "righteous anger" against any effort to interfere in China's internal affairs. If the United States demonstrated restraint about Taiwan, all the "wrath" and "hatred" stored up in China would fall upon the Soviet Union—which foolishly sought to detach "the four northern provinces of China."

It was a bravado performance. And it all went for naught. Later no doubt Acheson regretted having given the North Koreans a "green light" to invade, but had he been offered an opportunity to take back some of his words, the Secretary would still have had to say something to convince another audience, the Chinese Communists, that the United States did not intend to prod Syngman Rhee to invade North Korea so that an excuse might be created for a "reopening" of the Chinese civil war. It was also important to clarify the South Korean–American relationship because the United States had decided to establish atomic bomber bases on Okinawa and to go ahead unilaterally with a Japanese peace treaty.

American diplomatic officials abroad had been told that the decision about China was wait for the dust to settle, then the question of recognition could be discussed in a clearer atmosphere. Called the "Tito" option, this proposition demanded a great deal from pro-Chiang Americans, as well as an equal responsiveness (and understanding) from Mao Zedong. Clouds of vapor kept rising in the Formosa straits, however, constant reminders that Chiang Kai-shek still ruled if only on an island. He was an embarrassment. But for Acheson to do any more than he had already, or say anything beyond what he had said at the National Press Club, would expose the Administration, and him personally, to the charge that the United States had "put out a contract" on Chiang.

Whither Acheson's ruminations took him during these weeks no one can be sure, but certainly not that far. How much easier it was to think about Europe. The National Press Club speech, as a matter of fact, was one of a series devoted to a reassessment of all aspects of American foreign policy in the wake of the news that Russia had exploded an atomic bomb. Inside the State Department, meanwhile, the policy planners were at work on what would become National Security Council Paper, Sixty-eight (NSC-68), the basic outline of Cold War policy for years to come.

Boiled down to a few words, NSC-68 recommended increased spending on defense, not less than 10 percent of the gross national product, and, far less well-known, a political offensive, including covert actions, against the Soviet "empire." The peril-point, predicted its authors, would come in 1954, when the Russians would have approximate parity in atomic weapons. But speculations about whether, and where, the Russians might jump the gun, must have filled many lunch-hours. With no bombs in reserve, Truman had once promised to lay waste to all Japan unless a surrender was forthcoming. The Soviets did not have to have a bomb ready to deliver, then, to play the same game.

Atomic diplomacy had become a two-sided affair. With the Russians in possession of an atomic bomb, what became of the tripwire strategy? More important, what became of the rationale for NATO? A Russian atomic bomb severely weakened the political side of the alliance, by forcing back on itself the original operating assumption. Safe under the nuclear umbrella, Europeans could prosper. The umbrella reached wherever the NATO flag flew. The alliance provided in this way a sense of unity, yet room for national pride. It promised a huge "domestic" market across Europe, yet assured individual nations of internal stability. A Russian-American stand-off could well fragment the alliance, either by making Europeans afraid, or by inclining them inward again—back toward ancient ways and self-defeating xenophobia.

Odds were against such a dramatic loss of cohesion; but they evened out considerably when it came to prospects for completing what had been started, yet alone what had been scheduled for the future. Premised on an increasingly close economic relationship between recipient nations, the Marshall Plan could well evaporate, or find its place in textbooks close by the Kellogg-Briand Pact or the Dawes Plan. Already a severe recession was causing the industrial world to have a bad case of jitters, and statisticians to post some rather gloomy estimates about when, for example, the "dollar gap" might be brought under control. Until statesmen had a good reading on that problem, the chances for genuine economic cooperation in Europe were none too healthy.

The Berlin blockade, to take another example, had been lifted, but the basic German "issue" remained unresolved. One answer was to secure the Germans inside NATO, a thought that opened old wounds and stirred the deepest fears. Before the experience of "limited war," therefore, an atomic balance involved a crisis of confidence in American leadership—or so it seemed to anxious Washington policymakers.

So then, what new stimulus to Western unity was there that might check the corroding effects of these acids? On March 21, 1950, Secretary of State Acheson met with Republican Congressman Christian Herter. He was deeply troubled, Herter began, by the false sense of security that pervaded the land. To check the deterioration of the world situation before it got any worse, he went on, the United States should make one final offer to negotiate Soviet-American differences. If the Russians refused, "we should label them the barbarians they are," force them out of the United Nations, and break off diplomatic relations.

Acheson did not feel that matters had reached quite that point, but the past six to nine months had witnessed a "trend" developing, which, if permitted to go on, could reduce the American position. The Russians were bent on world domination, but the United States could not afford to initiate policies that its allies found repugnant, leaving us "thoroughly confused politically and economically."

Well, replied the Congressman, what could be done to arouse the people short of breaking relations with Moscow? "I replied," minuted Acheson, "that I do not believe it will be necessary to create such a situation, the chances are too good that the Russians will do so themselves." Describing several ways this might come about, Acheson arrived in front of the Asian defense perimeter. "Finally, I referred to the possibility of an overall attack on Formosa from the mainland of China where we understand air strips are being built, Soviet planes are being furnished, and Soviet crews are training Chinese crews."

Joining Acheson in the State Department at this time was his successor-to-be, John Foster Dulles. Dulles was employed in the work of drafting a peace treaty with Japan, the expectation being that whatever he put his seal of approval on would be acceptable to Republicans. He did not intend to work in anonymity. "It seemed desirable for me to gain some political stature," he told Truman, "for myself in my own right." Promising only to support policies that met his requirements, Dulles apparently felt he could "negotiate from strength" with Truman:

> . . . it was important that there should be some early affirmative action in the field of foreign affairs which would restore the confidence of the American people that the Government had a capacity to deal with the Communist menace. My impression was that many Americans had lost

confidence as a result of what had happened, particularly in the East. It was this lack of confidence which I felt made it possible for men like McCarthy to make a deep impression upon the situation and to achieve prominence.

Some days later, in a memorandum to himself, Dulles elaborated on the power shift in Asia, and how it put at jeopardy American interests behind any defense perimeter one could devise. The very idea of a defense perimeter illustrated what was wrong. It was static, the world, dynamic. Disaster could only "be prevented if at some doubtful point we quickly take a dramatic and strong stand that shows our confidence and resolution."

As word came into Washington of the North Korean attack, the "dreary record of the past" (as Kennan had put it) faded like a bad dream. So did the idea of the "Tito" option. The first cable from Ambassador Alan Kirk in Moscow offered an instant analysis that no later policy paper changed. "Kremlin's Korean adventure," it read, did not signal a readiness to fight an all-out war, and "thus offers us opportunity to show that we mean what we say by talking of firmness, and at same time, to unmask present important Soviet weaknesses before eyes world and particularly Asia where popular concept Soviet power grossly exaggerated as result recent Soviet political and propaganda successes that area."

Truman was anxious to have additional confirmation that the Russians did not intend to involve themselves on the battlefield. Meanwhile, he gave the press a statement that amounted to a declaration of war on "Communism." "The attack upon Korea makes it plain beyond all doubt that Communism has passed beyond the use of subversion to conquer independent nations and will now use armed invasion and war." Phrasing the statement in this fashion permitted him to avoid the possible danger of a Russian "reaction" to American steps, including MacArthur's early decision to allow bombing raids north of the 38th parallel.

It did more. It allowed him to lump together a variety of "Communist" aggressions—the Philippines, French Indochina, and the Formosan strait—and to unfreeze the policy-making machinery that had gotten stuck over the China "issue" since the failure of the Marshall Mission. Acheson was delighted with a conversation he had with the Norwegian Ambassador Wilhelm Munthe de Morgenstierne, who was full of congratulations for the decision to defend South Korea.

"There have been skeptics in Europe," he said. "This action will sweep away the skeptics." Other European representatives in Washington commented that, since the China debacle and the Russian atomic bomb, there had been an increase in Communist "Fifth Column" activities in their countries.

Yes, nodded the Secretary to each comment, "the dangers of inaction were much greater than the dangers of facing the problem in Korea. . . ." "This situation has pulled us together," he went on,

> I said that the communist intention to take Formosa and Indo-China had been evident; that if they had been allowed to take Formosa, following this thrust in Korea, the effect on the Philippines would have been drastic; . . . Formosa is the traditional jumping-off place for attack on the Philippines.

> Ambassador Morgenstierne repeated that if Korea had been allowed to pass, then other areas would have followed. I agreed emphatically, stating that I thought Asia would have fallen apart.

> Ambassador Morgenstierne said it was a great moment in history. I said I thought it was a turning-point in world history.

Historians have generally agreed with Acheson: it was a turning point in world history. They differ among themselves, however, about timing. For some, the war itself was the turning point. Others see the war as simply confirming (and simplifying) analyses originating in a general concern about "slow suffocation." Either way, the confusion disappeared; but with it went important restraints upon a developing hubris.

About to leave "active duty" in the State Department, George Kennan gave an insightful and prophetic account of this rising pridefulness, born of paradox, mixing frustration and supreme confidence, blindness and far-sighted vision—that would one day lead Lyndon Johnson to try to carry the Great Society deeper and deeper into the Heart of Darkness, only to find no solid ground there to support it.

Kennan, of course, was already famous for "second thoughts," an attribute that displeased Secretary Acheson, who found it of very little use in dealing with either day-to-day problems or in formulating strategy. In this instance, Kennan was reviewing Dulles's work on the Japanese treaty. Asked if he approved of the draft, the former Ambassador to Moscow and head of the Policy Planning Staff decided that he would put down his thoughts on Far Eastern Policy, if only for purposes of clarification before taking his departure.

Kennan then proceeded to discuss the failure to define realistic objectives in Korea, the wide latitude given to General MacArthur, the potential conflicts ahead in China policy, the appalling position of guaranteeing the French in their Indochina undertaking, "which neither they nor we, nor both of us together, can win," and the perverse insistence upon leaving American forces in Japan, where they would only turn the Japanese against the United States and make a settlement with Russia still more unlikely. "The course upon which we are today moving is one, as I see it, so little promising and so fraught with danger that I could not honestly urge you to continue to take responsibility for it."

Acheson was not the sort to be "urged" into doing, or not doing, anything. Neither did his sense of the fitness of things allow him to overlook the implication here that Kennan had a superior understanding of policy requirements. For a time, Kennan's doomsday prophecies seemed laughable. After the early shock of the North Korean attack and the retreat to Pusan, General MacArthur launched a brilliant offensive, landing at Inchon on the coast behind North Korean forces. The objective of the war changed: it became "liberation." The fall of North Korea would signal to the world that the tides of power were now running against "Communism," and the defense perimeter, pushed back to a small corner of Korea, now expanded outward in such a triumphant manner as to render silent at last the government's critics.

Acheson could bid farewell to Kennan, and to all the others who had misgivings. He would need this respite.

Much debated afterwards, the decision to cross the 38th parallel occasioned little discussion in the event. This was not yet a time that tried men's souls. After Inchon, and the successful counterattack out of Pusan, it was simply assumed that a "real" victory in Korea could not be forgone. On August 17, 1950, even before Inchon, the American Ambassador to the United Nations, Warren Austin, had announced that North Korean forces should surrender in order that the country could be reunited by elections!

Neither Truman nor Acheson ever overlooked the political angle. What would Republicans say, if, having risked humiliation in the first days of the war, the Administration shied from an opportunity to put

the North Koreans to rout? Truman knew what they would say, and
he didn't want to hear it. But to stop there and look no more would be
a mistake. There was a very serious objective to be gained in crossing
that hated dividing line. In accepting the inevitability of a covenant
with power, Wilson had placed liberal hopes on a League of Nations.
Roosevelt had wrestled with the need to reconcile the war-making
alliance with a general postwar collective security system. Truman
had substituted the NATO protectorate. But that did not answer, not
completely anyway, the contradiction inherent in taking the lead in
setting up the United Nations, only to follow a unilateralist policy
with the Truman Doctrine, the Marshall Plan, and finally NATO
itself.

If America went its own way, what would happen to the liberal
concept—and, more important, what would the Soviets do? The
Russian veto resounded around the Security Council in these years,
hanging a border of crepe over its early debates, but that situation
might change. Americans never felt entirely at ease without a means
of legitimizing the use of coercive measures. At the time of the North
Korean attack, the Russians were strangely absent from the table, an
odd circumstance, but it gave Washington a chance to secure passage
of resolutions calling upon member nations to supply South Korea
with the means and men to resist the invasion.

Pursuit of the North Koreans back across the 38th parallel thus
became a duty, a fulfillment of Wilson's original conception of the
role of an international "state." The 38th was a psychological barrier,
a line separating past failures and future success. Unfortunately,
everything at stake in Korea depended upon things falling into place,
exactly into place. In his memoirs, Truman would write that he had
been anxious to meet with MacArthur to make sure that the General
fully appreciated the risks of Chinese intervention as the UN forces
approached the Yalu River, the boundary between Korea and Manchuria. When they finally met on Wake Island, in mid-October
1950, Truman did caution his military commander along these lines,
but by far the most time was spent on planning for Korea's reunification.

Soon after the conference opened, for example, Assistant Secretary of State Dean Rusk asked MacArthur whether or not in the
future it would be possible to turn over the responsibilities of the
American military advisory group to the United Nations. This was
followed by Averell Harriman's question about Korea's "psychologi-

cal rehabilitation." Ambassador Muccio suggested that this could be handled by using South Koreans north of the parallel. "We could set up a very effective system with a radio or loudspeaker in every school and village center."

Truman interjected a remark that sound trucks were a good idea, "I won two elections with them." But, as the President noted, the question was, how would Syngman Rhee take to the idea of an early election? He would not like it, said Ambassador Muccio. Discussion shifted to the possibility of having "local" elections in the North, held under the auspices of officials either appointed from the South or recommended by Rhee's government. As they pondered Asia's future in the light of this Korean success, the conferees cast about for some way to make it more permanent, perhaps a Pacific counterpart to NATO. Admiral Arthur Radford was the most insistent: "The peace will be upset again in six months if you do not take steps to stop it. We just have to face the facts of life. We must continue the policy followed in Korea to maintain the peace." "It" was the supposed Russian-sponsored Communist advance across Asia. Korea had shown that "it" could indeed be halted, but the issue would not always be so clear-cut. "The situation in Indo-China is the most puzzling of all as to what we can do or what we should do."

Truman agreed with Radford. The difficulty with coming to grips with the challenge in Indochina was the French "colonialist" attitude. Bolstered by MacArthur's military success in Korea, as opposed to European failures in fighting Asian Communists, the President vowed to have another try. "If the French Prime Minister comes to see me, he is going to hear some very plain talk. I am going to talk cold turkey to him."

The euphoria settled a bit when General MacArthur reminded the group that America was not entirely a free agent in the Korean War: recent UN resolutions calling for all-Korean elections had seemed to equate the puppet North Korean leaders and Syngman Rhee. If the Koreans should turn against America "as a result of some UN opposition to the Rhee Government," warned the General, that would be the "greatest calamity" of all. Truman thought so, too:

The President: This cannot be done and should not be done. We must insist on supporting this government.

Mr. Rusk: We have been working and explaining our point of view in the United Nations but there has been an effective propaganda campaign against the Rhee Government which has infected some of the UN delegations.

The President: We must make it plain that we are supporting the Rhee Government and propaganda can "go to hell."

What is so striking about this exchange is the new-found confidence in Syngman Rhee. In a moment of apparent military victory—and because Korea meant so much now on a panoramic view of the Cold War—local realities all but disappeared. What applied in Korea, also applied in Indochina, if the French could only see it, and other places as well. Later accounts of the Wake Island Conference and its aftermath, including Truman's memoirs, imply that political officials were somehow dragged behind General MacArthur's chariot wheels as he set off in a mad dash for the Yalu. Not at all.

Aside from the "liberating" effects of General MacArthur's sweep across the 38th parallel, Korea had a serendipitous fall-out in other areas. "Korea was perhaps the only conflict in history," asserts Eliot Janeway, "which moved the world economy closer to international equilibrium."* The "dollar gap" that only seemed to worsen as Western Europe recovered was practically closed in little more than a year. In 1949 America's trade surplus even in a recession year stood at $6.7 billion. With a year that line on the graph fell to $2.3 billion, as American purchases increased in nearly every category. Dollars paid to commodity-exporting countries as the nation shifted to "military" Keynesianism turned them into solvent customers for industrial products, not only from America, but also from Europe and Japan. Prosperity paid huge dividends also in providing a platform for an era of international stability that would last for nearly three decades.

But MacArthur's chariots never reached the Yalu. At 4:46 a.m. on November 28, 1950, the Pentagon received an urgent message from MacArthur's headquarters. "We face an entirely new war." A massive wave of Chinese had suddenly appeared in front of the General's forces, driving them back in a retreat that threatened to turn into a rout. Thoughts of liberation fled from policymakers's minds. The new mood bordered on panic. "We want to avoid getting sewed up in Korea," Secretary of Defense George C. Marshall said to a White House conference later that day, and discover a way to get out "with

---

* *The Economics of Crisis: War, Politics & the Dollar* (New York, 1968), pp. 236–37.

honor." Truman's hints at a press conference that he was considering the use of the atomic bomb only added to the picture of disarray in Washington, and brought British Prime Minister Clement Attlee scurrying to the White House on a mission to reassure Europe that a world conflagration did not depend upon saving MacArthur's reputation.

His usual aplomb badly askew, Acheson groped for reasons to explain Chinese unreasonableness. "Everything in the world" had been done to reassure them, "and I should suppose that there is no country in the world which has been more outstanding in developing the theory of brotherly development of border waters than the United States." He recovered quickly, however, and put the American "case" before the world. The sole purpose America had for waging war in Korea, and for its foreign policy in general, was "to create and to maintain the environment in which the great American experiment in liberty could flourish and exist."

> That is all we have asked of the world. We have no special interests that we want to achieve. We don't want to dominate anyone. We don't want territory. We don't want any of the things for which empires in the past have fought. We want only a world in which we can be free and in which everyone else can be free.

If Acheson's updated version of the Declaration of Independence boosted morale, the stalemate on the battlefield remained worrisome. Eisenhower won the White House for the Republicans because of his image as a liberator; but, beginning with the truce in Korea, he was successful in office because he did not live up to it. And, in fact, the only liberation that really concerned Ike and his dour Secretary of State, John Foster Dulles, was liberation from an albatross they imagined had been hung about America's neck by the foolish actions of its Allies in failing to meet the "Third World" challenge.

6

The Perils of Liberation

Before China intervened, Korea looked to be a splendid "limited" war. Only in retrospect did the fateful decision to cross the 38th parallel seem such a horrible mistake. It proved to be Truman's undoing. But not even his worst critics blamed the President for anything other than faulty military judgment, whether they thought it had been a mistake to go north with MacArthur, or to accept a stalemate by placing restraints on the General's conduct of the war. Eisenhower's skillful use of his credentials as a military leader further obscured the political content of American foreign policy in the years after Korea. These credentials made it possible for the Republicans to promise liberation, and to continue to mislead themselves as well as the nation about the objectives of foreign policy and the nature of the Cold War.

In the Eisenhower years no dents were made in the Iron Curtain. Congress passed resolutions demanding freedom for the "captive nations," and Radio Free Europe called upon the peoples of Eastern Europe to revolt. When they did, in the 1956 Hungarian Revolution, Eisenhower refused to intervene—citing the danger of nuclear war. It was an embarrassing moment. And it planted seeds of discontent at home, seeds that would bear bitter fruit a decade and a half later during a Polish crisis.

Secretary of State John Foster Dulles, who had written the original "Liberation" plank of the Republican platform, took it in his stride. He admired their courage, Dulles said of the "Freedom-Fighters," but the way chosen by the Poles (as of 1956)—"gradual evolution or inching their way"—was the only possible policy. What Dulles deplored most, it almost seemed, was the Russians' inability to handle the situation without making it a peril to themselves and the world. "When [Foreign Minister Andrei] Gromyko came to talk with me at my home," Dulles confided to an aide,

> I said to him: "You want to be surrounded by friendly states. We want that for you too. We do not want a cordon sanitaire around Russia. But the way you are going you will be surrounded by hatred." Gromyko said, "We know what we are doing, we do not want advice from you."

Actually, Dulles was in a poor position to give advice at the time of the Hungarian revolt. Even more embarrassing than what the United States could not do (or would not risk) to rescue the Hungarians cut off in the streets of Budapest by Russian tanks was what it failed to prevent in the Middle East. In an effort to reverse Egyptian nationalization of the Suez Canal, and to topple Gamal Abdel Nasser from power, an Anglo-French-Israeli force had launched an invasion. "Why did you stop?" Dulles reportedly asked of British Foreign Secretary Selwyn Lloyd a few weeks later. Even Lloyd admitted, however, that what this meant was, "Why did you make such a mess of it?"

At odds with his image as a Cold War moralist, and no doubt against the grain in other ways, having a chat with Gromyko, or a few words in the hall with Selwyn Lloyd, were part of a day's work for Dulles. Any good lawyer knew that. The better the system worked outside the courtroom, the fewer times a "trial" would be necessary. In a nuclear age the wisdom of avoiding such contests was obvious. An austere, Bible-reading man, the Secretary was also given to Old Testament-style prophecy. But the *real* Dulles was a cautious man, who had a New Englander's love for a wall—and his fear of "the frozen-ground-swell under it," that "spills the upper bowlders in the sun. . . ."

Revolutionary earthquakes, whether they occurred in Eastern Europe or spilled the bowlders in Africa and Asia, rendered the law useless. What Dulles felt it was incumbent upon him to do to convince *everyone* that "inching their way" was the only safe policy. In this context, liberation took on a meaning that was almost a polar opposite from what both popular conceptions of the day and later historical treatments of the Secretary's "brinkmanship" have suggested. Many of the worst gaffes Dulles made were the result of over-compensation—a point first made by George F. Kennan.

Kennan also was among the first to point out that the new Administration's policies were no more militaristic than those being pursued
with such vigor in the final years of its predecessor. A fellow Presby-
terian, Kennan saw Dulles's dilemma: "Mr. Dulles . . . did not want to
have me around. He knew very well that whatever he might say
publicly, he was going to have to pursue in reality in this coming
period pretty much the policy toward the Soviet Union with which
my name had been often connected."

Dulles was sensitive to Kennan's presence not simply because of
possible complications with the Republican right wing but also
because the latter was a constant reminder of the European emphasis of early Cold War policy. For different reasons, the new Secretary
found Kennan's attitudes about Japan and Asia just as unpalatable as
had Dean Acheson. "Containment" could not be worked in Asia if
the United States merely took up positions in support of the colonial
powers. Things were going to have to be said that would offend old
allies; it might be easier to say these things, and accomplish the goals
of "Liberation," if the bowlders were tapped in place with harder
rhetoric. As Robert Frost wrote,

> We have to use a spell to make them balance:
> "Stay where you are until our backs are turned!"

In this strange way Dulles became devoted to keeping the Cold
War walls well-mended. He was sure that without some "spell" he
would lose all control of the decolonization process. Dean Acheson
had seen all he wanted of this problem in the 1950–51 Iranian crisis.
He did not share, Acheson said after leaving the Department, the
view that there was a great contest going on "for this whole area." Its
importance from the point of view of the diplomacy of the United
States "comes from the terrific potentialities of trouble . . . between us
and our allies."

That was precisely the view that Dulles wanted to "liberate" Americans from, especially his fellow Atlanticists. He felt a great debt to
Woodrow Wilson, and a sympathy for that President's problems as
the first to have to deal with the "Third World" in a serious way.
Wilson, Dulles wrote a prominent political commentator, was "the
greatest public man I have ever known." On the question of colonialism Wilson's thoughts on the American occupation of the Philippines
were especially relevant, according to Dulles, who then quoted them
at length:

Liberty is not itself government. In the wrong hands, in hands unpracticed, undisciplined, it is incompatible with government. Discipline must precede it, if necessary, the discipline of being under masters. Then will self-control make it a thing of life and not a thing of tumult, a tonic not an insurgent madness in the blood. Shall we doubt, then, what the conditions precedent to liberty and self-government are, and what their invariable support and accompaniment must be, in the countries whose administration we have taken over in trust, particularly in those far Philippine Islands whose government is our chief anxiety? . . . . [sic] They can have liberty no cheaper than we got it. They must first take the discipline of law, must first love order and instinctively yield to it. . . . [sic] We are old in this learning and must be their tutors.

But Dulles had little time to do more than quote Wilson. Certainly no one believed that the speeded process of decolonization allowed policymakers leisure for reflection on what the Third World should do. Besides finding a way of fulfilling the new obligations of a tutor, moreover, the Secretary had to consider always America's role as manager of the "Free World's" economy, Inevitably, there would be conflicts. European unity, which the United States had encouraged (and prodded along) since the Marshall Plan, required an external outlet for European products. Pressure for increased East-West trade was already evident, as was concern for a strong "post-colonial" position in Africa and Asia.

Dulles had benefited greatly from his experience negotiating the Japanese peace treaty. He had come away from that assignment more aware than ever of the nature of the connection between European and Asian economic problems in a Cold War context. All of Western Europe, it now appeared, was faced with Germany's old choice, Eastern Europe or colonial Africa, while Japan confronted a similar decision, China or Southeast Asia. To put the position this way is, of course, to over-simplify. These were not "either/or" questions, however much they appeared so, but matters of emphasis. In Europe, for example, a certain amount of East-West trade was recognized as essential, even salutary, so long as it did not become a "morbid" preoccupation that debilitated Western unity and stamina. Obviously, the better the "Free World" economy worked, the less need for developing trade with Communist countries—and the less need for formulating a complex rationale to get around Cold War orthodoxy.

Testifying in favor of the European Recovery Program (the Marshall Plan), Dulles had looked ahead—into his own future responsibilities as it turned out—to consider the situation if East-West trade was never restored: "Africa is a continent of the future so far as Europe is concerned, and the resources of Africa are absolutely incalculable. It is just a mine of all sorts of wealth, mineral and agricultural, and the surface has barely been scratched." Dulles was on treacherous ground here. World War II had been many wars. In Europe, Germany fought Russia; in Asia, America fought Japan. Within Europe, left also fought right; within Asia, nationalists fought colonialism. And so on. The United States had hoped to avoid a postwar conflict between Europe and its former dependencies. What made the situation so perilous, argued State Department experts who had studied the impact of the war on the European empires, was not the spread of democratic ideas either through popular knowledge of the Atlantic Charter or the work of mission schools, but the destruction of prewar economic ties between the metropolis and dependent areas: "This suffering more than anything else served to fan the flames of nationalism. For the same conservative classes who formerly supported their foreign rulers now had to divert the upsurge of the masses into nationalist channels in order to maintain their privileged economic position."

Faced with rioting and fighting from Algeria to Annam, the imperial powers had offered a greater degree of political autonomy to their dependencies, hoping they might salvage their economic control. They might pull it off. More likely, they would not. They would not because a new element, Soviet Russia, had become involved in the situation. Russia's physical recuperation would take a long time, but its prestige and self-confidence would never be higher than now. Strengths and weaknesses were mismatched to the disadvantage of the imperial powers. If they were to fend off the Soviet challenge, they would need material proof of their ability to supply the wants of their dependencies. The Russians, on the other hand, were not expected to send economic aid. Marxism-Leninism was enough.

"What is to be done?," asked the experts. Russian success in filling the vacuum left by the departure of the colonial rulers would threaten "the very existence of the United States and would bring on inevitably a third world war."

It is certainly desirable to ward off these threats before they become really serious. To stand by passively while the Russians take over the colonial empires would be simply foolish. Yet if we back up the Western European powers (as Mr. Churchill recently suggested [in the Iron

Curtain speech]) we should be committing ourselves to the perpetuation of an unjust and unstable system, a system which is incompatible with every American instinct and tradition. We should find ourselves perhaps even forced to assist in putting down the rebellions of oppressed and famished peoples. Such a course would only be possible for the United States, when Russian ambitions have grown beyond all bounds.

Only America had both the moral prestige *and* the economic power to pursue a "third course . . . which, if it is followed energetically and quickly enough, may succeed in stabilizing the world balance of power and avoiding a third world war." What the experts did not foresee was the impact of the Cold War on European recovery, and the concomitant shift in attitude toward the "colonial question." Hence Dulles's testimony on Africa as a substitute for Eastern Europe; hence, also, his understanding that it would not be "enough."

Despite the promising beginning in the Marshall Plan, moreover, there was still a good deal of the "old" about postwar Europe. The British Labour Government headed by Clement Attlee and Ernest Bevin illustrated the almost paradoxical nature of the era. Internationalist in orientation, professedly "socialist," the Labour Government had taken the lead in organizing the agenda for the Marshall Plan and providing a stimulus for NATO. Much less helpful to American planners were the measures that the Labour Government took to sustain "socialism in one country," which, to Washington's dismay, looked very much like the measures Conservative Governments had employed to seal off the Empire from the ravages of world depression, measures, American policymakers always insisted, that only made matters worse and had contributed to the war. Labour's "eccentric" Chancellor of the Exchequer, Sir Stafford Cripps, it was now being said, had become the most skilled manipulator of currency and foreign exchange operations since Nazi Germany's Hjalmar von Schacht in the 1930s.

Washington had granted the Labour Government a $3.75 billion credit in 1945 with two purposes in mind: it had been hoped that the money would ease the transition from Lend-Lease to normal trade exchanges, and that the stipulation that sterling be made convertible by mid-1947 would rule out either a return to "Imperial Preferences" or a radical departure into socialist experimentation with the Commonwealth. Neither purpose was served. When the Labour Government fulfilled the promise to make sterling convertible, the drain on the British Treasury forced an immediate reimposition of stringent controls. Thus the huge sterling balances Commonwealth members had amassed in London during the war remained available only to finance British exports—not to further the goals of multilateral trade.

Cripps had found a way, moreover, to use Marshall Plan "counterpart" funds to add another prop under Britain's shaky export economy—now the main support of the Labour Government's "welfare state," where as once it had undergirded the foundations of industrial capitalism. Through a complex system of special drawing rights, London permitted its debtors to acquire sterling from funds supposedly set aside against dollar-aid receipts. Since sterling was inconvertible, and since Western Europe looked to be in a debtor position for some time, the net effect was to perpetuate a closed trading area.

When challenged, however, Sir Stafford had his answer ready. A downturn in the American economy—like the current 1949 recession—had its worst impact outside the United States. It was like a sudden storm that took you by surprise, and left in its wake an ugly path of destruction. Britain's economic problems were real enough, said the *Washington Post* editorial of July 1, 1949:

> But the question that has to be answered—the question that Congress will ask—is whether the United States is justified in continuing to cover the dollar deficits of countries that are retreating from, instead of advancing toward, a system of freer world trade by building up an isolated rival sterling trade area under the leadership of the chief beneficiary of the dollar-aid program.

When the 1949 British–Argentine Trade Agreement became known, the furor it caused reverberated through Washington from Foggy Bottom to Capitol Hill. Everything about it aroused concern. What immediately came to mind was Schacht's notorious campaign to strengthen Hitler's autarchic economic policies by negotiating narrow bilateral trade treaties. With its guaranteed quotas and barter-style pairings, the British–Argentine pact might have been written in German.

Labour's employment of such "reactionary" methods, however great the British workingman's need of Argentine beef to maintain his meager weekly ration, displeased the State Department and convinced critics on Capitol Hill that the "socialism" being constructed over there was a positive danger to the American export trade and national prosperity. Everyone agreed that, while British power had been reduced, the impact of such "unnatural" policies, whether pursued in the name of socialism or something else had broad ramifications. Should Americans go on paying for the perverse privilege of watching Sir Stafford Cripps pull more hare-brained schemes out of his attaché case? Or should Congress put an end to this trickery by shutting off Marshall Plan aid?

When a member of the Senate Finance Committee put those alternatives to ECA head Paul Hoffman, the latter replied with a cautionary warning. "I think," he said, "that the austerity that they have practiced would be as nothing compared to what they would have. My opinion is that the resentment that would come would not be directed against the Labour Party, but unfortunately against us." Did anyone believe that denying Attlee foreign aid would lead British voters to renounce socialism? Labour Party spokesmen still avowed, moreover, that their program was fully compatible with reduced trade barriers and genuine multilateralism, only it would take time. Granting the worst for the sake of argument—that Britain never took the road back to "capitalism"—it still behooved the United States to work for economic recovery.

"It seems to us," cabled the American Ambassador in London, "that the logic of the situation would compel Britain and other countries to move toward the development of at least a quasi-autarchic sterling area, embracing as many countries as could be brought or forced into it. Also, with the probable shrinkage of trade with the dollar area, would not these countries eventually have to consider a reorientation of their trade toward Eastern Europe and Russia?" Policymakers did not much concern themselves, therefore, with Congressional complaints that Sir Stafford Cripps was out to build British socialism on the already heavily burdened back of the American taxpayer. Their primary concern was to induce the Labour Government to become more deeply involved in economic plans for the Continent; and their deepest fear was that Labour (and its successors) might hold aloof, and attempt to build a self-sufficient system out of sterling balances.

The problem was well stated at an October 1949 meeting of American Ambassadors to European countries:

1. Britain cannot be left in the back yard if unification of Western Europe is to take place; and

2. Economic and political integration in Western Europe of some form is absolutely essential.

Doctrinaire socialists, it was further argued here, were convinced that their plans for nationalization of British steel required separation. "This is the fundamental contradiction of Socialism with the conception of economic and political integration of Western Europe." Listening to these presentations, John J. McCloy, High Commissioner for Germany, was struck by the thought that "too much emphasis had . . . been given to the increase of Russian power in the world and too little thought to the enormously important factor that is the collapse of the British Empire. This collapse may be more important than the problem of Russia."

McCloy thought the problem of British isolationism had been brought on, ironically, because the socialists were clinging to the remnants of the Empire like a man thrown out of a torpedoed boat. Thus did the psychology of Empire and safety persist, a Tory conviction become a Labour invention. Without British participation in Western Europe, McCloy feared that the "struggle for the soul of Faust" in Germany would become intensified. The creation of the West German state was a great event, but only one aspect of that struggle. A new offensive was expected from the East, one more threatening than the institution of the blockade. East Germany had several propaganda advantages—for example, the dream of unity. "Then there is the vision of the enormous hinterland of unknown markets and trade outlets to the east."

East-West trade was a conundrum for American policymakers. They were certain, as McCloy had reasoned, that British absence from Europe would further complicate, and intensify, demands for its expansion. Only weeks earlier they had confronted other aspects of the puzzle, and failed to resolve them. The Paris Foreign Ministers' Conference of June 1949 ended the Berlin blockade and confirmed the existence of "two Germanies." For the American delegation, the key question was how to approach the Russians about restoring "natural German trade"—necessary to the safety of the political regimes of both Germanies. What if the Russians proposed trade pacts between West Germany and their Eastern European satellites? And then, continued this hypothesis, suppose the Russians argued that these would make German participation in the Marshall Plan (and, of course, NATO) unnecessary?

It was too soon, as it turned out, for the Russians to use that particular lever, or for the West Germans to be sure enough of themselves to respond. One did not have to be an alarmist, however, to point out that surplus German production had to have outlets— now more than in prewar years. German prosperity and German reintegration into the community of liberal states were inseparable objectives.

French reactions to this hypothesis were conveyed to a member of the American delegation, John Foster Dulles, by Foreign Minister Robert Schuman. This was a question of tomorrow or the day after, he said, not sometime far off in the future. Neither France nor Great Britain could stand too much German competition. Up until this time Americans had prided themselves on having avoided the postwar folly of the World War I era, when Germany had been forced to desperate measures by Allied shortsightedness. Yet, warned Schuman, the division of Germany had re-created certain aspects of that unhappy time. German industry in the West would have to work all the harder, he told Dulles, because the Cold War had cut off agricultural sectors in the East:

> They did not have enough land to sustain themselves agriculturally and their products would have to go somewhere abroad. Also, these could not be armament products. If their peacetime products could not go either East or West, there would be wholesale unemployment, the situation would be like that of 1932, and it would be impossible to prevent the rise to power of another Hitler.

Or, what seemed far more likely under the circumstances, another Lenin. "We are in a position," Secretary of State Dean Acheson concluded, "where we have to be proponents of increased East-West trade."

Over the next several months the question of what to do with excess German production engaged the energies of Schuman's compatriot Jean Monnet, the principal architect of the European Common Market and Community. Monnet's starting point was his apprehension that, once begun, a policy of diverting German trade to the East could not be easily reversed. It would lead to political agreements, the re-formation of cartels, and put France back "in the old rut of limited, protected production."

Yet this need not be. Disaster could be avoided if France would now take the lead in establishing an international authority to regulate coal and steel production. Acheson greeted this proposal with astonishment. Here was a plan for the most grandiose cartel in history. Almost at once, however, astonishment turned to ardor. This kind of imaginative thinking just might overcome the "dollar gap" as well as the continuing pariah status suffered by Germany.

A leading French socialist, André Philip, had arrived at a similar conclusion. There existed a great demand in the newly developing countries for manufactured goods, the export of which could bring Europe "considerable prosperity." Imperialism had produced wars in the past, and had not been profitable, Philip implied, because of European "nationalism." Now, however, was a perfect time, when empires were crumbling and nationalism obsolete, to take a new look at the possibilities. To take advantage of the situation required enormous capital spread over a great number of industries to reduce production costs. There could be no future for Europe unless this large "standardized" market was set up so as to permit export resumption on a profitable basis: "Unless this is done, and done quickly, 1952 will see a crisis of exceptional severity, accompanied by social unrest which might bring the Communist parties into power and mean the Russian domination of our continent."

Charles de Gaulle agreed. "One is almost dazzled," he would write, "by the perspective of what could be given the qualities of Germany and France combined, the latter prolonged into Africa. There is a common field of development there which could transform Europe. It is a matter of taking up again on modern foundations, economic, social, strategic and cultural, the enterprise of Charlemagne."

Charlemagne was remote enough to cast an heroic aura over the project. It might sound very different if he had talked about the dreams of, say, Bismarck or Theodore Roosevelt. To Robert Schuman, then, fell the responsibility of convincing the French National Assembly. "Europe will be able," the Assembly was told, "with increased resources, to pursue the realization of one of her essential tasks, the development of the African continent."

The Schuman Plan formed the core of practically all later thoughts on European unity. From its inception, not surprisingly, Franco-German economic cooperation was regarded with a somewhat jaundiced eye in Great Britain. The Labour Government, and no less the Conservatives who returned to power in 1951, saw it as forcing their hands: The Commonwealth or Europe. Ernest Bevin even accused Acheson of "having conspired with Schuman to create a European combination against British trade with the Continent. . . . He bristled with hostility to Schuman's whole idea."

But Washington was delighted. If the momentum toward economic unity in Western Europe continued, it would do far more toward neutralizing the impact of British socialism than Congress could ever accomplish. It would reduce the tension between Congress and the Administration by alleviating trade pressures on the American domestic market. And it would ensure that Europe played a constructive role in the inevitable process of "decolonization." Having suffered through two "civil wars" in the first half of the century, Europe had come into its own, at last, as a liberal capitalist power. As such, like the United States, it would not require formal imperialism to survive. Not, perhaps, since Thomas Paine had advanced the notion in 1776 that it was "common sense" to believe that America could remake the world, had the power of a "liberal" example seemed so self-evident.

It took several more years for the vision to be realized, and a great deal of American diplomatic pressure. And by the time the French National Assembly agreed to German rearmament in 1954, the "colonial" question had come to a crisis point in Asia. Some of the connected issues were a direct result of the Korean War. Others were more remote.

After Chinese intervention in that war, the United States had succeeded in having Peking branded an aggressor in the United Nations. It was the last clearcut victory Washington would have in that body. Despite being thus stigmatized, however, China steadily gained prestige within the Third World. With the rise of a so-called neutralist bloc, led by Egypt, India, and Yugoslavia, the "destabilization" of the Cold War became a disturbing fact of life. Secretary of State John Foster Dulles roundly condemned neutralism as immoral, but no one knew better than he what it would take to meet this challenge.

His experience with the Japanese peace treaty had convinced him that the Cold War would be determined in Asia. It was not that Communist China was a military threat. Russia's presence in Eastern Europe was far more formidable, in that regard, than China's in Southeast Asia. The difference was that Russia had come into Eastern Europe as a result of the war, and did not enjoy the same honored position culturally in Europe as China did throughout Asia.

Burdened with Stalinism, and with the clear evidence of day-to-day suppression in Eastern Europe available to the world, "Communism's appeal" was on the wane. Dulles predicted that Stalin's death in 1953 would leave the movement bereft even of the ability to command by fear. China revived Marxism, just as it was about to expire, and married it to nationalism.

"I'm not absolutely sure we can win this contest," Dulles confided to an aide. "You know, it's like getting a bunch of people who are suffering from malnutrition, rickets, all sorts of congenital ailments —who are weak—and saying, 'What you ought to do is play rugby football. Come on, get in there, out on the field. Tackle each other. Be rough and tough. . . . Have a competitive system.' And they say, 'Good god, there must be a better way of doing things.'" It was a tremendous difficulty to win souls for political freedom when the devil had so much on his side.

One had to outsmart the devil. Acheson had talked about negotiating from strength, a pre-condition that effectively removed the necessity of talking at all. Dulles talked about the "rollback" of Russian power in Eastern Europe, which, had it actually taken place would have frightened him to death. Yugoslavia had slipped free from Moscow's grasp, and look what happened there. Marshall Tito's independence had become a cross to bear not only in Moscow but also in Washington. On the surface everyone welcomed Yugoslav independence, but Tito's strong assertions and association with India's Nehru and Egyptian leader Gamal Abdel Nasser gave "national" communism too much respectability. Besides, suppose Tito or some successor finally provoked the Russians to move against Yugoslavia. What kind of contingency plan could one write to meet that emergency?

Putting, or attempting to put, capitalist systems into Eastern Europe risked war; allowing more independent socialist Peoples' Democracies would add new numbers to the neutralist bloc, strengthen China's position, perhaps, and, as a consequence, prod Russia into the "competition" to lead the revolution of rising aspirations in the Third World.

Dulles's well-known reluctance to have Eisenhower engage in personal negotiations with his Russian counterparts was not, in this view, a result of narrow moralism but a pragmatic way to preserve things exactly as they were. The Eisenhower and Dulles record yields remarkably few instances of any effort to pursue "Liberation" in Europe seriously, except when it came time to claim victories—such as the Austrian State Treaty in 1955—for domestic political purposes.

Testifying before the Senate Foreign Relations Committee in executive session that year, Dulles was notably circumspect about calling for an all-out offensive against Soviet positions. Asked if he had anything to say about the internal situation in Eastern Europe, the Secretary commented on the persistence of poor economic conditions: "My guess is that if you open up this new frontier between Austria and Hungary, things are going to happen in Hungary.... All of that combines to produce a result of which we can only see now partial manifestations and the full thing is not unveiled yet, and there is room for a great deal of speculation as to what it is."

What it was, Dulles did not really want to know. The Hungarian Revolution a year later was no surprise, perhaps, but a genuine shock. Afterwards, the Administration saw to it that Radio Free Europe did not make any more foolish promises about Western help for such uprisings. Eisenhower's special adviser on psychological warfare was stunned at the seeming indifference to the plight of the Hungarians. Surely the United States could make its feelings known without risking war, and it could take appropriate actions. "Everything that all of us have said about our side of the Iron Curtain," he wrote the President, "will turn out to have been a ghastly lie, and I do not know how we will ever manage to erase the bitterness." Eisenhower assured C. D. Jackson that the measures used to put down the uprising were "just as distressing to me as they are to you. But to annihilate Hungary, should it become the scene of a bitter conflict, is in no way to help her." And it would risk atomic self-destruction.

It would be difficult to separate such fears from a growing belief that Eastern Europe under Russian rule provided the West with a new form of *cordon sanitaire*: one that kept the Soviets locked in ideologically and checked their expansionist capabilities. The Hungarian situation was brought before the United Nations, but American leadership was lacking. The first debate on Hungary in the Security Council ended inconclusively, wrote Anthony Eden in his memoirs, and for five days the British worked to schedule a new session: "The United States representative was reluctant, and voiced his suspicion that we were using the Hungarian situation to divert attention from Suez. The United States Government appeared in no hurry to move. Their attitude provided a damaging contrast to the alacrity they were showing in arraigning the French and ourselves."

Eden's efforts at self-justification should not obscure an important point: the only consistent liberation policy pursued in the Eisenhower years was the attempt to detach American support for the Schuman Plan from anachronistic Anglo-French "colonial" policies. The Korean War had guided Europe into the American-led system even more effectively than the Marshall Plan or NATO. But the extension of the Cold War geographically into Asia raised up a host of new problems.

Korea posed the issue, for example, of a "Pacific Pact" to complement NATO. American policymakers were intrigued by the possibility of such a symmetrical solution to halting "Communist" expansion. So, in his own way, was Ernest Bevin. When the British Foreign Secretary visited Washington in April 1949 he brought with him a memorandum that explored the possibilities of a "common front" in Southeast Asia:

> If a common front can be built up from Afghanistan to Indo-China inclusive, then it should be possible to contain the Russian advance southwards, to rehabilitate and stabilize the area, and to preserve our communications across the middle of the world. A stable South East Asia may also eventually influence the situation in China and make it possible to redress the position there.

Bevin's inspiration—like his vision of a spiritual federation of the West that led to NATO—was Wilsonian to the core. When Wilson first imagined the covenant with power he had had in mind the role military force would play in preserving the hard-earned ideological victory over German autocracy more than what had happened on the battlefield. Where Wilson had once talked about providing an opportunity for the new states of Europe, even those athwart the Berlin to Baghdad route, to stand on their own—and to exercise a healthy influence on political institutions inside the "new" Germany—so now Bevin posed the modern counterpart to "influence the situation in China and make it possible to redress the position there."

Presumably, as we have seen, one of the key reasons for not abandoning South Korea in 1950 was because it represented precisely the kind of "demonstration project" in Western "liberal democracy" essential to either a "containment" or a "liberation" policy in Asia. But the British had difficulty with another American attitude. In several discussions of the idea of a Pacific pact or common front, there finally arrived a time to discuss Indochina. If a solution to that problem could be found, American policymakers would observe pointedly, Indochina could become "a bastion in the path of a southward rolling Communist tide."

The more State Department planners examined Bevin's proposal, the more questions they had. It was hard for them to see, whatever the Wilsonian origins of Bevin's idea, that what he had in mind, in a practical way, was anything more than yet another "special relationship," this time between a Britain afraid of losing Dominion support and American strength. In fact, concluded the Far Eastern experts in the Department, "the British are reluctant to have a rival to the Empire in this part of the world," and that explained Bevin's proposed solution.

For a time, however, Americans were stymied in efforts to achieve a Pacific Pact by the embarrassing "alliance" between South Korea and Chiang Kai-shek. In that sense, the Korean War simplified matters. Korea became the recipient of American funds and military support directly, while Chiang was isolated (by American action in placing the Seventh Fleet between him and the mainland), thereby leaving open the possibility of a Southeast Asian Pact. One of the principal purposes, American officials stressed in conversations with the British, would be the integration of Japan economically into a Western-oriented, liberal capitalist economic system. Whenever discussion turned in that direction, noted these officials, their British counterparts found great difficulties in the way of proceeding very far.

During the April 1949 discussions with Bevin on the British memorandum, Secretary Acheson had once again brought out Washington's concern about the limits of East-West trade. Unless something were done to integrate the underdeveloped countries into the Western economic system, a process terribly complicated by decolonization and the need to keep Japan solvent, the capitalist nations of Europe would quickly fall out among themselves. Far worse, they would become rivals for Eastern European trade favors. Acheson put it as plainly as he could:

As the President [Truman] sees the problem, if no new markets are developed after the termination of ERP [the Marshall Plan] in 1952, friction will occur and an unbalance will take place in the bargaining position of the West with the East. The Eastern countries would be in a strong position to exploit barter arrangements by their rigid production controls, but if there are other places than Europe to which the Western European countries can look, they will be in a better position vis-à-vis the East.

Anglo-American discussions soon revealed, however, that Bevin was less interested in "influencing" China than in protecting British Far Eastern trade; and, secondarily, in warding off a resurgent Japan. It thus became clear that the British were actually eager to extend recognition to the new regime in China, and saw the solution to *their* Japanese "problem" in that direction. "While we had suffered a terrible blow in China," said Bevin, he thought "we could get along without it. . . . After all, Great Britain had got along by letting the U.S. go its own way in earlier times."

The analogy held many unpleasant implications so far as American planners were concerned. Held in abeyance for a time, the Pacific Pact became one of John Foster Dulles's earliest priorities. At the time of his work on the Japanese peace treaty, the future Secretary of State had told the Senate Foreign Relations Committee that he thought it essential to associate the Asian Commonwealth nations, Australia and New Zealand, with Japan in a collective security arrangement. It would not have to be a formal treaty, only some way to provide an air and sea "shield around them."

After Dwight Eisenhower became a candidate for the Republican nomination in 1952, he wrote Dulles a long letter which reinforced the latter's beliefs. America must take the lead in promoting collective security, said the General: "We must face facts; which means that any thought of 'retiring within our own borders' will certainly lead to disaster for the U.S.A."

> The minimum requirement of these programs is that we are able to trade freely, in spite of anything Russia may do, with those areas from which we obtain the raw materials that are vital to our country. Since it is just as tragic for us to lose one of those areas to Communism by political action as by marching armies, our programs will not satisfy our minimum requirement unless they protect us and the areas in which we are concerned from both kinds of aggression—that is, military and political. This means that we must be successful in developing collective security measures for the free world—measures that will encourage each of these countries to develop its own economic and political and spiritual strength.

Where Acheson had been reluctant to put too much pressure on the European metropolitan countries to speed up the decolonization process, Dulles (with Eisenhower's full backing) assumed from the outset that a genuine collective security arrangement with Third World countries would have to be based upon "measures that will encourage each of these countries to develop its own economic and political and spiritual strength." For him that was the ultimate rationale for "Liberation."

British foot-dragging, the Secretary would complain, almost ruined the Southeast Asia Pact, now called SEATO, before it began. Not until the "First Indochinese War" ended in 1954 with the Geneva Agreement would London agree to participate. Dulles was determined to prevent the British from standing in the way in the Middle East as well. Shortly after he became Secretary of State, Dulles set out upon a fact-finding tour of that troubled region. European influence, he reported to the President—not without a tinge of satisfaction—had so deteriorated that it was beyond repair. Indeed, the longer the Europeans persisted, the more forlorn were their hopes, and the greater the risk of instability. Association with the old imperialism, and support for Israel, he concluded, were the biggest "millstones around our neck" in trying to accomplish anything.

In Dulles's mind there was a solution, however. He envisioned a Middle Eastern security treaty centered on Cairo, and drawing strength from the Egyptian revolution. The energy presently being wasted because of Arab feelings toward Europe and Israel could be converted into the main power source for an anti-Communist dynamo of almost unlimited potentiality. But whether an alliance actually materialized or not, Dulles was determined to gain full credit with the nationalist forces. To that end he pressured the British to speed up their evacuation of the Suez Canal. Eisenhower's Ambassador to the United Nations wanted the President to do even more, wanted him to make a public statement disassociating the United States once and for all from the colonial Colonel Blimps. "The colonial powers have really nowhere else to go." They would have to remain silent, in other words, because they needed America. That assumption was about to be tested to the fullest. Dulles's ardent wooing of Egyptian leader Colonel Gamal Abdel Nasser raised suspicions in Paris and London that the Americans simply had it in mind to displace the old imperialism with "foreign aid." Perhaps that was bad enough, but the Europeans also believed that Dulles was in far over his head and would take them all down with him.

Over-inflated by Washington's encouragement, they feared, Nasser's Pan-Arabist ambitions would turn the Middle East into a seething caldron of troubles. Once the Anglo-Egyptian agreement on Suez was finalized, Americans poured into Cairo with promises of economic aid and requests that Nasser consider a Middle Eastern counterpart to NATO. NATO was explained to him as a way of giving European nations an opportunity to band together as "equals." Nasser replied that he wondered what France, for example, would say about the restrictions of such "equality" in, say, ten years?

His goal, asserted the Egyptian leader, was to make Egypt truly independent, "with no Lawrences of Arabia" directing affairs "from the back rooms." The Colonel did not feign any desire to play the role of surrogate, yet the Americans continued to believe that Egypt would welcome the opportunity to be the leader in a Middle Eastern pact, indeed could not resist the temptation, and, most important, had to have outside aid for development projects. "If we give him the economic aid he wants," Miles Copeland, a doubter, was told, "he's damn well going to have to give some consideration for our interests. If he won't go along with us, there are others who will." But what if he lined up those others? persisted Copeland, "I mean, the way a labor union lines up the workers to face management with a united front." "He's too late. We've already got Iraq, Lebanon, Jordan, Saudi Arabia, Turkey, Iran and Pakistan."

To prove the point, and to demonstrate that Europe could achieve more without imperialism, there was the Aswan Dam. British, French, and German firms had created a consortium to undertake the building of a great dam on the Nile River. It was a project that Nasser believed would go far toward ending Egypt's bondage to famine, as well as to the outside world. Though fearful of Nasser's political ambitions, the governments of the European nations involved had agreed to support their bankers. But because of the huge sums, the World Bank had to be brought in to assist. Behind the World Bank stood the United States. By the end of 1955, negotiations were said to be very nearly complete.

Early the next year Dulles drafted a statement for a NATO ministers meeting concerning the right way to deal with leaders of the Third World. It was absolutely necessary, he planned to say, that close economic relations develop, so that leaders in these parts of the world could see that prosperity would result from association with the

West. Communism already ruled 800 million people. Twice that many lived in the free world. But a billion people lived in the underdeveloped areas. If they were won over to the Moscow-Peking side, the draft ended, the ratio of free to unfree would become intolerable —"given the industrialized nature of the Atlantic Community and its dependence upon broad markets and access to raw materials."

The statement was never used. As negotiations for the Aswan loan got snagged, Dulles apparently decided to postpone the lecture. The snags occurred because the World Bank placed certain restrictions on its willingness to participate, clauses that would have prohibited Egypt from undertaking any other major financial obligations. Nasser believed these to be political conditions of the very sort the British had once imposed on King Farouk and his predecessors. The effect of the conditions would have prevented Egypt from entering into any long-term contracts with the Soviet bloc. Instead of signing, Nasser threatened to bolt. And when he took a special "guest" to witness the last British soldier depart the Suez base, D.T. Shepilov, the Russian Foreign Minister, Dulles decided that he had better close down the show. A reverse bandwagon effect was soon under way, with everyone anxious not to be the last off.

On July 19, 1956, Dulles informed the Egyptian Ambassador that the United States had decided to withdraw its support from the scheme. The manner and method represented a considerable advance, perhaps, over those of the nineteenth century, but echoes of Disraeli and Salisbury filled the room. A week later, Nasser announced the Suez Canal would be nationalized. Though they had grown dubious about the Aswan project, British and French leaders were aghast. What was Dulles trying to do?

Dulles's handling of the Aswan situation lent weight to an interpretation that, whether by design or clumsiness, the Americans were out to destroy Europe's independence by depriving it of any role outside the NATO area. This was an exaggeration, but it fueled determination to redeem the Anglo-French position in the Middle East. The nationalization of the Canal was at most a final straw.

British reverses had really begun with the 1950–51 oil crisis in Iran, when the properties of Anglo-Iranian had been nationalized by a revolutionary government. Bad news kept on coming. On March 1, 1956, for example, Jordan's King Hussein dismissed Sir John Glubb, the legendary creator of the Arab Legion. The last of the "Lawrences" had been given his walking papers. The blow was primarily to British pride, but it hurt future prospects as well as diminished past glory. In their frustration, British leaders magnified Nasser's power and influence. He was a Mussolini. Worse, he would open the doors of the Middle East to the Russians. The French despised Nasser no less, and feared him equally. In February 1956 the new Prime Minister, Guy Mollet, was greeted with jeers and rotten tomatoes from the French inhabitants of Algeria. Mollet returned to Paris determined to do whatever necessary to crush the F.L.N. independence movement. His advisers told him that the first thing to do was to knock out their supply base: Nasser's Egypt.

Dulles made it clear to London and Paris that the United States had no intention of sending a battleship to Suez. When it came to discussing alternatives, however, the Secretary displayed none of the crisp decisiveness he had promised the Republicans would bring to foreign policy questions. His answer to a reporter's question about whether Egypt's "physical possession" of the Canal, with guarantees, would be unacceptable, was typical: "As I say, that is not a matter which is primarily of United States concern but primarily of concern to the many countries—about 20—whose economies are vitally dependent upon the Canal."

Well, at least, the British and French now knew how far "Liberation" went. Dulles did not mean this as a signal that he would keep hands off while Nasser met his justly deserved fate. Almost the opposite. He meant that the United States would not be maneuvered into a confrontation by the Europeans.

Thus Paris and London were left to choose: to decide whether to abandon the last vestige of their power, the symbol-laden Suez Canal Company, where it all began in the nineteenth century, or to risk everything on one throw of the dice. In considering these choices, recent parallels came to mind: Iran and Indochina. In the former instance the oil properties were restored, but not to British ownership. An international consortium was established that gave the United States a major share of what had been a strictly British enterprise. In Indochina the Americans took over after the fall of the French fortress Dienbienphu and installed their own man, Ngo Dinh Diem, even calling him a "George Washington" for Southeast Asia.

What drove the French and British toward this tragic farce, however, was not nostalgia but the awful realization that they stood alone. Dulles was hardly the sinister figure conjured up by his opponents. Subconsciously he may have "willed" them toward the edge, if only to prove what America could really do if it was at last free from the clutches of the old world. But he, too, was undergoing an "agonizing reappraisal" of his own policies. While Dulles studied his options, the dice were thrown. On October 29, 1956, Anglo-French-Israeli forces invaded Egypt. The invasion lasted a week. It seemed much longer, especially to Americans.

Told by the Americans that they needed a security treaty to protect themselves against the Russians, the Egyptians were invaded instead by America's NATO allies. To make matters worse, from Washington's perspective, the Russians now claimed a share of the credit for forcing an end to the invasion by virtue of Khrushchev's blustering missile-rattling at the height of the crisis. Unable to bring down Nasser, the Europeans had to suffer the further humiliation of standing at attention in the UN for a dressing down on the evils of colonialism—backed by an American threat of economic coercion.

Dulles and Eisenhower were furious. The Europeans had given the Russians an opening into a previously "safe" area; they had set back Western prospects, perhaps fatally, for any sort of co-operation. In this outburst of self-righteousness, there was little self-reproach for a dubious assumption that, going back to the Korean War, led Americans to believe they understood the dynamics of Third World nationalism better than anyone else. "We are in an awkward position," lamented C. D. Jackson, "of having to cheer for freedom with one side of our mouth and deplore most of the juvenile delinquencies of these new nations with the other side: and if we have any mouthroom left, tell our European allies that it is all a terrible pity and that we are all for them in their efforts toward orderly decolonialism."

Some months after the Suez debacle, Eisenhower and Dulles resumed the dialogue over "colonialism" at a Bermuda meeting with the new British Prime Minister, Harold Macmillan, and his aides. Macmillan complained that Americans had a tendency to move too fast and must take on themselves a share of the blame for a climate of opinion that held the old colonial powers responsible for everything in the world that was wrong. Macmillan made a special plea for unity. This met a curious response, a mixture of sympathy and sermon. Dulles even launched into a discussion of how colonialism at Hong Kong had compromised British policy toward Red China, preventing Western solidarity on the vital issue of recognition.

Suez was the last time, however, that the original Wilsonian commitment to self-determination—however diluted over the years—

would find expression in this way. Henceforth the shoe would be on the other foot, as America discovered itself the target of European criticism of neo-colonialism in the Caribbean and Southeast Asia. And where Dulles had once held up Nasser as a seeming paragon among Third World leaders, he now denounced him in terms not unlike those used by the British and French themselves. The Democrats, so recently the objects of Republican criticism for the stand-pat nature of "containment," were pleased to see the final denouement of "Liberation," a jumble of contradictory statements and policy confusions.

Even Eisenhower's sunny disposition had clouded over as he wrestled with what had not been accomplished. On March 26, 1958, the President wrote Dulles, "about your conclusion that I was becoming a pessimist." Eisenhower was frankly worried about the "costs" of security, under which he included the danger of "a dangerous degree of regimentation" of the American economy. Military power seemed to him only a temporary solution. "Security through arms is only a means (and sometimes a poor one) to an end. Peace, in a very real sense, is an end in itself."

But there was the difficulty of arriving at reliable agreements with the Soviets, he went on, a difficulty made more intractable by American failures:

> It is, of course, quite comforting to recite all of the international difficulties that have, over the five years, been either surmounted or ameliorated. I've personally recited these in a number of speeches.

> But these specific successes cannot blind us to the most potentially dangerous of all the situations now developing. This is the credence, even respect, that the world is beginning to give to the spurious Soviet protestations and pronouncements. As their propaganda promotes this world confusion, the tone of Soviet notes and statements grows more strident. The more the men in the Kremlin come to believe that their domestic propaganda is swallowed by their own people and by the populations of other countries, including some we have counted upon as allies, the greater the risk of American isolation.

"We must never confess," he warned, "that we have gotten to the bottom of the barrel in searching for ideas to stem and turn the tide of Soviet propaganda success." As the decade drew to an end, Washington was overhung with clouds of fretfulness. Democrats denounced a Republican-caused torpor which, they argued, had seen Communism advance to within 90 miles of the American coastline. It was not ennui that characterized those final days of Eisenhower's incumbency, however, but a nervous uncertainty: about Castro in Cuba, about the U-2, about the economy, and about what John F. Kennedy proposed to do to get America moving again.

"I personally believe," Eisenhower had written Dulles in that March 1958 letter, "that one of the main objectives of our own efforts should be to encourage our entire people to see, with clear eyes, the changing character of our difficulties, and to convince them that we must be vigilant, energetic, imaginative and incapable of surrender through fatigue or lack of courage." Those were to be the watchwords of the Kennedy administration as well, and of its successors. At their one meeting after his election, Eisenhower told the young President-elect that America could not permit a Communist take-over in Southeast Asia—at any cost. Fearing what he now believed had come out of the covenant with power—the over-militarization of American society—Eisenhower nevertheless recommended, and Kennedy adopted on behalf of the General's heirs, a policy sure to make it even more dangerous for American institutions and national safety.

7

Vietnam:
The Whole World Is Watching

Three European leaders attempted to warn John Kennedy against becoming involved deeply in Indochina. Harold Macmillan was the first. "I had warned him of the danger of being sucked into these inhospitable areas without a base," the Prime Minister would recall, "without any clear political or strategic aims and without any effective system of deploying armed forces or controlling local administration." But nothing Macmillan said weakened Kennedy's resolve to build up a world order from the Indochinese peninsula, an order that would stand as "a bulwark against the Soviets."

The next was Charles de Gaulle, who received Kennedy in Paris a few days before the latter was to sit down across the table from Nikita Khrushchev in Vienna. "You will find," the French leader began with a usual display of hauteur, "that intervention in this area will be an endless entanglement. . . . The ideology which you will invoke will make no difference. Indeed, in the eyes of the masses it will become identified with your will to power." De Gaulle continued:

I predict that you will sink step by step into a bottomless military and political quagmire, however much you spend in men and money. What you and we and others ought to do for unhappy Asia is not to take over the running of these States ourselves, but to provide them with the means to escape from the misery and humiliation which, there as elsewhere, are the causes of totalitarian regimes.

"I tell you this in the name of the West," the Frenchman ended. Jack Kennedy was particularly sensitive about who spoke for the

West. After the Bay of Pigs fiasco, where Cuban exiles, with American support, had failed to invade Cuba, he was doubly determined to appear firm, and not the callow youth de Gaulle's patronizing demeanor seemed to suggest.

When Kennedy arrived in Vienna a third warning awaited him. Khrushchev had wanted to talk about Berlin and European affairs, but Kennedy took him on a country-by-country world tour. "All right," the Russian finally replied to repeated references to "miscalculation," but "how could we work anything out when the United States regarded revolution anywhere as the result of communist machinations? It was really the United States which caused revolution by backing reactionary governments."

It was up to the super-powers, he went on, to allow revolutions to take their course, and not worry about so-called changes in the balance of power. "The worst thing for the United States to do, he warned, was to start guerrilla warfare against regimes it did not like; no undertaking was more hopeless than guerrilla action instigated from outside and not supported by the people."* But Kennedy would not let go. At one point he said that even the "loss" of Taiwan to the "communist camp" would upset world equilibrium. The theme of the 1961 Vienna Summit, on the American side, was simply an extension of JFK's presidential campaign.

"Our frontiers today are on every continent," Senator Kennedy had announced upon undertaking the race. "For our future and that of the rest of the people of the world are inseparably bound together, economically, militarily, politically." Kennedy proclaimed the New Frontier. But the American experience in Vietnam would yield only sadness and tragedy. No homesteads awaited eager young Americans there, no bonanzas of untold wealth. Yet policymakers stayed with the frontier idiom and watched it become anathema to the war's critics. "Well, we're not the French," a cornered Vice President Hubert Humphrey would retort, trying again to make a distinction between what Americans had wanted and what others once sought in Asia, "we're not the French, with all respect to that fine nation. . . . We are not colonialists. We have no empire to save. We are not fighting against a whole people. We are fighting for the freedom of that people."

Lyndon Johnson pushed the new-old frontier analogy all the way

*Arthur M. Schlesinger, *A Thousand Days: John F. Kennedy in the White House* (Boston, 1965), pp. 362–365.

to paradox, challenging his liberal critics to prove that their opposition to his Vietnam policy was not rooted in racial prejudice, and an unwillingness to spend lives and money to give Asians a chance at a better life. In truth, LBJ had hit upon a soft spot, because Vietnam was indeed a "liberal" cause—at least at the outset. It was the military counterpart to the ruling belief in Keynesian management of the economy. Just as the business cycle could be tamed, so also would the revolution-reaction peaks and valleys that disturbed international stability gradually be evened out. Secretary of Defense Robert McNamara had no doubt of it. He held in his hands the proof, the print-outs from the Pentagon computer, which told him: "Every quantitative measurement we have shows we're winning the war."

Policymakers constantly talked about not losing "credibility." But before it was over the Vietnam War had done more to destroy American credibility than any event in the nation's history, bringing on the most divisive debate over foreign policy since the Declaration of Independence. A decent respect for the opinion of mankind became the taunting epithet of the anti-war movement: the whole world is watching.

Forebodings about entanglement in Indochina went back to World War. From the moment the Japanese occupied the French colony in 1941, Roosevelt knew that he would one day have to face the question of whether or not it was to go back to France. He had vowed that Indochina should not go back to its former rulers. And throughout the war he repeated his words on a number of occasions. But his plans for the colonial areas were never very well defined, probably because he knew full well that no solution would be easy to impose. Asia would be the scene of conflicting forces long after the Japanese had been expelled. The greatest effort FDR made was to bolster the chances for China to assume at least some of the stabilizing functions the Japanese had performed, however perversely, but without the militarist implications.

On a visit to Washington in September 1944 an American diplomat in China, John Paton Davies, learned from Roosevelt's closest adviser, Harry Hopkins, that things were not going according to plan—not at all. The hopes for China's postwar development, so high at the Cairo Conference a year earlier, had given way to pessimism. When Davies confirmed Hopkins's impression, the latter "then wryly observed that this did not seem to give much scope for the rosy plans which were being drawn up for expansive post-war economic development of China by the United States." Roosevelt was still convinced that France could not be "permitted to have Indochina," but the British were busy lining up the French and Dutch to resist American interference in the restoration of the colonial empires. The Russians were sympathetic to Roosevelt's attitude, concluded Hopkins, but "they had no genuine interest at this time in what was taking place that far away."

Chinese weakness, Russian lack of interest, Roosevelt's failing health, and myriad other complications shrank whatever grand design American planners had for solving the colonial problem by war's end. Dean Rusk would recall in 1963 that Roosevelt was weary of hearing about Indochina. When asked by the Joint Chiefs for a policy statement, said Rusk, the President's only reply was: "I don't want to hear any more about Indochina." Neither, in fact, did Harry Truman, who made no effort to implement any policy beyond a desultory monitoring of French promises to increase autonomy.

The monitoring was carried out, for the most part, by middle-level desk officers in the Department of State. On September 5, 1945, for instance, they received a representative from the French Ministry of Colonies, who had asked for an opportunity to explain de Gaulle's plan for a French Union, patterned somewhat after the British Commonwealth. American private investment would be welcomed, indeed encouraged. The Americans assured him that this was a most satisfactory statement, one "in harmony with the trend encouraged by the U.S. with respect to dependent areas."

But doubts about French policy grew when fighting broke out between French troops and the Vietminh guerrilla forces. The nationalist leader, Ho Chi Minh, had been contacted during the final days of the Pacific war by advance units of the United States Army, including specially trained OSS (Office of Strategic Services) intelligence officers. Ho made a good impression on the OSS cadre, portraying his movement as a moderate middle-of-the-road attempt to rein in extremists, yet dedicated to resisting French "reconquest." He felt certain, Ho told the Americans, that if the American people could only know the facts, their moral support would be assured: "This is all I ask, that news of Indo-China be given to the world."

State Department experts split over Indochina. Everyone in Washington was distressed by the "slow progress" being made to settle the Indochina "dispute." But there was little agreeement about who was to blame. Secretary of State George C. Marshall voiced the dominant position, however, in a telegram to Paris on May 13, 1947. The key to the American approach, he said, was "our awareness" that in respect to developments affecting the position of the Western "democratic powers" in Southeast Asia, Washington was in essentially the same boat as the French, British, and Dutch. The telegram went on:

> In our view, southern Asia in critical phase its history with seven new nations in process achieving or struggle independence or autonomy. These nations include quarter inhabitants world and their future course, owing sheer weight populations, resources they command, and strategic location, will be momentous factor world stability. Following relaxation European controls, internal racial, religious and national differences could plunge new nations into violent discord, or already apparent anti-Western Pan-Asiatic tendencies could become dominant political force, or Communists could capture control. We consider as best safeguard against these eventualities a continued close association between newly-autonomous peoples and powers which have long been responsible their welfare.

Marshall thus wrote finis to Roosevelt's grand design, but he had no real policy of his own:

> While we are still ready and willing do anything we can which might be considered helpful, French will understand we not attempting come forward with any solution our own or intervene in situation. However, they will also understand we inescapably concerned with situation Far East generally, upon which developments Indochina likely have profound effect.

The internal struggle to control policy toward Indochina ended in 1949, when the new Secretary of State, Dean Acheson, overrode all objections from the Southeast Asia experts to issue a statement in support of the French puppet, Bao Dai. A bitter concession of defeat came from SEA (Southeast Asian Affairs), combined with a warning that Acheson had been shielded from reality by WE (Western European Affairs):

> What has happened is that SEA's policy has been junked; nothing effective is being done to promote a non-Communist solution in Indochina. . . . This is the culmination of three years consistent effort on the part of WE to set aside all considerations of our position in Asia and to keep a free hand for the French. This has been done on the grounds that

a stern attitude on the part of the US would cause the French Government to fail. We have been gagged by this consideration beyond all reason, in so many contexts that the thing has become a joke.

French internal security was only one reason, however, for Acheson's decision. He shared WE's general distrust of an avowed Communist, Ho Chi Minh, leading a supposedly nationalist movement. Even were it otherwise Acheson could not imagine the Vietminh being any more hospitable to the white man in Asia than had been the Japanese militarists before the war. And finally, the Secretary feared revolution anywhere.

Formal military endorsement of the French effort in Indochina came in President Truman's initial reaction to the outbreak of the Korean War. At the very end of the announcement of the steps he had taken to turn back the North Koreans, the President himself widened the war against "Communism" to all Asia. The conflict on the Korean peninsula itself was to be kept limited, all the better to respond to other Soviet thrusts on the perimeter of the Free World. Truman pledged aid to the Philippine Government in its fight with local insurgents, and to the French to defeat the Vietminh.

Lacking a UN mandate outside Korea, American policymakers had to find a means to bring other areas in under the protective roof. Acheson had little faith in revolutionary nationalism. To support these men against old friends was only storing up trouble for the future, both in Europe and Asia. Dulles took a different view, of course, one predicated upon some sort of alliance with what he always called the "dynamic" forces in the world. While American leaders pondered prospects for a Pacific Pact, a complement to NATO, French policy in Vietnam moved steadily toward defeat. Whatever was decided in Washington could not be built upon yet another "lost" country in Asia. Concern was at its greatest in the spring of 1954, when the fate of the world seemed to turn on the besieged French garrison at Dienbienphu.

We can't go in alone, President Eisenhower told the National Security Council. That would look like an attempt to police the world: "We should be everywhere accused of imperialistic ambitions ... the concept of leadership implied associates. Without allies and associates the leader is just an adventurer like Genghis Khan." Eisenhower and Dulles had in mind joining the colonial powers with "independent" Asian nations in some combination of a trusteeship system and military alliance to watch over the emerging countries of Southeast Asia. This revamped idea of an Asian treaty organization ran into difficulty right at the outset. British leaders feared Dulles was driven to seeking a confrontation with Communist China, perhaps to make up for the inconclusive ending to the Korean War, while the French saw only too clearly that they were being eased out under the guise of Cold War necessity.

The stakes were so high, nevertheless, that for a few weeks in that spring of 1954 the Administration did consider taking over the fighting in Indochina. Eisenhower studied the "Genghis Khan" option, but finally said no. The consequences of defeat, the President told a press conference, "are just incalculable to the free world." He pictured a row of dominoes, the first knocked into the next, and so on down to the last. And he spoke about the Japanese "connection," and what would happen to that economy. "It takes away, in its economic aspects, that region that Japan must have as a trading area or Japan, in turn, will have only one place in the world to go—that is, toward the Communist areas in order to live."

Dienbienphu fell on May 7, 1954. The French defeat came at the opening of the Geneva Foreign Ministers' Conference, a meeting co-chaired by Great Britain and Russia. Americans did not relish attending a conference at which Communist China would also be present, let alone under such dreadful circumstances as military defeat. Considering the magnitude of that defeat, the West came away from Geneva in surprisingly good shape. Negotiations with Indochinese representatives led to an agreement that Laos and Cambodia would become independent, and that Vietnam would be divided temporarily at the 17th parallel. All-Vietnamese elections to determine the future government were to be held within two years.

That deadline could not be met, American policymakers feared, without adding political defeat to military defeat. It would have been better, perhaps, if the Vietminh had won a complete military victory. The consequences of the first "elected" Communist government were fully as great, indeed greater, than the economic loss. Asked about these four days after the fall of Dienbienphu, Dulles responded this way to a question positing the election of Ho Chi Minh. "I said that I thought that the United States should not stand passively by and see the extension of communism by any means into Southeast Asia. We are not standing passively by."

The Secretary was mainly worried whether he would have time to build any sort of political structure before the scheduled elections in 1956. There were three essential tasks, as he saw it: (1) the final removal of the "taint" of French colonialism; (2) the creation of an international structure to support Vietnam from the outside; and (3) the establishment of a viable government in the area below the 18th parallel. The first task was the easiest. "We have a clean base there now," Dulles told an Eisenhower aide, "without a taint of colonialism. Dienbienphu was a blessing in disguise." The second was accomplished, or at least a start in that direction, on September 8, 1954, when SEATO (Southeast Asia Treaty Organization) came into being. It was not everything Dulles had desired—for example, Taiwan had been excluded from membership because of British and French objections—but for the first time bilateral colonial relations had been replaced with a "League." The SEATO pact contained a protocol which extended its benefits to Cambodia, Laos, "and the free territory of Vietnam." "The Indochina Armistice created obstacles to these three countries becoming parties to the Treaty at the present time," admitted Dulles. "The Treaty will, however, to the extent practicable, throw a mantle of protection over these young nations."

The "free territory of Vietnam" thus became almost immediately one of "three . . . young nations." If SEATO worked, moreover, it was clear that it would supersede the Geneva Agreement which prevented these "three countries" from joining "at the present time." Only one loophole remained, and Dulles corrected that at an early meeting of SEATO ministers in February 1955.

"One little thing," Dulles prompted reporters at a "background" press conference after the SEATO meeting,

One little thing I might mention. You'll find the words "international Communism" are mentioned in the communiqué—a hurdle which some people found a little hard to take. They were not in the communiqué that came out from the working group. The word Communism never found any mention at all. I called attention to the fact that it seemed rather extraordinary, when we were making all this effort to combat something, that we couldn't even give it a name. And so the words "international Communism." I think that from now on it will be respectable in this circle to talk about International Communism.

No longer one country temporarily partitioned, Vietnam had become instead a "divided" nation on the order of North and South Korea, East and West Germany. Divided nations enjoyed a special status, and were entitled to protection against both the overt and covert manifestations of "international Communism." In the case of East and West Germany, NATO and the Warsaw Pact served the two purposes of Western policy well. From this perspective, indeed, it was almost disappointing that the Russians did not follow suit by creating an Asian treaty organization to match SEATO, composed of China, North Korea, and North Vietnam. If they had, Dulles may have thought later, both super-powers might have been spared the troubles of neutralism.

But the Secretary had more than enough to do without worrying about Cold War asymmetry. The American choice for Vietnam's "Founding Father" turned out to be Ngo Dinh Diem, an expatriate who had lived for several years in the United States, but who had genuine nationalist credentials. Over French objections, Diem was installed as Bao Dai's Prime Minister. It was four years since the Wake Island conference and Truman's promise to talk "cold turkey" to the French about Vietnam. Dulles was equally determined that the 1956 elections not produce a "legitimate" Communist government. Nothing, literally nothing, could be worse.

Traveling to Saigon to assure the Indochinese elite that Diem had America's confidence, the Secretary was met with questions about French opposition to his selection. "We never deny the possibility of a change," quipped Dulles. "There is always the possibility of changing the status of a country. France no longer has a king." How the Secretary must have delighted at this opportunity to get on the right side of revolution, and to remind everyone that with American aid the Vietnamese now had an excellent chance for self-determination. It was as if Hanoi and Ho Chi Minh were a million miles away.

He knew that was not the case, of course. But at least the dominoes were now falling the other way. "We granted independence to the Philippines," the Secretary said on another occasion, "and now after they get their independence they in turn are helping another country, Vietnam, to become independent. There is a certain drama about it which appeals to me, at least, and it is having an excellent effect in Vietnam. President Diem [*sic*] spoke to me about it there when we had lunch together in Saigon."

Asked about French and British reactions, Dulles began talking about trade. The French might lose some trade, that was so, but nothing that would disturb their economy. After all, Japan had to have an outlet. "It may not be pleasant for some individual concerns in France, but by and large the impact on the French economy will not be serious. . . . [T]here is no desire on the part of the United States to try to displace French influence in that area. A certain displacement is, I think, inevitable."

As for the British, well, they now understood that it would be better to face Japanese competition in Asia than at home. It does no justice to Dulles, who had clearly in mind the world-system the United States was trying to build, to criticize American policy in these years as sleep-walking into a quagmire:

> If the reciprocal trade agreements act is extended [by Congress], as I hope it will be, and when we carry through our negotiations under that act, and when we have got operating our more complete economic program, for Southeast Asia and South Asia, which will be geared to promoting trade with Japan to that area, I think the combination of those things will really pretty well take care of the Japanese economic problem. That, of course, assumes that the Southeast Asia and South Asia area does not go Communist.

Because American policymakers "thought" it ought to work did not mean that it would, or that the system they were proposing was free from contradictions. Dulles faced a skeptical NATO ministers' meeting in Paris during May 1955. The idea that Japan should find its major outlets in Asia excluding China was, after all, not really an appealing prospect to statesmen who hoped that the "end of empire" did not also mean the end of prosperity. One reason the French opposed Diem, for example, was that a militantly nationalist government in South Vietnam dimmed chances that they would ever be able to resume valuable economic relations with North Vietnam.

To overcome European doubts, Dulles led off his presentation with a lengthy series of comments on the China problem. China represented a great population mass, he began, that would naturally exert a powerful pull on Asian countries, besides which China enjoyed among its neighbors a cultural prestige which the Russians lacked. The Chinese Communists, on the other hand, were more belligerent. At China's disposal, and that was what would happen if Japan could not trade with "Free" Asia, Japanese industrial might would be a formidable weapon. "If you like the kind of U.S. you see here," he concluded, "you should give it your confidence, as we apply the same policies in Asia, and join us if you will."

In March 1956 Dulles arrived at the Saigon airport bringing congratulations to the Vietnamese people, who, "under the inspiring leadership of President Diem, have made striking progress toward the consolidation of a strong and free country." Two years earlier, odds against getting this far with South Vietnamese nation-building had been set at 10 to 1 against. The Geneva Agreement had called for all-Vietnamese elections, which, through a series of maneuvers had been transformed into a referendum on Diem's leadership. The French were gone, and that was another reason for celebration.

Hanoi's overtures for carrying out the Agreement were turned aside with scathing criticisms of Ho's "totalitarian" regime. Elections were held only in the South, because, said Diem, "the Communist regime in North Vietnam does not allow each Vietnamese citizen to enjoy the democratic freedoms and fundamental rights of man." South Vietnam's economic performance, as measured even by pre-World War II days under French rule, sagged. Without large-scale American aid, the situation would have been almost desperate. South Vietnamese deficits, occasioned by a fall in rice exports, unsuccessful attempts to gain more of the world rubber market, and an ineffective agricultural reform program, had to be made up by Washington. The South Vietnamese themselves criticized the United States for not extending more aid, not demonstrating any real interest in matching North Vietnamese industrial progress. Dulles admitted in October 1957 that serious problems confronted the new "nation." "There is a measure of deterioration in some of the heavily populated Asian countries where it is being discovered that there does not exist in adequate measure what George Washington called the necessary props of a popular government, namely, religion and education. Therefore, there is a trend toward the alternative which Communism seems to offer of a dictatorial form of government directing the energies of the people."

Diem's response to the rising insurgency in the countryside mocked Dulles's words, for the trend in Saigon was certainly toward a "dictatorial form of government." Portents of crisis were generally visible throughout the area, as Dulles noted in his remarks concerning George Washington's list of essentials. Having "presided at its birth,"

as Senator John Kennedy put it in 1956, the United States was bound
to be held accountable for Vietnam's future welfare. Kennedy had
other analogies besides dominoes. South Vietnam represented "the
cornerstone of the Free World in Southeast Asia, the keystone to the
arch, the finger in the dike."

South Vietnam's intensifying difficulties were an additional burden
to the Republicans, who were coming under increasing criticism for
the poor state of the American economy, the launching of *Sputnik*
ahead of any United States space orbiter, and the obvious failures of
"Liberation" in Hungary and at Suez. Elder statesmen in the Democratic party, leaders in the original Cold War generation, had been
concerned about the supposed "drift" in national affairs and were
eager to pounce on Dulles's "credibility gap" wherever it appeared.

The Secretary gave the Democrats a marvelous opportunity to
have it both ways: condemn him for a rigid and doctrinaire approach
to the complicated issues posed by the rise of the Third World and
neutralism, while at the same time berate the Administration for its
inability to do anything about Soviet expansionism. Typical was
Averell Harriman, who, in his brief memoir *America and Russia in a
Changing World*, published later in 1971, pursued the former line. He
could never understand, Harriman commented there, "why Dulles
took over from the French their role in South Vietnam in 1954." In
the 1950s, however, he was a vigorous critic of Republican softness.
He had worried that "they're in a mood to surrender." At a private
gathering of former Truman administration officials during the Dienbienphu crisis, Harriman declared, "I want to go on record here that I
think we ought to take steps to get troops—American and as many
others—into Indochina, the Red River Delta, before this thing begins
to go."

Eisenhower should act. "Only one fellow can do it and that's Mr.
Eisenhower, and Mr. Eisenhower stands up and says 'this is it boys'
and the country is going to follow him. . . ." In the summer of 1959
Harriman had a series of interviews with Nikita Khrushchev prior to
the Soviet leader's visit to the United States and his talks with
Eisenhower at Camp David, where the two attempted to resolve the
Berlin issue. Harriman's report on these talks was published in *Life*,
under the title, "My Alarming Interview with Khrushchev." Selecting
the most flamboyant of the Russian's statements, Harriman said that
there was a good deal of bluff and mere acting involved: "But it would
be a grave mistake to believe it is all bluff. The present situation is

dangerous, for the Russian premier might well overplay his hand."

Appearing before the Senate Foreign Relations Committee, Harriman stressed the need of assisting the underdeveloped countries. Asked about his article, and what, in his opinion, the Russians really wanted from America, Harriman replied: "They would like to have us leave them alone, go back to Fortress America or isolationism, or whatever you want to call it, and leave them alone in the world. . . . [T]hey would like to have us leave them alone, *and then their revolution will take over*" (Emphasis added).

Dean Acheson always had grave doubts about getting bogged down in Asia. Having gone through the Korean experience, he was skeptical of the mess "Foster" had gotten himself into in Indochina. But he agreed with Harriman that the principal danger was that American leaders would yield to their fears at the most likely testing place—Berlin, he thought—and bring American troops home: "Berlin stands out as both the symbol and the prelude of the collapse which Mr. Khrushchev hopes to bring about." Acheson addressed NATO legislators in November 1959, telling them he wanted to adopt the perspective of the future historian: "I believe that that historian would say as he looked at the year 1959, the conclusion of this decade, that events were hurrying to a decision, that the moment was coming which would be decisive."

Acheson feared that the "high priests" of negotiation were threatening to take charge within his party, and that the campaign of 1960 might also see an "isolationist" Nixon as the Republican standard-bearer. A replay of the 1932 Hoover-Roosevelt campaign was a far-fetched notion, but the Democratic party, at least, had already given signs of the split that would occur during the Vietnam build-up. The Democrats were divided over how to respond to the Dulles-Eisenhower policy, with Stevenson "liberals" anxious to take advantage of the "brinkmanship" issue and Eisenhower's bumbling over the U-2 spy plane incident that ruined the follow-up summit to the Camp David talks. Cold War "stalwarts" (some of whom would eventually change party allegiances during the Reagan years) were just as eager to press the Republicans on Eisenhower's mishandling of every foreign policy issue since Suez, when, to Atlanticist horror, the United States and the Soviet Union had appeared to stand together against Britain and France.

Party affiliations mattered less, however, than a perceived slippage in America's will to realize its destiny. Dulles was dead, Eisenhower in his dotage, and the Republicans were about to nominate Richard Nixon. If the Vice President alienated the "intellectuals," if he turned to the Fortress America wing of the party for support, everything that had been accomplished in educating the people to their world role would have gone for naught. Among Republicans, Nelson Rockefeller had raised much the same question about Nixon. His protégé, Henry Kissinger had written a study, *Nuclear Weapons and Foreign Policy* (1957), that served as a foreign policy manual for those in both parties who yearned for a doctrine and detailed instructions to face tomorrow's likely crises.

Americans were a paradoxical people, Kissinger argued, Calvinist in economics, they were reluctant to abandon a "business" style prudence about defense budgets. Politically they recoiled from the use of power, forcing them to turn every war into an all-out moral crusade. They altogether lacked an appreciation for nuance, for ambiguity—and its requirements. Lacking these, they were ripe for disaster:

> We are certain to be confronted with situations of extraordinary ambiguity, such as civil wars or domestic coups. Each successive Soviet move is designed to make our moral position that much more difficult: Indo-China was more ambiguous than Korea: the Soviet arms deal with Egypt more ambiguous than Indo-China: the Middle Eastern crisis more ambiguous than the arms deal with Egypt.*

In this analysis the primary mistake made by Dulles and Eisenhower was one of education. The American people had not been educated to ambiguity. What Nixon would do to the nation's foreign policy, well, one could only pray. The worst thing that could happen, probably, was that the national "debate" over foreign policy would return to a 1930s' framework, with everything lost that had been gained.

Nixon would be the first "Republican" elected since Hoover, Eisenhower having succeeded in a non-partisan Presidency for eight years. If foreign policy was put in his hands, Nixon would immediately stir up old memories, pit liberals against an Administration that tried to conduct a forward national security policy, and undermine the consensus that had grown up around the need for the United States to fulfill its obligation to the world. In short, Nixon could neither

---

* *Nuclear Weapons and Foreign Policy* (New York, 1957), pp. 427–28.

correct mistakes made in the 1950s, nor carry through a successful
foreign policy in what looked to be a much more unstable era to
come.

As it happened, there was already a "new" Nixon, one who could
describe the Kremlin's principal challenge as economic not military.
In a speech delivered in San Francisco immediately after the Soviets
launched *Sputnik* in 1957, the then Vice President declared that the
Russian achievement proclaimed that a slave economy could outproduce a free economy: "It promises the developing areas of the
world that the Communist system can do more for them in a shorter
time than the system of private enterprise which is the economic basis
of the free world."

And during the 1960 Presidential debates, Nixon effectively an-
swered Kennedy's overly excited comments on Cuba, and chastised
the Democrat's choice in favor of arms aid to Cuban exiles. The point
is not whether Nixon was sincere in expressing concern for America's
image, but rather that, coming from him, it was not believed, and, it
could be argued, protests against the interventionist policies Kennedy
and Johnson would follow were muted in comparison to the uproar
that would have been occasioned by a Nixon "Bay-of-Pigs."

The Democrats talked about other isues besides Cuba. But that
concern took pride of place in their campaign, which attempted to
have the American people settle Cuba's future with their votes.
Kennedy's inaugural combined militant Cold War rhetoric with a
nostalgic whiff of Wilsonian idealism: "If a beachhead of cooperation
may push back a jungle of suspicion, let both sides join in creating a
new endeavor, not a new balance of power, but a new world of law,
where the strong are just and the weak secure and the peace
preserved."

How soon those words "beachhead" and "jungle of suspicion"
would come bouncing back to the White House! Kennedy's aides
prepared a "white paper" on Cuba that drew a sharp distinction
between legitimate and illegitimate revolutions, part of an education
process designed to explain in advance the need for covert activity
against Castro. Long after the New Frontiersmen, most of them, had
become disenchanted with this "mission," General William Westmoreland would explain Vietnam in similar fashion, but in far fewer
words: "Our own revolution has ended the need for revolution
forever."

Given the Administration's final go-ahead, the hapless Cuban exile army waded ashore at the Bay of Pigs on April 17, 1961. They had counted on their American sponsors to come to their rescue if the invasion went awry. No one came. No airplanes, no ships, no men. Kennedy ordered a stand-down, took on his shoulders the blame for the ill-fated expedition, and vowed to make amends for falling short of the promise held out in his inaugural. Three days after the humiliation of Brigade 2506, Kennedy stood before the American Society of Newspaper Editors. "Let me then make clear as the President of the United States that I am determined upon our system's survival and success, regardless of the cost and regardless of the peril!"

America under siege, that was Kennedy's theme. As he spoke of Cuba, the President also mentioned "the rising din of communist voices in Asia and Latin America." Task forces had been appointed to study ways of countering the Soviets at every level on the escalation ladder, and at every point on the globe. "We dare not fail to see the insidious nature of this new and deeper struggle," Kennedy told the news editors. "We dare not fail to grasp the new concepts, the new tools, the new sense of urgency we will need to combat it—whether in Cuba or South Vietnam. . . . The complacent, the self-indulgent, the soft societies are about to be swept away with the debris of history. Only the strong, only the industrious, only the determined, only the courageous, only the visionary who determine the real nature of our struggle can possibly survive."

The next President to issue such a summons to the American people to restore the nation's will would be Ronald Reagan, in the aftermath of Jimmy Carter's "Bay of Pigs," the Iranian hostage crisis. The campaign rhetoric about the somnambulant Eisenhower administration had become a terrible half-reality, with Kennedy a victim of his own inventions. But not entirely his own. Eisenhower's reputation for having opposed the introduction of American ground forces into Indochina had perhaps not prepared the younger man for "Ike's" emotional counsel about Laos. Eisenhower told his young successor that "we must not permit a Communist take-over . . . . it was imperative that Laos be defended. . . . unilateral intervention would be our last desperate hope."

Kennedy's motivation for making Southeast Asia the Administration's counter-insurgency "test" area was more complex certainly than simply a response to the advice of his elders, whether Dean Acheson, Averell Harriman, or Dwight Eisenhower. Kennedy's first mentor on foreign policy questions had been Winston S. Churchill. Where Churchill once declared that he had not become the King's minister to preside over the liquidation of the British Empire, Kennedy now warned Khrushchev that "he had not become President of the United States to acquiesce in the isolation of his country. . . ."

But that is exactly what happened. Vietnam blighted the Kennedy promise and withered the achievements of Lyndon Johnson's Great Society far more effectively than American defoliants exposed enemy positions. Worse, American ability to lead, economically or morally, was undermined by an isolationism that resulted from preoccupation with the war and a disregard for any opinion other than those promising victory. According to neo-conservative critiques, on the other hand, the media and domestic dissenters must bear the onus for the nation's humiliation, and the depressing aftermath in Iran and Latin America. The radical fringe could not have succeeded, it is argued, had it not been for a mistaken liberal premise that mandated from the outset an impossible task.

The task was "nation-building," which came at the expense of an effective war effort, and which opened American policy to criticism. The only dissent within the Kennedy administration as the American build-up began, observes Norman Podhoretz, "came from those who argued that military measures would fail unless we also forced the South Vietnamese government to undertake programs of reform."* Vietnam policy was controlled by closet "doves" all along, thereby assuring eventual defeat. Such a complaint would have surprised Dulles, because nation-building was his proudest claim for South Vietnam. And if one looks back to the original Eisenhower commitment to Diem, American aid was always conditioned upon the latter's achieving "standards of performance . . . in developing and maintaining a strong, viable state. . . ." To the extent that Diem's overthrow was an American responsibility, moreover, the justification was his failure to meet Eisenhower's standards. What hurt was the inability to find a successor for Vietnam's impotent Founding Father. As a result, nation-building did become a preoccupation. Kennedy's favorite General, Maxwell D. Taylor, bore the brunt of this effort as the head of the American mission to Saigon. Ambassador Taylor recalled that of sixty "Mission tasks" given the Embassy in 1965, only

---

*Quoted in Harry G. Summers, Jr., *On Strategy: The Vietnam War in Context* (Washington, D.C., 1981), p. 105.

nineteen had a direct military component. Most of the money spent by Mission agencies, he notes, went toward solving political, economic, and social problems, rather than military. "If we made a mistake this period [1964–65], it was in trying too much in the civil field before an adequate level of security was reached. . . . We should have learned from our frontier forebears that there is little use planting corn outside the stockade if there are still Indians around in the woods outside."*

In General Taylor's world-view, America's oldest and newest frontiers merged into one long saga. Yet there is more to be said. The American penchant for "nation-building" goes to the heart of both ideological and "strategic" reasons for the involvement in Vietnam's agony. From the time of the Bay of Pigs to the Cuban missile crisis of October 1962, Kennedy constantly stressed the theme of "legitimacy." Failure in the original attempt to topple Castro was equated with illegitimacy, betrayal of the nation's mission to the world, so much so, in fact, that Kennedy in his speech to the newspaper editors even denied the obvious by insisting that Americans had no responsibility for the failed invasion: "While we could not be expected to hide our sympathies, we made it repeatedly clear that the armed forces of this country would not intervene in any way."

Although the Cuban missile crisis alleviated Kennedy's ideological anxiety, by forcing Khrushchev to admit that the Russians had secretly put missiles on the island, and by allowing him to take America's "case" to the proper authorities, the first crucial steps toward a military involvement in Vietnam had already been taken. At each step of the way, each addition to the "Mission tasks," was a concern spoken of by George W. Ball. "It was both the best and worst of times," Ball wrote of the United States on the eve of the Kennedy inaugural. Economic growth, or the lack thereof as seen in Democratic eyes, was not sufficient to match the increase in the American labor force and in productive capacity. Unemployment had reached the dangerously high (for then) figure of 6 percent, a peril point for political support of an international economic policy of the sort envisioned by the New Frontiersmen.

Eisenhower had talked of bringing home soldiers' dependents from Europe to ease the balance of payments deficit. That deficit was far more serious than the temporary estrangement of military families.

* *Swords and Plowshares* (New York, 1972), pp. 339–40.

But another thought had begun to trouble the restless centurians along the New Frontier. The most dangerous assault on their positions, the greatest threat to "our system's survival and success," was not from a boatload of Cuban revolutionaries landing in the dark of night on the coasts of Latin America but from what was happening in broad daylight. Ball entitled his chapter on this menace, "Assisting and Resisting the Third World." The Third World countries, he notes, were organizing for a frontal assault on the markets of the great trading nations. Past solutions would not be enough:

> For some Americans foreign aid has served as an excuse for denying Third World nations free access to our markets. It is politically easier to obtain foreign-aid appropriations than to keep open our markets for Third World products, even though that has meant depriving poor countries of the chance to earn their living in the world economy.*

Later the dilemma would get a name: the North-South split. But Kennedy's concern was with building an international economy that would not produce such tensions as either to force the United States into an isolationist-protectionist posture (the internal threat to legitimacy feared since New Deal years) or a wholesale defection to East-West economic bartering (the external threat since the days of the Marshall Plan and NATO). Here again Vietnam impinged upon all other calculations. Economic "world-building" was, in this view, one of the oblique forces propelling the United States into a deeper and deeper involvement throughout Southeast Asia, and the reason why nation-building could not be separated from fighting the war.

The prospect of leading the Third World "into the twentieth century," muses Ball, offered an almost unlimited scope for experimentation. Not only did Kennedy fashion the Green Berets to make secure the "infrastructure," but there were economists, sociologists, psychologists, city planners, agronomists, political scientists, and experts in chicken disease. "It was the golden age for development theorists." Ball was, as events were to demonstrate, the most prescient of the "Best and Brightest."

> A story current at the time told of the professor who boasted that he occupied "The Pan American Chair of Development Economics." By that he meant a first-class seat on Pan American Airways to any destination in the world.

---

* George W. Ball, *The Past Has Another Pattern: Memoirs* (New York, 1982), pp. 187–88.

But the most presumptious undertaking of all was "nation-building," which suggested that American professors could make bricks without the straw of experience and with indifferent and infinitely various kinds of clay. *Hubris* was endemic in Washington.*

Over the next half-decade policymakers repeatedly pondered the question, and wrote memorandum after memorandum to understand "Why we are in Vietnam." What emerged was very little different from what Vice President Lyndon Johnson had said in 1961 upon his return from a Southeast Asian mission. All the leaders of the "Free World" in Asia were watching, he reported to Kennedy, to see what the United States was going to do. "The battle against Communism must be joined in Southeast Asia with strength and determination to achieve success there," read the key sentence, "or the United States, inevitably, must surrender the Pacific and take up our defenses on our own shores." Putting troops ashore would not solve the basic problem, Johnson cautioned, at least by themselves. The momentary threat of Communist military success should not obscure the graver peril—the persistence of economic conditions that bred Communism at the village level. Johnson's conclusion was a strange, yet accurate codicil to American notions of nation-building. "It would be useful to enunciate more clearly than we have—for the guidance of these young and unsophisticated nations—what we expect or require of them."

As the American military presence in South Vietnam grew—it reached the 15,000 level late in 1963—it was made clear to President Diem that in future he would be expected to pay more heed to American advice. Particularly troublesome were the Buddhist protests against religious and political discrimination, especially as they became a favorite subject for American TV cameramen. Self-immolations by Buddhist priests did more than any other reports of corruption and ineptitude to cause the American public to question policy. It became dangerous for Diem to continue. He had betrayed the sacred trust; worse he was losing control. In 1954 John Foster Dulles had promised that the United States would not stand by and allow South Vietnam to vote to disappear behind the "Bamboo Curtain." Now Kennedy vowed that South Vietnam would not be destroyed by one who had turned out to be a bogus George Washington.

* *Ibid.*, p. 183.

Word was passed to Diem's generals that Washington would not interfere to prevent any action they deemed necessary to save their country. "We are launched on a course from which there is no respectable turning back," cabled Ambassador Henry Cabot Lodge from Saigon on August 29, 1963, "the overthrow of the Diem government." Still uncertain, the generals canceled the first coup attempt. But they would not be allowed to dither for long while the monks burned. On October 2, 1963, Kennedy announced a policy of economic sanctions against Diem, forcing the generals to undertake what was expected and required. Convinced that they could not carry on the war without Washington, the generals acted. Diem was overthrown and assassinated on November 1, 1963.

Three weeks later Kennedy was dead, himself the victim of an assassin in Dallas. All efforts should go ahead, cabled Lyndon Johnson to Saigon, and should be concentrated so as to "turn the tide not only of battle but of belief. . . ." Nation-building would go on, said the new President, and the war would go on. Johnson ran the next summer as the "peace" candidate against Republican Barry Goldwater, whose reputation as a quick-trigger man apparently frightened many voters. Just as the campaign got under way, moreover, Johnson got his chance to demonstrate his aptness at the "crisis manager" role Kennedy had pioneered during the "Ten Days of October," the Cuban missile crisis. An attack on American warships in the Gulf of Tonkin by North Vietnamese PT-boats, followed by a second encounter of less precise origins, enabled Johnson to ask Congress for a resolution to protect American forces in the area. It was a beautiful bank-shot off his opponent's hawk-perch, that wound up in the pocket labeled Kennedy political "cool."

Many who voted for the Gulf of Tonkin Resolution in August 1964 were convinced that they were only backing Johnson's maneuver to keep the "radical right" at bay. They hardly imagined they were giving him a warrant for a massive "search and destroy" mission across the swamps and jungles of Indochina. LBJ did nothing to correct that impression. Inside the Administration, the policy-planners picked up the pace of "option" making, deciding what measures would cause the North Vietnamese to give up supporting the Vietcong guerrillas. Bombing raids—Operation Rolling Thunder, they were called—soon began on a tit-for-tat basis. Once started, the bombing could not be stopped, even though evidence piled up that it was having absolutely no effect on North Vietnam's fighting capacity or weakening its will to win. It became necessary to bomb in order to convince Saigon of American determination to stay the course. While this "boomerang" effect intrigued policy "intellectuals," the President's military advisers warned that airpower alone would never suffice, no matter at what level. It was a matter of demonstrating one's willingness to prevail, even at the cost of suffering casualties in large-scale ground warfare. And in this regard, it was equally necessary to show both Hanoi and Saigon what Americans were really made of. Saigon would not make progress toward a stable government without such a commitment; and Hanoi would doubt American seriousness until it was done.

In May 1965 a Gallup Poll indicated that the public had little confidence in South Vietnamese ability to establish a stable government, and, more important, that a majority of Americans felt, in that eventuality, that American forces should be withdrawn. At the same time, the "teach-in" movement had begun to spread across the nation's college campuses. Taylor's successor in Saigon, Henry Cabot Lodge, was impatient with his countrymen's fickleness: "It is obviously true that the Vietnamese are not today ready for self-government, and that the French actively tried to unfit them for self-government. . . . But if we are going to adopt the policy of turning every country that is unfit for self-government over to the communists, there won't be much of the world left."

Lodge had even greater doubts about South Vietnamese ability to determine whether the Americans should leave or stay: "The idea that we are here simply because the Vietnamese want us to be here . . . that we have no rational interest in being here ourselves; and that if some of them don't want us to stay, we ought to get out is to me fallacious." All the Vietnamese needed to be told, it appeared from the Ambassador's comments, was that it was all for their own good. Lodge returned to Washington for the decisive National Security Council meeting of July 28, 1965, at which Johnson approved the sending of 100,000 ground troops.

The debate ranged over a number of issues. Secretary of Defense Robert McNamara suggested at one point that the very success of the Vietcong/NVA military campaigns would become their undoing—if the American troops were sent—because the war was fast approaching the "Third Stage," when, according to guerrilla war specialists, the enemy would break out of the jungle ready for the climactic fight for the cities. American troops, agreed a State Department official, would "hopefully stop the erosion of security, at some point push the VC back into the jungle, and, sooner or later, make them more amenable to a political settlement."

LBJ wondered if that was really so. Could Westerners win a war against Asians in the jungle rice paddies? Were these "Indian wars" winnable? Henry Cabot Lodge had no qualms at all, about any of the questions raised, not even the problem of Saigon's persistent instability:

> There is not a tradition of a national government in Saigon. There are no roots in the country. Not until there is tranquility can you have any stability. I don't think we ought to take this government seriously. There is simply no one who can do anything. We have to do what we think we ought to do regardless of what the Saigon government does.

"As we move ahead on a new phase," ended Lodge, "we have the right and duty to do certain things with or without the government's approval." If the Saigon elite could be thus ignored, American policy-makers felt it even less important to inquire deeply into the nature of the enemy. According to General Maxwell Taylor—the "thinking-man's general" of the Kennedy administration and later Ambassador to South Vietnam—at the time of the military build-up, "we knew very little about the Hanoi leaders other than Ho Chi Minh and General Giap and virtually nothing about their individual or collective intentions."

As the war grew bigger and bigger, Johnson's perspective narrowed and his language hardened into a visceral meanness that surprised even those accustomed to his blunt style. At one press conference he blurted out that any hint of a willingness to back off in Vietnam would put the whole world on the scent, like sharks after a blood trail. That was softened later in printed versions to say nothing more than America had what the world wanted. Even before the Vietnam situation turned into a daytime nightmare, Johnson was squeezing the Winning of the West motif to fit his own experiences. "Hell, Vietnam is just like the Alamo. Hell, it's just like if you were down at that gate and you were surrounded and you damn well needed somebody. Well by God, I'm going to go—and I thank the Lord that I've got men who want to go with me, from McNamara right on down to the littlest private who's carrying a gun."

In 1966, two years after he sponsored the Gulf of Tonkin Resolution, Senator J. William Fulbright, chairman of the Senate Foreign

Relations Committee, held hearings that put the Administration "on trial." The following exchange, that began in response to a question by Idaho's Frank Church, cut to the core:

Secretary Rusk. Senator, I think it is very important that different kinds of revolutions be distinguished. We are in no sense committed against change. As a matter of fact, we are stimulating, ourselves, very sweeping revolutions in a good many places. The whole weight and effort of the Alliance for Progress is to bring about far-reaching social, economic changes.

Senator Church. That is change sought, Mr. Secretary, without violence. History shows that the most significant change has been accompanied by violence. Do you think that with our foreign aid program we are going to be able, with our money, to avert serious uprisings in all of these destitute countries in future years?

Secretary Rusk. Not necessarily avert all of them, but I do believe there is a fundamental difference between the kind of revolution which the Communists call their wars of national liberation, and the kind of revolution which is congenial to our own experience, and fits into the aspirations of ordinary men and women right around the world.

There is nothing liberal about that revolution that they are trying to push from Peiping. This is a harsh, totalitarian regime. It has nothing in common with the great American revolutionary tradition, nothing in common with it.

Senator Church. The objectives of Communist revolution are clearly very different indeed from the earlier objectives of our own. But the objectives of revolutions have varied through the centuries.

The question that I think faces this country is how we can best cope with the likelihood of revolt in the underdeveloped world in the years ahead, and I have very serious doubts that American military intervention will often be the proper decision. I think too much intervention on our part may well spread communism throughout the ex-colonial world rather than thwart it.

Now, the distinction you draw between the Communist type of guerrilla war and other kinds of revolution, if I have understood it correctly, has been based upon the premise that in Vietnam the North Vietnamese have been meddling in the revolution in the south and, therefore, it is a form of aggression on the part of the north against the south. But I cannot remember many revolutions that have been fought in splendid isolation. There were as many Frenchmen at Yorktown when Cornwallis surrendered as there were American Continentals.

Senator Pell tells me more. I accept the correction.

In any case, it seems to me that the Communists have not changed the rules of revolution by meddling in them, regardless of how much we disapprove of their goals.

When we were an infant nation we stood up for the right of revolution, and I am afraid . . .

That unfinished sentence summed up the American mood as Vietnam forced its way into every aspect of the nation's life. By 1968 Washington had sent 500,000 Americans to fight, with victory nowhere in sight. Although the VC/NVA February Tet offensive "failed," it probably sealed Lyndon Johnson's political fate. The strategic hamlet resettlement program was wrecked, the most visible sign that the anti-guerrilla "reforms" did not work. In the wake of Tet, Johnson revised a stand-fast speech to the nation, transforming it completely into a public "letter" of resignation. He would not seek re-election, he said, but peace.

"I thank the Lord," LBJ had once declared, "that I've got men who want to go with me. . . ." But they didn't—not any more. Robert McNamara had left to become head of the World Bank, where he hoped to try out a new strategy for promoting "liberal" revolution. The littlest privates came home to an America struggling to understand what had happened during Tet, to understand itself after Kent State, and the rest of the world after two centuries—1776–1975—of calling itself the last, best hope of humankind.

8

The Burden of Richard Nixon

"The establishment has a guilt complex. They can't stand the fact that I, their political opponent, am rectifying their mistakes." Richard Nixon's obsession with the eastern liberal establishment was a visible scar. One could not miss it. It marked him forever with a glowering countenance and, as in this excerpt from the Watergate tapes, forced out of his lips endless self-justification. Nixon is an irresistible subject for psychohistorians. Yet he cannot really be set apart in this fashion, assigned to walk a long, lonely path on the cliff-edge of our history, forever muttering to the chasms below.

No, that won't suffice. Did Nixon's feelings run any deeper than Lyndon Johnson's brooding suspicion that behind every closed door in the Executive Office Building huddled Kennedy men, working only for the return of the Camelot days? And after Nixon both Jimmy Carter and Ronald Reagan won election as self-proclaimed "outsiders," men chosen by the people to challenge the monster bureaucracy that had grown up in Washington since World War II.

During his first term, Nixon had staged a "candid" photograph of himself walking meditatively along the beach, a California version of John Kennedy sailing off Cape Cod. It was a ghastly mistake. He looked instead like T. S. Eliot's confused "J. Alfred Prufrock," trying to remember his few lines:

> Shall I part my hair behind? Do I dare to eat a peach?
> I shall wear white flannel trousers, and walk upon the beach.

Nixon had craved the establishment's approval. Always. It could even be argued that the dominant reason Nixon appointed Henry

Kissinger his National Security Adviser was a desire to demonstrate that he, too, could manage intellectual hired-hands with the same aplomb and effectiveness as a Harvard-educated President. Kissinger was also a "loner," however, if of a different temperament. In a not-so-Freudian slip he compared himself, in an interview, to Gary Cooper standing straight and tall in *High Noon*—standing straight and tall after the local establishment had lost its nerve.

Like Nixon, Kissinger firmly believed that the American establishment had not only lost its nerve, but lost its way as well. Those who had led the nation during the most creative erea of its foreign policy now seemed paralyzed before the uninformed bawlings of a Spock-spoiled generation of college "radicals." It was Kissinger, in fact, who targeted Daniel Ellsberg, the man who leaked the "Pentagon Papers," as a representative example of the very worst features of the protest movement. In Oval Office discussions, the National Security Adviser excoriated Ellsberg's private life, fanning "Richard Nixon's flame white-hot" about counter-culture and the threat to national security: "Time after time Kissinger warned about the dire consequences of 'letting them get away with this,' of having Ellsberg running around loose and of permitting the Government 'to leak like a sieve'."*

The notion that the country was more threatened from within than without had been growing as the war in Vietnam dragged on month after month, year after year. It began with the accusation that war-protesters were largely responsible for Hanoi's intransigence, for the Vietcong's belief that it could "win" in America politically what it could not win on the battlefield. The media were also to blame. And so were disloyal civil servants. The list got longer as the war got worse.

It was hardly surprising, then, Nixon-era memoir writers tell us, that the White House should consider a break-in anything more than a necessary "Plumbers'" job to plug national security leaks. Nixon blamed "Watergate" on a dying establishment's unwillingness to accept defeat, and its unwillingness to forgive him personally. It was really all about the Alger Hiss case, he told associates, as the Watergate tide crept closer to the Oval Office. Hiss had destroyed himself by lying, Nixon would say, but the establishment never forgave him: "The establishment is dying, and so they've got to show that despite

---

* John Ehrlichman, *Witness to Power: The Nixon Years* (New York, 1982), pp. 301-2.

the successes we have had in foreign policy and in the election, they've got to show that it is just wrong just because of this [Hiss]."

The Hiss case and Watergate are bookends; they mark the span of Richard Nixon's political career, the generation of Cold War consensus. No one, ironically, was more aware of the impending and inevitable changes than Nixon himself. He perceived a world where a new vision of Wilson's old dream had begun to take shape. "It is a time when a man who knows the world will be able to forge a whole new set of alliances," he told Garry Wills, "We are now in a position to give the world all the good things that Britain offered in her Empire without any of the disadvantages of nineteenth-century colonialism."

As everyone soon had reason to know, Nixon was much too optimistic—about ending the war, and about the economy. Lyndon Johnson had refused to make a choice between guns and butter. The consequences of the Vietnam inflation would plague his successors even more, perhaps, than the supposed loss of military credibility. The Tet offensive in 1968, for example, set off a wave of speculative gold purchases in the United States. And the anticipated severity of the international monetary crisis looming ahead played a crucial role in the decision not to grant General William Westmoreland's request for yet another 200,000 troops: "But even those in policy-making circles who welcomed the reversal of the Vietnam policy were horrified by the realization that U.S. foreign-policy options were being dramatically restricted by the weakness of the dollar."*

Far from discouraged, Richard Nixon believed himself to be in a perfect position to extricate the nation safely from Vietnam— without any loss of prestige—and to rebuild a solid political base for launching *The Spirit of '76* around the world once again.† He seemed very close to that goal early in 1972, sitting across from China's Mao Zedong. "I like rightists," the aged Communist leader quipped. That gave Nixon an opportunity to be what he had always wanted to be, cool and sophisticated: "I think the most important thing to note is that in America, at least at this time, those on the right can do what those on the left only talk about."

---

* Fred L. Block, *The Origins of International Economic Disorder: A Study of United States International Monetary Policy from World War II to the Present* (Berkeley, 1977), pp. 193–94.

† Nixon renamed *Air Force One*, the Presidential airplane, *The Spirit of '76*, on the eve of his trip to China in 1972.

Nixon's words are all the more striking if compared with the strident lecture John Kennedy delivered to Nikita Khrushchev a decade earlier in Vienna. The opening to China startled Nixon-watchers, supporters and critics alike, forcing them to come to terms, as historians now must, with a much more subtle reality than they had previously known or expected. Nixon and Kissinger sometimes referred to their foreign policy design as "The Structure of Peace." So long as the United States enjoyed overwhelming nuclear superiority, it had been possible to insist that the Sino-Soviet split did not exist, or made no difference. But that luxury existed no more. "Let's put it in plain words," Nixon told NATO Council Ministers in April 1969. "The West does not today have the massive nuclear predominance that it once had, and any sort of broad-based arms agreement with the Soviets would codify the present balance." Unlike his successors, however, Nixon did not reject arms negotiations that assured "the present balance." What the situation required, he concluded, was a closer working relationship between the United States and the European NATO countries.

Approaching the situation by another path, Henry Kissinger agreed, adding that it was essential for the unity of the West for America to take the lead, but the lead in détente: "We found ourselves in the paradoxical position that we would have to take a leadership role in East-West relations if we wanted to hold the Alliance together and establish some ground rules for East-West contacts." At the center of the paradox was the "German" question. West Germany's new leader, Social Democrat Willy Brandt, was initiating a policy, *Ostpolitik*, that, like Gaullism (past and present), threatened Western cohesion and, unlike Gaullism, already raised fears about German reunity. Brandt's tentative opening to the East arose out of a number of concerns. Prominent among these was the desire for expanded economic relations, whether for themselves, or as adjunct to other desired ends.

From the time of the Berlin Wall, erected in 1961 to put an end to East German emigration, the Russians had been on the moral defensive in Central Europe. For a decade no Berlin negotiations had been necessary between East and West, but with *Ostpolitik* rising in the background, Nixon agreed to a four-power understanding about the old German capital that would have left orthodox Cold Warriors aghast. By promising that the Federal Republic (West Germany) had no intention of trying to make Berlin the capital again, the Soviets could be assured that NATO wanted to maintain the status quo.

Kissinger fretted that *Ostpolitik* could easily get out of control, could lead, in hands less capable than Brandt's, to an unhealthy economic competition that would only redound to Russia's benefit. Beyond that possibility, heavy with the danger of a fragmented Europe, lurked something even worse. Consciously or unconsciously, Brandt had set his foot upon the road Germany had traveled before, with disastrous results for the world. However unlikely it was that *Ostpolitik* would lead to a new German effort to play the "balancer" between East and West, the thought haunted policymakers. Willy Brandt was no Bismarck, but that was hardly comforting. The Social Democrats had a serious problem, Kissinger warned President Nixon privately, and that was how to control a "process," which, "if it results in failure could jeopardize their political lives and if it succeeds could create a momentum that may shake Germany's domestic stability and unhinge its international origin."

However carefully Brandt must be watched lest the détente business get out of hand, neither Kissinger nor Nixon were so foolish as to believe that only Europeans needed guidance along these strange new paths. Kissinger had in mind a set of geopolitical ground rules for the post-Vietnam era, rules that came down from the time of the French Revolution written by men who had sought to restore the classical balance of power. But those were already insufficient to the needs of the Industrial Revolution. Since that time Cobden had written, Marx had prophecied, and Keynes had come to dominate capitalist thinking. None of them offered much support for the National Security Adviser's belief that self-discipline should replace the dictates of the marketplace.

The Vietnam protest movement, paradoxically, had opened a breach in the Cold War consensus that allowed economic policymakers to start looking for a new ideology that would incorporate the new "liberalism" into a policy that would help to overcome the very real ills suffered because of America's distraction in Southeast Asia. At the top of the list was the great advantage that the war had bestowed on commercial rivals, West Germany and Japan, whose booming export economies had done far more damage than *Sputnik* to America's self-image and Hertz-like confidence, "We're Number One." On these matters, moreover, Kissinger was much less well informed than Nixon, who had spent his "exile" years among New York's elite managerial class. In the years that Nixon "apprenticed" in a prestigious New York law firm, American direct investments abroad more than doubled, from just under $32 billion to more than $78 billion. The decade 1960–70 also saw a stupendous growth in manufacturing investments abroad, from $11 billion to over $32 billion.

Even so, Kissinger was contemptuous of Democratic liberals, who, he said, were the ones ready to make the Soviets a "gift" of eased trade restrictions without regard for "linkage" considerations, i.e. political good behavior. The claim that the Cold War was over was a naïve view in the National Security Adviser's mind, as was Senator Walter Mondale's contention that trade restrictions "hold back economic growth in the U.S., not in Eastern Europe." The tabletalk Nixon heard, however, demonstrated that American economic leaders rather than Democratic "softies" had developed their own notions concerning the structure of peace. It was from these he had elaborated a neo-Wilsonian "internationalism," his belief that the time was right to forge a whole new set of alliances, that America was ready to offer the world something better than the *Pax Britannica*.

The chief economist for the U.S. Council of the International Chamber of Commerce, Judd Polk, believed that the world was already witnessing a new industrial revolution—similar to the one that had produced a national free market in nineteenth-century North America: "For the first time, men are in a position to treat the world itself as the basic economic unit." Polk did indeed mean the whole world. Testifying before Congress, the economist asserted that it was time to think of the LDCs (less developed countries) and the "centrally planned ones" (Russia, Eastern Europe, and China) as component parts of the "emergent world economy." Western Europe and Japan were ahead of the United States in this regard, he said, and we had better catch up.

"I have always said," noted Republican Senator Charles Percy during hearings on foreign economic policy, "that European countries look on us as suckers when they see restrictions by the U.S. Government on our doing business with Eastern European countries. . . . They are amazed that we have such blinders on. In our ideological battle, what we forget is that what we lack is gold, and what we need is trade."

What Kissinger perceived as a loss of nerve, or liberal naïveté, then, was in large part the confusion attendant to the formation of a post-Cold War worldview. The situation was not unlike that in the

1945–47 era, when "containment" emerged as the dominant outlook, and stragglers hurried to catch up with the pace of events. A sign of the times was Defense Secretary Robert McNamara's May 18, 1966, speech to the American Society of Newspaper Editors. Immediately dubbed the "Montreal" speech, it enraged President Johnson, who demanded to know who had cleared the Secretary's remarks. He discovered that it was his own close adviser Bill Moyers. The firmest advocate of the Vietnam build-up in 1965, McNamara now showed another side of his personality. Much of the speech was taken up with a discussion of the North-South global split between developed and undeveloped nations; other parts were concerned with the construction of a structure of peace that would include developing countries, America's allies, and the Communist nations. Relations with the last, he said, called for realism:

> But realism is not a hardened, inflexible, unimaginative attitude. The realistic mind is a restlessly creative mind—free of naive delusions, but full of practical alternatives.

> There are practical alternatives to our current relationships with both the Soviet Union and Communist China.

Eighteen months later McNamara would leave the Defense Department to head the World Bank, completing the transition from architect of war to practical philosopher of economic development. Various rumors accompanied his departure. Lyndon Johnson said that McNamara had gone soft on him. It was true that he had lost faith in the bombing policy as a solution to Third World problems, but McNamara had not nested with the doves. Instead, he had become convinced that the hawks had blinded themselves to reality.

In the wake of the Tet offensive, the so-called Council of Wisemen Johnson called to the White House surprised him by reaching the same conclusion. After deliberating for two days on disarray within the Democratic party, the growing strength of the antiwar movement, and the perilous situation created by a $20 billion gap in America's balance of payments, the Wisemen delivered their verdict: "We had better start looking for another way to get this war settled."

Isolated for so long from any serious dissent in White House circles, Johnson could not really quarrel with those arguments. He had planned a speech calling for perseverance. That was changed into an announcement that he was ordering a partial suspension of bombing raids against North Vietnam. He also announced that he was taking himself out of the Presidential race to clear the way for other men to deal with the Gordian knot Vietnam had become. Still, it would be wrong to assume that LBJ had given up all hope of "winning" the war. The momentum in favor of expanding America's role on the ground had been checked, but not been replaced with a clear-cut decision to withdraw. A cable sent out from Washington on the day of Lyndon Johnson's speech noted that the partial suspension might end within four weeks. It was a testing period: "Hence, we are not giving up anything really serious in this time frame. Moreover, air power now used north of 20th can probably be used in Laos (where no policy change planned) and in SVN."

Nixon vowed that he would not allow the war to destroy him as it had Johnson. He recalled that Eisenhower's success had depended upon ending the Korean War quickly, yet without compromising America's "credibility." "I'm not going to end up like LBJ, Bob," Nixon told H. R. Haldeman, "holed up in the White House, afraid to show my face on the street. I'm going to stop that war. Fast. I mean it!" The Eisenhower parallel had in fact captivated Nixon. The mysterious plan for ending the war he announced in the 1968 Presidential campaign turned out to be his variation on Eisenhower's threat to use atomic weapons if the Korean stalemate continued. He lacked Ike's military credentials, but he thought that his long career as a bitter anti-Communist would serve to convince the North Vietnamese that he meant what he said: "I call it the Madman Theory, Bob. I want the North Vietnamese to believe I've reached the point where I might do *anything* to stop the war. We'll just slip the word to them that, 'for God's sake, you know Nixon is obsessed about Communism. We can't restrain him when he's angry—and he has his hand on the nuclear button'—and Ho Chi Minh himself will be in Paris in two days begging for peace."

But that was not all. A year before the Presidential campaign began in earnest, Nixon had written in *Foreign Affairs*, the premier establishment journal, "We simply cannot afford to leave China forever outside the family of nations." Post-Vietnam Asia, he said, held unlimited possibilities. "In a sense it could be said that a new chapter is being written in the winning of the West: in this case, a winning of the promise of Western technology and Western organization by the nations of the East."

Almost as soon as he arrived in the White House, Nixon instructed Henry Kissinger to pass the word: the Madman Theory was in operation. But he also wanted it known that, if the North Vietnamese were willing to enter into "legitimate" peace negotiations, he was prepared to make a generous offer of financial aid. Moscow was to be informed, in addition, that possibilities existed for Soviet-American economic co-operation. Simultaneously, Nixon began to follow through on a plan for ending China's "isolation."

Thus Nixon's plan owed as much to Robert McNamara as it did to Eisenhower. It could be argued, therefore, that the mix itself lacked credibility. The Madman Theory worked only if the other side could be made to believe that Nixon had taken leave of his senses. Hanoi's leaders could afford to gamble on Nixon's sanity, even if, as happened, the President's growing frustration led him to widen the war to Cambodia and Laos, and to unleash new destruction from the air.

On June 8, 1969—even before Henry Kissinger had ever met with his North Vietnamese opposite number—Nixon made a coolly calculated decision to withdraw 25,000 American troops. Later announcements were timed to blunt the peace movement's offensives, now capable of sending hundreds of thousands to Washington. These were not the acts of a madman. They only succeeded in increasing demands for a definite timetable for final evacuation. And the overall impression created in America was of madness, yes, but it created the opposite of the desired effect: The Administration knew it was going to lose, and was wasting lives thrashing about, flailing the earth with bombs and poisonous chemicals, oblivious to everything save its own frenzy.

Vietnamization, the rationale for the Nixon policy, depended (as had America's policy since 1954) upon success in "nation-building." It could not work otherwise. The only alternative to "nation-building" was endless war. Indeed, the Nixon administration required a stable regime in Saigon more than any other time since Dulles, despite the neo-conservative critique of Kennedy-minded liberals in charge. How else would it be possible to create an effective South Vietnamese military? With American aid and urging, South Vietnamese armed forces climbed from 600,000 in early 1968 to over a million in 1971. The South Vietnamese air force, with over a thousand planes, became the world's fourth largest. Vietnamization implied, indeed dictated, the "incursions" into Cambodia in 1970 and into Laos a year later.

When Kissinger forwarded to the President in late 1969 a Central

Intelligence Agency study of growing pessimism in South Vietnam, derived from a fear of an overly hasty American withdrawal, he received this reply: "They must take responsibility if they are *ever* to gain confidence. We have to take risks on that score." Added to this psychological imperative was Kissinger's own belief that the war could not be won so long as the South remained in a defensive posture, reacting to the other side's initiatives. The only way to open options at the negotiating table was to create military problems for one's adversary on the battlefield.

Of a piece with Vietnamization was Nixon's "Guam Doctrine," announced on his first official tour of the Far East and Southeast Asia. Several versions of the "doctrine" exist, an indication of the several audiences Nixon was somehow trying to reach with a statement about future policy in Asia. In its original formulation, the President promised to honor all of America's treaty commitments to SEATO nations and others, but he qualified this by saying also that so far as "internal security" problems were concerned, "except for the threat of a major power involving nuclear weapons," the United States had a right to expect Asian nations to handle this responsibility by themselves.

That was close to an admission that the original basis for American participation in the Vietnam War, and the elaborate variations on the Munich analogy spun out by Johnson administration witnesses on Capitol Hill, were, at the very least, overdrawn responses to a localized conflict. Or it could be read differently, of course, to mean that Vietnam was a special case and to reassure the world that Richard Nixon did not intend to go rushing into civil wars. Either way, and in the context of a program of troop withdrawals, the effect was quite dramatic. It also underscored the President's ever increasing willingness to consider a "coalition" government in Saigon, though not named as such in his speeches, as a solution to the deadlocked peace negotiations.

The Guam Doctrine, however interpreted, was a strange way to persuade the other side of the Madman Theory. Still less would Nixon's hints at a coalition solution mark him with a lunatic's brush. On November 3, 1969, the President stated, as if it had been American policy all along, that the "Communists" could participate in the "organization and conduct of the elections as an organized political force." Not only had the Johnson administration refused to countenance any such recognition of Vietcong "legitimacy," the whole history of the Cold War, on the American side, denied the possibility. The Greek Government in 1947, for example, had never been required to permit the Communists to share in the electoral planning and process. Quite the opposite, in fact.

By this "concession," moreover, the Nixon policy undermined another fundamental of the American position in Vietnam: the claim that Saigon was a sovereign government. How was it, if South Vietnam was independent, that Washington could make such an offer? But neither the offer of a coalition, nor the willingness to shorten the stay of American forces after a formal truce, nor even, finally, the oblique suggestion that a standstill truce would meet American requirements, instead of an immediate North Vietnamese withdrawal, budged Hanoi from previously stated positions.

As Nixon's frustration mounted, it grew upon him that the establishment enjoyed his agony—a suspicion fed by Kissinger's tattling reports on members of his own staff—and was pleased that his efforts at peace had met with failure, that it was, in fact, backing Hanoi's play: "North Viet-Nam cannot defeat or humiliate the United States. Only Americans can do that." He pictured himself as Wilson's true heir; risking political defeat for a decent peace:

Fifty years ago, in this room and at this very desk, President Woodrow Wilson spoke words which caught the imagination of a war-weary world. He said: "This is the war to end wars."

His dream for peace after World War I was shattered on the hard realities of great-power politics, and Woodrow Wilson died a broken man.

On April 30, 1970, moreover, Nixon announced the Cambodian "incursion" in words and sentences that sounded like he had decided on martial law at home to end dissent:

My fellow Americans, we live in an age of anarchy, both abroad and at home. We see mindless attacks on all the great institutions which have been created by free civilizations in the last 500 years. Even here in the United States, great universities are being systematically destroyed. Small nations all over the world find themselves under attack from within and from without.

If, when the chips are down, the world's most powerful nation, the United States of America, acts like a pitiful, helpless giant, the forces of totalitarianism and anarchy will threaten free nations and free institutions throughout the world.

The "wedge" that Wilson had so feared Nixon called anarchy. Nixon did not ask for martial law, of course, but he tried to unloose government agencies against an enemies hit list, and he plotted ways of circumventing the Constitutional rights of war-protestors. Whatever snares he set for others, it would be Nixon who got caught. Before Watergate he was stuck before a logical obstacle, which, he rationalized, could not be overcome except by indirect methods. Already engaged in an innovative effort to persuade Americans to the need to grant legitimacy to Communist China, and, less certainly, to the Vietcong and North Vietnam, he felt he could proceed only by assaulting the legitimacy of his domestic opponents.

To accomplish this feat, Nixon had drawn into his inner circle Henry Kissinger, a genuine conservative, but, for the President's purposes a shield against "egg-head" attacks on his left flank. Locked in tandem, and with each suspicious of the other, Nixon and Kissinger suffused an Administration already given to intrigue with the atmosphere of an Italian Renaissance court.

Observing all this with a surprisingly sympathetic eye was Dean Acheson, who rallied to an old sworn enemy's defense. Like Nixon, Acheson feared anarchy, feared it as an evil product of Communism, feared it perhaps more than the power of the Soviet Union. At one point during the Korean War, Acheson had written words of solace to the father of an American soldier, trying to explain why it was necessary for his son to be there. Americans found it hard, the Secretary had written, to believe that such evil as the Communists had unleashed upon the world really existed. But it did, and it twisted and tormented every human soul. It was a strange letter, not really addressing the father's complaint, and better understood in retrospect.

Acheson realized that, whatever his faults, the establishment could not heap upon Nixon's head responsibility for what was taking place, without damaging itself in the process. Nixon-bashing was a dangerous exercise, as it degraded the Presidential office. If America succumbed to the war-protestors, if America came home to isolationism, what was there left? A civil war in Europe that began in 1914 and ended in 1945, he told a *New York Times* interviewer, had destroyed all the empires. England was unable to accept its new status, a bankrupt people conducting a banking business they should get out of. France was deeply divided, Italy hardly a country, and the West

Germans on the verge of a political crisis. Russia had invaded Czechoslovakia in 1968 out of fear, not strength. Nationalist China was finished, the Communist Chinese weak, and so were the Indians.

If America was to exert the leadership the world so obviously required, the nation must support its Presidents: "I think we're going to have a major constitutional crisis if we make a habit of destroying Presidents. We'll have the situation we had after the Civil War, when the Presidency practically disappeared—from Andrew Johnson to McKinley." It was the time for students, liberals, and intellectuals to cease and desist: "This is why Dr. Spock gives me a pain, why Bill Coffin [William Sloane Coffin]—a hell of a nice fellow—by being a Protestant clergyman [thinks he] knows everything about international affairs. He doesn't. When I was a trustee at Yale I wanted to give him a hemlock cocktail to relieve him of some of his responsibilities."

Acheson's jests were never idle. More conservative than other Johnson stalwarts during the Vietnam War, Acheson was also more forthright in insisting, as a special member of the 1968 Council of Wisemen, that the President must de-escalate. Throughout a long career in office, Acheson had always viewed Asian policy as a means to some other desirable end. He was a true empire-builder in this respect, as in others. America had accepted Japan's challenge, not to save China, but to demonstrate the white man's right and ability to dominate the Pacific. He had cared very little about Korea, except to demonstrate the Truman administration's ability and right to lead Europe back to political health.

Vietnam was a disaster. But it must not be compounded into the end of the American Century. The United States was losing face in both Asia and Europe. Like others, Acheson viewed the drift towards *Ostpolitik* (and later neutralism) as the result of a European feeling that America had too little time and energy left over to attend to alliance needs. Nixon did not need to hear this from either Kissinger or Acheson, however, as he recalled other voices in his memoirs. "Thank God you are here," West German Chancellor Konrad Adenauer had greeted him in 1967, though what Nixon could do about the internal crisis in the alliance and the threat of rising support for the Communists was hard to say. Italian Foreign Minister Amintore Fanfani was equally distraught, blaming the situation directly upon America's preoccupation with Vietnam: "America is like the man

confronted with a small fire in his barn when his house is falling apart
for want of repairs."

The final crisis would come, Adenauer predicted, when Charles de
Gaulle left the scene. De Gaulle frightened his fellow conservative
leaders. He had challenged the notion that safety in numbers—the
NATO formula—was their only sure guarantee against internal enemies as well as against Russia. Returning to power as America went
deeper and deeper into Vietnam, de Gaulle's ascendancy looked to be
a case of double jeopardy for traditionalists, a quirk of fate that might
bring them all down. FDR once said that de Gaulle suffered from a
Joan of Arc complex. The voices de Gaulle heard were closer at hand,
however, than the Maid's inspiration. Jean Monnet was his guide. All
the General did was to push Monnet's vision as far as it would go.
Having ended the Algerian War successfully, de Gaulle asserted a
French claim to mediate between Europe and the Third World.
Europe must find its own way again, he would declare over and over,
without super-power interference.

Doubters thought the General was fishing in troubled waters, and
would pull in a catch loaded with stingrays. He risked Europe's
future, they said, simply to take advantage of an American "mistake."
Supporters thought otherwise, of course. Vietnam was no mistake,
and America had no qualms about risking Europe's future in the
Third World for the sake of the *Pax Americana*. De Gaulle had
warned Kennedy not to go into Vietnam. Beginning in 1965 he sought
to impose "sanctions" on Washington—public denunciations of the
war and economic measures. Perhaps he saw this as poetic justice,
after all that had been said against France between 1945 and 1954 for
imperialist failings that imperiled "Free World" interests in Asia; or
perhaps he undertook to place himself in the frontline of America's
critics simply as a guise, behind which he would work to free Europe
from American hegemony. Probably it was a bit of both, and more
besides. But what if he miscalculated? He could taunt Americans into
"isolationism," some said, or he might undermine political stability
from within. Eventually, during the May Day student uprisings in
1968, General de Gaulle had a premonition of the latter—and stepped
aside.

Whatever his motives, de Gaulle's trenchant criticism of the war
and his alternative vision for Europe's future became as much of a
constraint on American actions, arguably, as Russian supplies of

weapons to North Vietnam. At the time of the Cuban missile crisis in 1962, if not earlier, the General had concluded that Washington's defense policies no longer gave first priority to Europe but were instead holding Europe hostage to pay for an adventurous attempt at world empire. The Vietnam War he took as final proof.

What was the evidence? Well, for one thing, Lyndon Johnson had refused to raise American taxes to pay for the war, a sinister means of shifting the burden to the backs of Europeans. How? By depending upon deficit spending, the American President took advantage of the dollar's "reserve currency" status to transfer—through inflation—a percentage of the war costs to the unwary European who still believed the dollar was worth its weight in gold. If this trend kept on, de Gaulle predicted, Europeans would find themselves with stacks of green paper in their vaults, while Americans kept all the gold. But that was not all. Since the dollar's value remained relatively higher outside the United States, it became easier for American capitalists to "use" Vietnam to colonize European industry. Simply put, a million "domestic" dollars would buy more in Europe.

So the General declared France's "independence." The first shots fired came when he presented several hundred million dollars to the U.S. Treasury for redemption in gold. Then at his annual press conference, on February 4, 1965, he sounded a warning to all Europeans that the dollar was already a dangerously inflated currency, worth so much more outside the United States than inside that there followed "a growing propensity to invest abroad which, in many countries, amounts to no less than a sort of expropriation of such and such enterprises."

A few weeks later, during talks with Soviet Foreign Minister Andrei Gromyko, de Gaulle made a public attack on American policy in Vietnam, using the opportunity to contrast France's attitude toward former colonial areas: "While we are helping them, the Americans are using all their brilliant new technological inventions to exterminate in the most horrible ways thousands of these poor long-suffering Vietnamese, who merely want to be left alone. And look what they are doing at San Domingo [the Dominican Republic] . . . And I'm afraid this isn't the end yet. *L'appetit vient en mangeant.*"

In 1967 de Gaulle rejected Britain's new bid to join the Common Market, repeating a frequent charge that to admit the British was to welcome an American Trojan Horse. Even for de Gaulle, this press conference of November 27, 1967, marked a new high in anti-Americanism. The United States had ignored his call for big power negotiations to settle Middle Eastern questions, he went on, a foolish refusal that had prompted Israeli adventurism that both America and Israel would come to rue one day soon. He even demanded that Canada grant its French-speaking province, Quebec, a sovereign status, so that it might "stand up to the invasion of the United States."

From Paris he saw an "outside element, artificial and unilateral," that stood poised to strike down "our national patrimony. . . . It is quite remarkable that the total of the American balance-of-payments deficit for the last eight years is precisely the same as the total for American investment in Western European countries."

Some Nixon advisers, meanwhile, as well as a good many war critics, would urge the new President to imitate de Gaulle's successful solution of the protracted Algerian War: Get out, at once, make a clean break with the past. Possibly, if de Gaulle had not made so much of his *coup de paix*, had not thrown it in American faces quite so often, this would have had significant appeal, but probably not, given American obsessions with "credibility," which had become the sole refuge for war-defenders, and an awesome reverence for Parson Weems versions of history. In that latter view, the Vietnam War syllogism went as follows. The war in Algeria was a colonial war. America did not fight colonial wars. If America lost in Vietnam, that war became (by definition) a colonial war, like Algeria, where the only solution was defeat.

Vietnamization, it soon became apparent, was no substitute for victory. Later versions, including, of course, Nixon's own, held that a victory was won in Vietnam in 1972—only to be thrown away by Congress and the "trendy" media. Henry Kissinger argues a similar case, but at least he admits to doubts in describing Hanoi's Le Duc Tho's comments about Vietnamization:

> He cut to the heart of the dilemma . . . All too acutely, he pointed out that our strategy was to withdraw enough forces to make the war bearable for the American people while simultaneously strengthening the Saigon forces so that they could stand on their own. He then asked me the question that was also tormenting me: "Before, there were over a million U.S. and puppet troops, and you failed. How can you succeed when you let the puppet troops do the fighting? Now, with only U.S. support, how can you win?"

Kissinger's readers are not told what Le Duc Tho had to say, if anything, about the balance-of-payments crisis, which was worse than Tet, and which, along with the other economic "dilemmas" threatened the ultimate humiliation for Nixon. Grant that war critics disguised their moral objections with statistical tables, there was no gainsaying what the Council of Wisemen had told Lyndon Johnson in 1968: the war was gutting America's international economic position and destabilizing the economy at home.

There was an understandable tendency to insist that the war was not the real problem but rather European and Japanese "protectionism." To be sure, America's industrial partners in the "Free World" had displayed a disappointing lack of concern about their obligations to resolve the balance-of-payments by accepting more imports, or picking up the costs of American military establishments. Kissinger's expertise left off inside the realm of such work-a-day capitalist concerns. That was more in John Connally's line. Appointed Secretary of the Treasury in late 1970, the tall Texan was the first Cabinet officer to penetrate the "palace guard" around Nixon, or to pre-empt Kissinger's place in the public eye. The National Security Adviser doubted Connally (or anyone else) could put things back on the shelf, at least in the same order, but he recognized a kindred spirit. "He was convinced that the best way to transcend the malaise of Vietnam," Kissinger recorded of the Treasury guardian, "was for our leaders to be visibly engaged in a tough defense of the American interest."

Connally did not beat around the bush. In Munich, on May 28, 1971, he told NATO's finance ministers that from now on they would have to carry more of "the common burdens."

And, to be perfectly frank, no longer will the American people permit their government to engage in international actions in which the true long-run interests of the U.S. are not just as clearly recognized as those of the nations with which we deal.

Connally's words had a strange ring. Where was the Kremlin master design to rule the world; what had happened to the Kennedy promise to pay any price for freedom? Connally sounded like an "isolationist" midwesterner out of the 1930s. Either that or one of George III's ministers upon surveying the state of the empire in 1763. It had seemed only fair then for the American colonies to share in the common burdens of imperial defense. After all, they were on the frontier of freedom. And after all, the costly war against the French had been fought as much for their benefit as for the mother country.

At the time Connally "put it on the line" in Munich, American gold stocks had fallen to just above $10 billion, lower than at any time since 1936. The payments deficit was running at more than $20 billion, almost twice the record figure of 1970. On August 15, 1971, Nixon announced his equivalent of the Stamp Act—a 10 percent tariff surtax and an end to dollar-gold convertibility. Bolder than his military initiatives in Vietnam, more risky than the Cambodian or Laotian "incursions," Nixon's New Economic Policy faced Europe and Japan with the choice of accepting a paper "dollar standard" or of plunging the world into economic chaos. Four days later in Dallas, the President singled out the philosopher William James (of all people) as the guiding spirit of his future policy. James had predicted that the fate of civilization would depend upon finding a moral equivalent for war. Nixon took him up. An insidious line of propaganda was afloat, the President said, that held it did not matter if America was number one:

> My comrades of the Veterans of Foreign Wars, the history of civiliza-
> tion is strewn with the wreckage of nations that were rich and that fell
> before people that were less rich and considered to be inferior to them
> intellectually and in every other way, because the rich nations, in their
> maturity, lost their drive, lost their desire, lost their dynamism, lost
> their vitality.

It felt right to him, this New Economic Policy, and Nixon could not resist quoting de Gaulle. The General had said not long before his death that France was "her true self only when she was engaged in a great enterprise." Well, concluded Nixon, that was also true of America. It felt right for Connally, too: "We have a problem and we're sharing it with the world—just like we shared our prosperity. That's what friends are for." Two years later, in the fall of 1973, the Egyptians launched a military attack against Israel on the eve of the Yom Kippur high holy days. Nixon ordered a world-wide military alert to put the Russians on notice not to intervene, and found, to his amazement, that the NATO allies had banned their territory for the use of American forces destined for the Middle East. It was Suez in reverse—or something worse. European fears that the Arab world would retaliate for American intervention in the Yom Kippur War by embargoing oil to the industrial world had produced a major schism between Europe and the United States. The war came to an end without either Russian or American intervention, but the fear of an oil embargo proved justified as the war became the "take off stage" for OPEC (Organization of Petroleum Exporting Countries), the first successful counter-offensive by a raw materials combine since the Industrial Revolution separated the world into developed and under-developed areas.

After OPEC, Connally's words sounded more like Lord Grenville's premature crowing over the Stamp Act. Be that as it may, Nixon had entered upon an odyssey that would take him all the way to the Great Wall of China and back, a journey that would enable him to shuck off a cumbersome Cold War ideology that had confined American poli-cymakers for too long. Americans had always assumed that they had a special role to play in China. But no President had ever gone there, let alone to listen and learn. Yet it was not enough. The trip to China had resulted in a memorandum that all but eliminated Taiwan as a major barrier to Sino-American relations, but in doing so, the trip also refocused attention on the Soviet Union as the malevolent force behind the agony in Vietnam—and everyplace else.

Perhaps only novelists like Robert Stone have succeeded thus far in revealing to us what the Vietnam experience was all about, and how it reshaped America internally; corrupted government; made us all "Dog Soldiers" in an insane war against ourselves, running in packs after a blood scent. In any case, the events of the first Nixon administration could not be absorbed (perhaps even by the Presi-dent), or sorted out in a coherent fashion, by a nation that had been promised nothing less than a world of its own.

Nixon imagined a second term free of Vietnam, a time to reflect, a chance to build upon the "structure of peace." Even without the Yom Kippur War and OPEC, odds were against him. Democratic candi-date George McGovern was asked by *Time* to comment on détente and Nixon's achievements. He replied, "It's a little like telling a man that he was in fine physical condition, except for a malignant tumor in his lungs." Nixon had correctly judged that McGovern would be the easiest Democrat to beat, and so he was, but the "radicalism" which alienated so many old Cold War liberals and eventually drove them into Reagan's ranks was an ominous sign. Perhaps the right could not, as Nixon had assured Mao, do what the left only talked about. Perhaps Nixon was afraid of what he saw around the next turn on the Great Wall.

The Cold War "masks" worn by actors on the world scene, however inadequate for the future, were less frightening in the end, than what he saw ahead.

What strange voices whispered to him in the Oval Office? What self-destructive urges produced Watergate; what enemies did he imagine he must risk so much to prove wrong—finally and terribly wrong? The furies that pursued Nixon so relentlessly were not figments of his damaged psyche. Despite all the self-congratulatory talk before Vietnam about how Americans had at last accepted their role, their world responsibilities, the Cold War had, in fact, enabled the policymaking elite to go on convincing the nation that Americans lived apart from the rest of the earth's peoples. And it allowed the elite to imagine a world, in turn, which could be reduced to alternative options of an NSC memorandum.

So it was appropriate, after all, for Nixon to call upon William James, and to warn Americans of the difficulties attendant on forging a post-Cold War political consensus. Unfortunately, as the election of 1972 neared, Kissinger gave a press conference that made it appear "peace was at hand" in Vietnam, and that the transition to a new world-view had been accomplished. The supposed agreement evaporated, largely because at the last moment the United States could not make the South Vietnamese accept the terms, except at the high cost of a final break with Saigon. There followed a depressing sequence of events that left the President isolated politically and morally. The already troubled interaction between détente and the Vietnam War became outright contradiction with the so-called Christmas bombings of Hanoi and Haiphong. If the Soviets were responsible for North Vietnam's continuing obstinacy (even though it was Saigon that originally rejected the agreement), then what use was détente? If they were not, then what use were the bombings?

For eleven days American B-52s waged the most intensive raids of a campaign that had already seen record tonnages dropped. Over two thousand strikes were carried out against North Vietnamese cities. Administration sources were not even sure of the purpose of this final "brutalizing" of the enemy. Immediately controversial, the bombings were said by some to be necessary to bring the South Vietnamese in line, by convincing them that the United States would never stand by and see the Communists take over their "country." Others averred that the real reason was psychological, a warning to would-be aggressors that America would not be mocked. Still others saw it as a pre-emptive strike against American conservatives who had cried out for so many years that what was wrong with the war strategy could be cured in a short time if the politicians just got out of the way of the generals.

Many things remain in dispute about the bombings, including even their short-term efficacy in bringing the North back to the negotiating table. The changes in the final agreement signed in 1973, whatever was claimed for them, did not permit the South anything more than a "decent interval" to set its affairs in order. The key provision in this regard was the stipulation that North Vietnamese military forces could remain in place in South Vietnam during the creation of a new Government of National Reconciliation. And what was the Government of National Reconciliation except the coalition arrangement long demanded by the North, and resisted with heaven-witnessed oaths by the South and its American "advisers."

The other side of the bombing ledger revealed a very short list of presumed gains. True, Hanoi gave up its demand that the Thieu Government be "overthrown" and replaced immediately with a Provisional Government of the Vietcong, neutrals, and Republic of South Vietnam officials. American negotiators always insisted that the bombing made North Vietnam offer a satisfactory solution of the POW question, though the speculative nature of this claim suggests that it was made in part to enhance the Korean "parallel," and Eisenhower's threat to use atomic weapons. In this view, only Watergate made the agreement a bad one, wiped out the Korea-like victory for containment, and made the document into a Munich-like exercise. Watergate shackled the "President" (now a separate concern from Nixon's fate), making it impossible to fulfill promises to use military force against military force should the North Vietnamese resume efforts at conquest.

To the contrary, the Christmas bombings actually reduced Presidential options, depriving the executive of "credibility" with all the groups he was so concerned to influence. Conservatives could be satisfied only by victory. Liberals found a rallying point in opposing Nixon. Word spread that Nixon was indeed unbalanced. One journalist claimed that the President had confided to a chosen few that he did not care if the whole world thought he was crazy, for then "the Russians and Chinese might think they were dealing with a madman and so better force North Vietnam into a settlement before the world was consumed in a larger war."

What had befallen Nixon, however, was explainable only as the culmination of Cold War irrationality. In the 1950s John Foster Dulles had boasted that the art of diplomacy was going to the brink of war to preserve peace. During the 1961 Berlin crisis, Dean Acheson had recommended that Kennedy convey to the Russians a total implacability, irrationality even, so as to impress them with America's commitment to preserving things as they were. The illusion of negotiation from strength, which Nixon knew no longer obtained in his world, made it all the more important not to negotiate détente from weakness.

No office wielded more power in the history of civilization than the American Cold War Presidency, yet none was more bound to a disabling world-view. Little wonder that Nixon always yearned to strike a decisive blow at the "enemy." Early in the Administration he considered ordering retaliatory attacks on North Korea for the downing of an American plane. The attacks on North Vietnamese sanctuaries in Cambodia—a policy that was later listed in the bill of impeachment prepared by Congress before he resigned—was undertaken to demonstrate to domestic enemies that he could play "hard ball" as well as Jack Kennedy in the Cuban missile crisis, or LBJ during the Gulf of Tonkin "crisis." Nixon had some justification for feeling that he was a scapegoat for a generation, a role once played by Alger Hiss, and most recently by Lieutenant Calley.

Probably the most convoluted explanation of the relationship between Vietnam and détente was supplied by Washington's last Ambassador in Saigon, Graham Martin, who suggested that détente would be of little use to Peking and Moscow if the United States demonstrated any lack of will in carrying out its avowed commitments. Vietnam was a psychological battlefield for Martin, recalled a CIA analyst, and he imagined the American Embassy as an extension of the White House, where only the world crisis mattered: "I believe our successfully completing the job has an enormous effect on the perception of the United States, on the will of the United States, on the value of the commitment of the United States in Peking and Moscow."*

The May 1972 Moscow Summit Conference was taken as evidence of the soundness of this theory. The spring offensive by North Viet-

*Frank Snepp, *Decent Interval: An Insider's Account of Saigon's End Told by the CIA's Chief Strategy Analyst in Vietnam* (New York, 1977), p. 75.

nam during that year had been met with daring boldness, a decision to mine Haiphong harbor—despite the risk that the Russians would call off the Summit. When four Russian merchant-ships were damaged by American bombers in raids on the North Vietnamese harbor, the Russians launched a protest against these "gangster activities." But that was it. Furthermore, Soviet leader Leonid Brezhnev confessed (as it were) that Moscow did not have a great deal of influence over Hanoi. As interpreted in the Oval Office, the Russian reactions both justified the use of the bombers in Ambassador Martin's ambiguous sense that "the value of the commitment" was demonstrated and in the more abstract and subtle conviction that the Russians were actually becoming afraid of the consequences of their own Marxism —leaving it to the United States to set the limits.

Whether or not Nixon needed the bombings (then or later) to look at himself in the mirror of détente, or to buy insurance policies against the conservatives made uneasy by the very thought of a new "Yalta," then, American policymakers took the Soviet response as confirmation of the value of the covenant with power, the final resolution of the contradictions in the original Wilsonian worldview. At Moscow the entire range of East-West issues came under discussion, including the difficult SALT-I agreement. But Nixon and Brezhnev signed a twelve-point statement of basic principles that further underscored the conviction that perseverance in Vietnam had served the cause of world order. The second and third points concerned the need for mutual restraint so as to avoid nuclear war. "Accordingly," they read in part, "they will seek to promote conditions in which all countries will live in peace and security and will not be subject to outside interference in their internal affairs." Further down the list, at point eleven, appeared this statement: "The USA and the USSR make no claim for themselves and would not recognize the claims of anyone else to any special rights or advantages in world affairs. They recognize the sovereign equality of all states."

Did these "pledges" require the Russians to refrain from "causing" new Vietnams, or did they merely codify, however vaguely, a live and let live super-power understanding about respective spheres of influence? Kissinger writes that, "we interpreted [it] as a denial of the Brezhnev Doctrine." In 1968 the Soviets had intervened to crush a Czechoslovakian regime that sought a "liberalization" of party rule, claiming a special right to protect the socialist bloc against outside interference. Hence the "fraternal" Brezhnev Doctrine. To take the

Moscow pledges for anything other than "window dressing" was uncharacteristic for the confirmed geopolitician, Henry Kissinger, especially since the realist complaint had always been that Nixon's predecessors had been taken in by such transparent devices.

When the President addressed Congress on the results of the Summit on June 1, 1972, nevertheless, he pictured its accomplishments as lasting achievements, and not preludes to disappointment as after past "euphoric" episodes in Soviet-American relations: the Eisenhower "Spirits" of Geneva and Camp David, Kennedy's "Spirit" of Vienna (which did not belong in the list), and LBJ's "Spirit" of Glassboro. All had evaporated, leaving nothing but the harsh reality of Cold War. Having thus dismissed the failures of past diplomacy (including those of his mentors Dulles and Eisenhower), Nixon reached too far. Referring to the statement of principles, he asserted of the Russians, "They disavow any intention to create spheres of influence. . . ."

How many sitting there that day heard echoes of another speech after the Yalta summit? The Yalta Agreements, Franklin Roosevelt had declared, meant an end to all the old expedients that had been tried and found wanting: balance of power, spheres of influence, and all the rest. Despite the passage of a quarter-century, Yalta had left a deep imprint. It was condemned by conservatives, excused by liberals. It was never viewed as anything but a failure, and, by some, a treasonable act against the United States.

Nixon's domestic support, observes Henry Kissinger, began to erode soon after the Summit. Leaks about SALT-I were partly to blame, rumors that Nixon had given away America's strategic edge to get an agreement: "We were involved in a delicate balancing act: to be committed to peace without letting the quest for it become a form of moral disarmament, surrendering all other values. . . ." America's foremost memoir writer hints that the President he served was not secure enough within himself to travel across this highwire in safety. A few weeks later came Watergate, where the President's men bungled a "nickel-and-dime" robbery, but succeeded in collapsing the "structure of peace." No safety net below, Nixon plummeted into political oblivion.

Different lessons were drawn from Watergate. Kissinger, joined soon by a rising chorus of lapsed liberal intellectuals, put the investigators on trial. Their exposures, it was asserted, achieved nothing but the weakening of the President's power and therefore the nation's resolve in meeting the Soviet challenge. The mistake in Vietnam had been made at the outset, but once in, America had to prove it could not be driven back from the farthest frontiers of freedom, lest the old "isolationist" urge reassert its control over a shaken public opinion. Nixon's gravest offenses, in his view, were that he brought the "executive" into disrepute, and, it was now being suggested, that he sought agreement with the Soviets to save his own skin.

Ironically, in the Watergate affair was, for others, the potential for the post-Cold War vision Nixon had reached for with one hand, while the other gripped Henry Kissinger's shoulders for support. The disparities between self-image and reality had been brought home by Vietnam and Watergate. Together they had forced a re-examination of foreign policy, covert intelligence activities, and the growth of the policymaking system. Richard Nixon had confronted these, obliquely, and tried to avert the coming danger. He tried to make Wilson's ideas fit his own narrow conceptions of world order. When that would not work, neither he—nor Kissinger, who landed on two feet—undertook to build a post-Cold War constituency. Asked if he thought the former President and he had "oversold" the term détente, Kissinger replied with some asperity, "Nixon was running for re-election—I wasn't." In later years Nixon became a "futurist," writing of the *Real War* (1980) in such a way as to expunge his own record or to blame détente upon the liberal establishment; Kissinger wrote his minute-by-minute memoirs, and waited for the call to action in Cold War II.

9

On Board the *Pequod:* The Search for a 1980s' Foreign Policy

Experienced commentators have already provided a list of historical antecedents for the "Reagan Revolution." Theodore White, the chronicler of Presidential elections, found it necessary to take the long view, rather than his usual approach, and he entitled his new work, published in 1982, *America in Search of Itself: The Making of the President 1956–1980.* In it he writes, "Thus in 1980 I had to consider Ronald Reagan and Jimmy Carter. Neither seemed to me to carry in his personality the vitality that moves history. It seemed rather that they were both men who were carried up or borne down by forces outside themselves."

Pointing to the low voter turnout, other observers wondered if indifference was not the most powerful force in determining the outcome. It was not a "revolution" at all but simply a case of "throw the rascals out"—a common occurrence in American politics. Nation-wide the voter turnout was the lowest since 1948, a time when blacks were still disenfranchised in many areas of the South. Only a little more than half of the eligible voters went to the polls, and Reagan won the Presidency with the support of less than a third of the total electorate.

Nonvoters have become the largest "party" in America, notes political scientist Walter Dean Burnham, a distressing sign that liberal democracy is in deep trouble: "Whether ideological or not at the grass roots, the election will be put to ideological ends by those who won it."* Ronald Reagan favors a comparison to Franklin D. Roosevelt and the New Deal, which, in an important sense, confirms the Burnham thesis, for voter turnout in 1932 was only a percentage point or two above that of 1980. The New Deal became the closest approximation of European-style class politics in American history, and the beginning point for all later discussions.

Since the New Deal, Republicans had "won" only two Presidential elections, 1952 and 1968, if one counts re-elections as a reward for services rendered, and in each instance the result had been continuity, not change. From a conservative perspective, Richard Nixon was the most promising, and ultimately the most disappointing, chance to reverse the political tide. Few conservatives expected to undo the New Deal; what they did look for was a leader who would halt the New Deal-based liberalism of a Kennedy or Lyndon Johnson, whose spending policies threatened to create an inertial inflationary force that could not be stopped short of socialism.

"Reagan is different from me in almost every basic element," declared a beleaguered Jimmy Carter on September 2, 1980. "And I might add parenthetically that the Republican party is sharply different under Reagan from what it was under Gerald Ford and Presidents all the way back to Eisenhower." Republicans had found an "electible" conservative, and his backers could give absolute guarantees that *this time* there would be no swerving to the middle-of-the-road. Carter, meanwhile, had survived a challenge from Teddy Kennedy, but the Democrats were hopelessly divided.

Four years earlier Jimmy Carter had emerged from Plains, Georgia as the "common sense" candidate, who, if anyone could, would silence the ideological turmoil within his party. Gerald Ford, even with Henry Kissinger still at the helm over at the State Department, appeared befuddled and out of his depth. Against a series of major setbacks that began with the Yom Kippur War in 1973, continued with a string of losing wrangles with Congress over control of "warmaking" powers and détente, Ford had but a single "victory" to his name: the defeat of the Cambodian "navy" in the Mayaguez affair. *Time* magazine did what it could with that triumph, a full-color spread of a shirtsleeved Ford directing strategy sessions inside the Pentagon. But there just wasn't enough there.

*"The 1980 Earthquake," in Thomas Ferguson and Joel Rogers, eds., *The Hidden Election: Politics and Economics in the 1980 Presidential Campaign* (New York, 1981), p. 110.

Things got so bad that in the Ford-Carter television debates of 1976—the Bicentennial Year of the American Revolution—Ford blurted out that there was "no Soviet domination of Eastern Europe." That slip may have cost him the election. What it revealed, however, was general unease. Ford was well aware of the real predicament (perhaps even more so than Jimmy Carter): that neither Russia nor the United States had developed an alternative to the Cold War. Carter neatly skewered Ford on the President's impressions of Russia's role in Eastern Europe, but his own ideas about world affairs did not congeal into a working hypothesis during his entire four years in office. And if his memoirs are an accurate guide to his thinking, each day seemed to bring a "surprise," topped off, of course, by his almost apologetic statement to the nation in the wake of the Soviet military occupation of Afghanistan that he had learned more about the Russians in the last twenty-four hours than in the previous three years.

"I don't use the word détente any more," President Ford told an audience at the outset of the 1976 campaign. "I think what we ought to say is that the United States will meet the Super-Powers, the Soviet Union and China, and seek to relax tensions so that we can continue a policy of peace through strength." Congressional confusion, as Henry Kissinger insisted, was no less pervasive in those years. Hoping to prevent future Vietnams, the legislators hurled boomerangs down Pennsylvania Avenue toward the White House—with the inevitable result. A perfect example was the "Jackson Amendment," which vitiated a 1974 trade agreement with the Soviet Union. Senator Henry Jackson's efforts to limit the executive's ability to conduct economic diplomacy, and to secure the right of Russian Jews to emigrate, produced a stalemate instead.

With no incentive to opt into the "structure of peace," warned Kissinger, the Russians were almost bound to return to old Cold War ways. For a time, the National Security Adviser (later Secretary of State) saw himself as the sole support of the "vital center," upholding the pillars of order against onslaughts from the left and right. Brooding over the meaning of Watergate, Kissinger eventually arrived back at a pre-World War I overview—spread out below him was a spectacle of the apocalypse that had ruined the twentieth century once, and would certainly do so again. In this vision the great powers were led—or rushed toward (it mattered not)—a final confrontation by the irresponsible action of narrowly ambitious client states on the fringes of the "civilized world." The combination of external crisis and internal disorder created a milieu out of which desperate acts would lead not to the millennium but to mass destruction. He could almost pick out from the scene some young revolutionary about to rush forward in the footsteps of the Serbian patriot, bent upon striking a blow for freeedom.

The Yom Kippur War was Kissinger's first crisis as Secretary of State. He had been appointed on August 22, 1973, with Nixon issuing only a terse statement that his qualifications were well known. It was evident to everyone in Washington that the appointment had as much to do with Watergate as with any failings of Secretary of State William P. Rogers. Then came the Egyptian invasion on October 6, 1973. It came at a time when policy-planners were deeply concerned about the situation along the entire Mediterranean. Greek politics were unstable. A crisis was developing in Cyprus between Greece and Turkey. Italy was shaky, Portugal in danger. And in Spain and Yugoslavia the long reigns of Franco and Tito would soon have to come to an end. When the grim reaper had claimed his due, what would follow?

At first it was thought that Moscow had egged Egypt's Anwar Sadat into attacking Israel in the hope of expanding Soviet influence throughout the area. Later it became apparent that that was not the case, but it did not ease Kissinger's worries. The Yom Kippur War was celebrated in the Arab world as a turning point, a restoration of pride and self-esteem for countries submerged for a hundred years under the Ottoman Empire, then British and French hegemony, and, finally an American-Israeli suzerainty. But it was more than that. In the early days of the war, the Arab states dominating the organization of petroleum producers (OPEC) decreed a boycott against Israel's friends. What began as a war measure—at least on the surface—altered world politics overnight, and sent tremors through the finance centers around the globe.

In the American view always, détente required stability, often defined in terms of "restraint" and "linkage," both of which placed a burden upon Soviet-American relations. The essential view also held that Russia was behind difficulties between the industrial world and the developing areas, and that friction at North-South contact points would disappear if the Soviets called off their local agents who supplied guns and dogma. But the linkage that bedeviled American policymakers was an invisible psychological tie between American defeat in Vietnam and their perceptions of world affairs. The weakening of the Presidency could not have caused the Yom Kippur War, still less the supposed "sequel" in Iran six years later, but old patterns of thought reasserted themselves. The equivalent of the Cambodian "incursion" soon became a drive to increase defense spending across the board, and to develop a Rapid Deployment Force to stand ready to go into the Persian Gulf.

But what if no Russians showed up? For the first time since Vasco da Gama, explained a representative of the Group of 77, a loose organization of Third World states, a decision taken outside Europe or America could not be reversed by the industrial nations. The Yom Kippur War ended. But OPEC's pricing policies greatly intensified the downward momentum of the world economy, plunging it into recession. Attempts to split the OPEC nations from other raw materials producers failed, and this despite the fact that the high cost of petroleum products hit the undeveloped countries harder than others, sending the cost of vitally needed fertilizers soaring. Western unity shattered under the impact of OPEC's assault, despite Henry Kissinger's disparaging remarks aimed at nations that switched their allegiance during the Yom Kippur War.

OPEC rode high for a decade. Then, because of a combination of factors, its control of the world oil price lessened. The most important of these was the deep recession which curtailed demand, and, to American dismay, further exacerbated economic divisions within the capitalist world, and between the industrial metropolis and the periphery. The world recession was a powerful force, finally, in producing Cold War II, as conditions in Eastern Europe worsened bringing "crack-downs," and American fears of Communist "penetration" into the Caribbean basin.

In the short run, however, the North-South debates led Kissinger to put more emphasis on détente, on how to persuade the Soviets to co-operate with the "have" powers. Quite clearly that was the intent of the Secretary's September 8, 1975, message to the United Nations, although it was ostensibly directed to the non-industrial delegates. "The global order of colonial power that lasted through the centuries," he said, "has now disappeared . . . the cold war division of the world into two rigid blocs has also broken down and major changes have taken place in the international economy . . . therefore it is time to go beyond the doctrines left over from a previous century that are made obsolete by modern reality . . . the world economy is a single global system of trade and monetary relations."

The phrase "doctrines left over from a previous century" is an appropriately ambiguous one, but Kissinger must surely have meant also to remind the Russians of what they should have remembered from the 1972 Moscow Summit, that the consequences of Marxism in the Third World held dangers for them all. The vulgar derivatives of that "philosophy" practiced by Third World leaders, and the romantic attachment Western "radicals" now felt for revolutionary "celebrities" like Che Guevara, poisoned the intellectual wells at which both East and West must meet to carry on their dialogue.

Did he expect the Soviet Union to re-educate Third World leaders, or shut down the Moscow Foreign Language Publishing House so that works by Marx and Lenin would disappear? Not that, but he expected concrete evidence of restraint, in return for updating (and making more specific) the phrases in the Basic Statement of Principles issued at the 1972 Summit, phrases that implied not what Nixon reported to Congress of that meeting but a guarantee for the Soviet Union's sphere of influence. A few months after his speech in the United Nations, Secretary Kissinger and his chief aides met in London with U.S. diplomats posted to Eastern European capitals. Almost at once press leaks spilled the principal theme, developed by Helmut Sonnenfeldt, into an already boiling debate over détente.

Sonnenfeldt's remarks deploring the lack of an "organic" unity between the Soviet Union and Eastern Europe overshadowed Kissinger's message to the assembled cast of diplomatic spear-carriers: "We must draw the Soviet Union into relationships which are both concrete and practical and we must create the maximum incentives for a moderate Soviet course." He spoke about recent developments in Africa, about Portugal's slide toward Communism, and how decolonization had created problems along both the North-South and East-West axis of world affairs. The "Sonnenfeldt Doctrine" may have been leaked on purpose, however, to get across to the Soviets that, while they apparently felt free to meddle in Africa, either directly or through Cuban proxies, they should realize the danger of this course. Revolutions "let loose" in one place might come back to haunt their sponsors closer to home.

Whatever subliminal message was being conveyed to Moscow, the Secretary was anxious to make clear Washington's rising concern about "Eurocommunism." Long fearful that *Ostpolitik* might end with the "moral" barriers to Communist participation in Western governments sadly breached, Kissinger warned of a "shocking change" if that actually happened. It might still be possible to have parallel policies with Communist governments in the West, he admitted, if the Communist parties were as truly independent of Moscow as they claimed. But the alliance had always had an importance beyond military security: "The United States would be alone and isolated in a world in which we had no relations by values to other countries."

In this sentence, Kissinger summed up the ethos of American foreign policy in the twentieth century. Since the time of the Spanish-American War, at least, the threat of a foreign "invasion" had never been worth a second thought. The nation's ideological and economic frontiers were a different matter. And the public response to the Sonnenfeldt Doctrine was an indicator that alarm bells were sounding along those lines. Seized upon by liberal critics as well as despairing (of Nixon-Ford) conservatives, the Doctrine was denounced bitterly as unconscionable by the former and as Yalta II by the latter. Instead of rededicating America to the cause of freedom, the Spenglerian Dr. Kissinger and his ilk appeared actually to enjoy presiding over America's decline.

"There is an inconsistency perceived in the United States," Kissinger admitted in a rare understatement, "between our opposing Communist governments in Western Europe and our talking to them in Eastern Europe. We must overcome this problem in the public's mind." He would find it very difficult indeed to explain the Administration's attitude toward *Ostpolitik*.

Under Willy Brandt's guiding hand the Federal Republic of Germany had moved quickly in late 1969 to achieve better relations with Eastern European capitals. These overtures, which were accompanied by large credit offers, were warmly received. On a visit to Warsaw the German Chancellor took with him Berthold Beitz, chairman of the supervisory board of Krupp, the steel company, "whose trading activities in Poland and other East European states had paved the way for the restoration of diplomatic links." Also accompanying him, said the *New York Times*, was Gunter Grass, whose literary works had provided another bridge between West and East. The most interesting aspect of the *Ostpolitik* policy was Brandt's ability to negotiate an agreement with Poland settling an old Cold War dispute, the frontier question. The Russians had imposed the Oder-Neisse line in 1945, allotting Poland more than 40,000 square miles of prewar Germany in compensation for what it had lost to Russia in the east. West Germany now agreed to recognize that line, and Poland agreed to allow nearly 100,000 ethnic Germans to emigrate—to West Germany.

These arrangements were then given Moscow's imprimatur in a blanket pact between West Germany and the Soviet Union renouncing the use of force and recognizing all European frontiers as "inviolable." American policymakers were never sure how they felt about *Ostpolitik*. On the one hand, Brandt's initiative could pay, quite literally, large dividends by opening Eastern Europe to trade and investment. And, as it happened, American bankers were eager to seize the opportunity, at times with the fervor of a California gold rush. But there was another side, worth pondering about. For one thing, *Ostpolitik* leapfrogged, at least at this stage, the German Democratic Republic. Poland's arrangement to allow ethnic Germans to emigrate to West Germany was potentially unsettling to the German Democratic Republic. Like John Foster Dulles, who actually cared more for stability than "Liberation," the Nixon-Ford administration was concerned that the Soviets not do anything that might stir up trouble, even—and perhaps especially—within their own sphere.

A much deeper psychological concern, however, was the difficulty of accepting an "independent" European policy, whether led by Charles de Gaulle or by Willy Brandt. France's "eccentricities" might explain de Gaulle. Germany was always a different matter. Neither Brandt nor his successor, Helmut Schmidt, indulged in Gaullist outbursts; nor did they display any desire to rid West Germany of NATO bases or to send American troops home. To the contrary, but that was all the more disturbing, because Washington was being expected to "pay" for *Ostpolitik* by guaranteeing West German security while it felt free to go its own way.

Circles within circles, a dizzying journey to the center of a maze, was that where détente led? Kissinger had paid even less attention to Latin America than most of his predecessors, but now, in the context of Eurocommunism and *Ostpolitik*, the threatened election of a Marxist in Chile, Salvador Allende Gossen, stirred him to action. He was not moved by complaints of American investors, who stood to lose millions (or thought they did), but by other considerations. Addressing the Chilean Foreign Minister in 1969, who had confronted Nixon with an accusation that Latin America returned to the

United States 3.8 dollars for every one it received in aid, he declared, "Mr. Minister, you made a strange speech. You come here speaking of Latin America, but this is not important. Nothing important can come from the South. History has never been produced in the South. The axis of history starts in Moscow, goes to Bonn, crosses over to Washington, and then goes to Tokyo. What happens in the South is of no importance. You're wasting your time."

Allende's appearance bent the axis of history, bent it badly. In March 1970 a special "40 Committee" approved $135,000 for anti-Allende propaganda. At a later meeting this sum was increased by $300,000, down payments, as it turned out, in a three-year campaign against the Marxist politician. "I don't see why we need to stand by," Kissinger was reported to have said, "and watch a country go communist due to the irresponsibility of its own people."* Various offers were made by investors, especially the International Telephone and Telegraph Company, to provide more cash to educate Chilean voters, but what concerned Kissinger was politics.

With the Mediterranean "arc" increasingly unstable, American policymakers were worried about the impact of a Marxist electoral victory in Chile because of traditional ethnic ties. Such an event could have a rebound effect on European politics, and, perhaps more significantly, stimulate a change in tactics by Communist parties in the "old" world. From that perspective the greatest danger was not that Allende's election would spell an end to democracy in Chile, but that it might not, that he might be voted out at a later date, thereby "regularizing" the participation of Communists in the electoral process.

Allende was overthrown in 1973, signaling an end to the electoral process and the institution of an era of military dictatorship. American responsibility for the *coup d'état* remains at dispute, though not the determination that Allende must go and the willingness to take extraordinary measures to that end. But if the Chilean apostasy was halted dead in its tracks, the last years of the Nixon-Ford era were ones of apparent retreat. Whether or not it was Kissinger who decided, and whether or not the motive was to conquer Vietnam "paralysis," the Administration's bid for legislative backing to intervene in an Angolan civil war met with a strong rebuff. On this

---

* Kissinger denies the statement, though many accounts, including the one cited here, Seymour Hersh, "The Price of Power: Kissinger, Nixon, and Chile," *The Atlantic Monthly* (December 1982): 31–58, feel secure in the assertion.

occasion Congressional conservatives joined with liberals in a united front to prevent aid to UNITA, a supposedly moderate force which enjoyed South African support, in its struggle with the government of that former Portuguese colony, now led by radicals and supported by Cuban troops. No amount of alarmist pentagon cajolery or White House arm-twisting could change the outcome. For the first time in three decades, going back to the beginning of the Cold War in 1947, Congress had dared risk such a refusal.

The stalemate of '76 marred the nation's 200th anniversary celebration, setting the stage, however, for Jimmy Carter's promised revolution in foreign policy: the Human Rights Campaign. Part old-time religious revival and part skillful deflection, the Human Rights Campaign was probably the only way Carter could reassert traditional liberal arguments for an active American role abroad, and at the same time cause the Soviets and the apparently burgeoning Euro-communists considerable embarrassment.

Where Kissinger appealed to the policy "elites" to stiffen their backbones for the long haul, put Vietnam behind them, and reclaim their accustomed authority, Carter sought to rekindle the burnt-out spirits of American liberalism with a torchlight parade all the way from Plains, Georgia, to Pennsylvania Avenue, Washington, D.C. Whether Jeffersonian or neo-Populist, this "grass-roots" approach soon spelled trouble for Carter. The President found himself trapped in the Nixon syndrome: he could never move fast enough to satisfy liberal critics, and conservatives were appalled by the damage done to staunch anti-Communist allies. Instead of bolstering confidence in American foreign policy, therefore, the principal effect was to highlight the worst aspects, present and past, of Cold War expediency— and to add a new burden, inconsistency, to the list of woes that had befallen the latter-day Presidents of the American Century. Finally, instead of ridding the national conscience of Vietnam, Carter's efforts to begin again produced a strong conservative backlash in 1980.

Pressure put on American allies in Latin America and Asia may have brought short-term results, and the Human Rights Campaign possibly had the desired impact on relations between Moscow and the Western European Communist parties. It added stimulus, in other words, for the latter to repudiate the Soviet political system, or risk alienating domestic support. On balance, nevertheless, the campaign was an amateurish exercise that would have embarrassed the

nation's Founding Fathers with its simplistic sophistries. When the
Russian crackdown on Poland began, the only lesson that could be
drawn was that the Human Rights Campaign was an utter failure,
except in countries that depended almost exclusively upon American
support. And it was in one of these that Carter's foreign policy came
undone. The United States had restored the Shah of Iran to his
throne twenty-five years earlier in a famous CIA caper, perhaps
ahead of the Guatemalan coup in 1954 on the agency's list of scalps in
the Cold War. In recent years, moreover, after the Yom Kippur War,
the Shah had become almost indispensable to Washington's Middle
Eastern policy. Among the Shah's assignments in this regard was the
task of proving that the Guam Doctrine had genuine substance, and
was not just a cover for defeat in Vietnam. The Shah was staunchly
anti-Communist, a committed disciple and advocate of pro-Western
modernization theories, and a sure guardian of his country's natural
resources.

But he had Caesar's ambitions. Iran's Manifest Destiny led him on,
much to the discomfort of many Americans who would have preferred that he not demand so much so soon, or seek arms from the
Russians as well. Iran was a 1970s' "boomtown," with all the attendant social problems and a dramatically uneven pattern of development. The Shah hoped to master these over the long run, but he relied
upon his security force, the CIA-trained SAVAK, for short-term
solutions. SAVAK swept off to prison thousands of the Shah's
subjects, multiplying his enemies and raising up in their midst the
powerful voice of religious prophecy. Yet, on New Year's Eve 1977,
Carter praised the Shah for having established "an island of stability"
in a troubled region. It was "a great tribute to you," he toasted the
occupant of the Peacock Throne, "Your Majesty, and to the respect
and the admiration and the love which your people give you."

Carter writes in his memoirs that he had spoken privately to the
Shah, urging him to ease off some on the strict police policies, but
to no avail. The Shah not only would not be budged, but he told
American reporters that what he feared most was the example of
"permissive societies" in the West. From this point forward, American policy toward Iran lurched back and forth, never coming to rest
for any length of time on any fixed position. With discontent rising,
spurred by the exiled religious leader, the Ayatollah Khomeini,
Washington put added pressure on the Shah to "liberalize" his
regime. As the crisis deepened, rumors abounded that the United

States had sent "instructions" to the Iranian military to support the Western-educated moderate, Shahpour Bakhtiar, who, having been appointed Prime Minister by the Shah, called immediately for the Shah to leave the country.

Again to no avail, as the Ayatollah returned in triumph to establish a theocracy dedicated to purging the land of the influence of the "Great Satan" in the White House. By January 1979, when the Shah finally fell, it was hard to find someone with knowledge about foreign affairs who did not believe either (a) that past policies of support for the Shah had brought on this disaster; or (b) Carter's simplistic approach to a friendly "authoritarian" regime made him unfit to conduct American foreign policy.

The Ayatollah's determination to exclude the hated Western culture-robbers from Iran was only partially, and primarily symbolically at that, responsible for the series of woes that followed in the wake of his return, but he quickly became the focus for American frustrations. Oil prices rose, inflaming the gold market, which then went off like a jet-powered rocket. The shock waves hit Congress a tremendous blow. Senator Frank Church of Idaho, a leading liberal critic, spun around, reached into his recently unused Kennedy holster, and pulled out a blazing condemnation of a "newly discovered" Soviet brigade in Cuba. Carter was flabbergasted. He recovered sufficiently in a day or two to declare that the Soviet presence was "not acceptable," only to backtrack when a more sophisticated intelligence investigation confirmed that the brigade was only a leftover remnant of the force present since the days of the missile crisis.

Almost providentially, it seemed, Moscow provided a real Cold War crisis on which to summons back the scattered foreign policy consensus. Throughout the nineteenth century Afghanistan had served as a buffer between Victoria's Indian Empire and the Tsar's outward pressure on Russia's southern frontiers. Once again Carter was astounded. Were the Soviets prepared to throw away the chance for SALT-II, not yet submitted for Senate ratification? It seemed that that was the case when, on December 27, 1979, reports reached Washington of a massive airlift of Russian soldiers.

Carter was certainly not responsible for the misconceptions that prevailed about the Iranian Revolution, or for the notion that Afghanistan was the beginning of an offensive drive to the south. Ironically, the trigger for the occupation of Afghanistan may have been Moscow's fear of a general Muslim uprising that could penetrate into discontented areas in provinces next to Iran. However that may be, the Russian move was not, as Carter said, "the gravest threat to world peace since World War II." He hurt himself the most with that statement, because whatever he did in response would be roundly condemned as piddling and cowardly. And when he placed an embargo on American grain sales to Russia, the charge of self-defeating was added.

But it was the hostage crisis that finally ruined the Carter Presidency beyond repair. It quickly conjured up the worst image of all: sheer incompetence. Even as alternatives for securing their release were being discussed, and discarded one by one, the atmosphere grew heavy with recrimination. Persuaded to accept the Shah into the United States for medical treatment at the behest of David Rockefeller and Henry Kissinger, Carter had chosen to honor a "moral" obligation to an old friend, even though he had been warned that militants would attack the Embassy compound in such an event. The dark shadow of the final days in Saigon, and American abandonment of "loyal" South Vietnamese, had fallen across the President's desk in the Oval Office. In Iran all but about seventy-five of the Embassy staff, which once numbered eleven hundred, had been evacuated, but nothing had been done to improve the security of those who had remained.

On November 4, 1979, Iranian student "radicals" overran the Embassy compound, making prisoners of the stranded Americans inside. The fate of these seemed attached to America's future in the entire area; and, in the popular mind, Iran and Afghanistan were linked with a Russian forward thrust that threatened to sweep down through Iraq, through Turkey, to the Red Sea and the Persian Gulf. Another part of the world, it now appeared was to be shut off behind a Russian barricade. Another part of the American spirit dimmed by an inability to respond.

Memories of the final days in Vietnam were also stirred by media reporting. Once again Americans saw, night after night, faces suffused with hatred—hatred for their government, hatred for them. One television network began each night's news report with a caption: Day 20 of the Hostage Crisis, Day 21 of the Hostage Crisis, . . . College campuses, once the scene of the "teach-in" movement during the Vietnam War, were covered with banners proclaiming a desire for revenge. "Nuke the Ayatollah" and "Make Iran a Parking Lot" were among the most popular.

Carter could find no one to negotiate with as authority in revolutionary Iran swirled around the Ayatollah, but even he seemed unable to shout down the wind. Iranian assets were frozen. An economic blockade was imposed. An appeal from the Vatican. None had the slightest impact. Contingency planning to use military force began within a week of the take-over. Almost as soon, the new National Security Adviser, Zbigniew Brzezinski, began keeping a "crisis diary." As the day approached for the rescue mission in mid-April 1980 the diary entries (as later reported by Brzezinski himself) edged over into fantasy, recording options for coping with failure that included the possibility of attacking Russian vessels in off-shore waters as part of a broad cover operation.

More than a "Freudian slip," Brzezinski's private musings suggested the intense frustration that gripped policymakers, pulling them constantly back to Cold War postulates. But the rescue mission of April 25, 1980, ended not with a bang, but a whimper. Heliocopters and transport planes got tangled in the midst of a night-time dust storm. Eight American soldiers died, and the mission was scrubbed in the desert. Back home Secretary of State Cyrus Vance, who had opposed the mission, resigned.

Disenchanted liberals began to form ranks behind Teddy Kennedy or independent John Anderson. Other Americans looked to Ronald Reagan, whose Cold War views were never complicated with intricate patterns like those Kissinger and Nixon had projected with détente. The Shah had not been unpopular. He had been subverted: "And part of this being overthrown was inspired by a radio station inside the Russian border that was broadcasting in Farsi, the language of the country, constantly against the United States. . . ." Abetting the revolutionaries, moreover, were the human rights "hypocrites." "I think this Administration is completely hypocritical. It talks human rights, but it has never found anyone guilty of violating them except a friend."

With Reagan pounding on Cold War themes from three decades ago after the "loss" of China, the hostages helped to shape history in ways they could never have imagined, sitting blindfolded so many thousands of miles away. Inside the Administration, Vance's resignation was not taken as a cautionary sign. If anything, it speeded momentum in a different direction. Vance's departure was dismissed, as Kissinger might have said, as a sign that more must be done to restore the elite's flagging self-confidence. Carter could not secure the release of the hostages during the election campaign; they finally returned home as Reagan was being inaugurated. But he could do something about restoring America's "image."

In the 1976 campaign, Carter had promised to cut the defense budget. He could lop off $5 to $7 billion, he said, without lessening American security by so much as a single computer chip. But the promise was taken to mean that his Administration would also re-examine the whole process of Pentagon budget-making—and the assumptions behind it. He turned down the plan for a B-1 bomber to replace the aging strategic fleet of B-52s, once again on efficiency grounds, but the idea persisted that Carter was applying standards other than mere cost-accounting. In his inaugural address, for example, he had pledged himself to move "a step toward our ultimate goal—the elimination of all nuclear weapons from this earth."

Carter's determination to lessen the chance of nuclear war, and decrease surplus weapons, was evident in an early proposal to the Soviets for deep cuts in each side's arsenal. But as he notes in his memoirs, he agreed with the Joint Chiefs of Staff that America's over-all military posture had been "long-neglected." Even before his inauguration, he had begun to receive briefings from the Joint Chiefs that convinced him there had been a growing disparity in American expenditures, down 35 percent in real dollars during the eight years of Republican rule, while the Russians had lifted theirs by about 4 percent annually.

The Russians turned down Carter's deep cut proposals in favor of an incremental approach. Plans were made for negotiating with Moscow on that basis, but, as summit confrontations with Leonid Brezhnev demonstrated, Carter even before Iran and Afghanistan had made up his mind about the root cause of the world's difficulties. "My concerns had not been alleviated by his words," Carter would recall, "because the fact was that when violence occurred in almost any place on earth, the Soviets or their proxies were most likely to be at the center of it."

What Carter "learned" from the Iranian-Afghan imbroglio was that nuclear weapons could not be eliminated, that they had to be integrated even more securely into the covenant with power. This was codified in 1980 with the formal announcement of a new strategic doctrine, P.D. 59, that recalled (as did Carter's response to Brezhnev) Kennedy "counterforce" strategies. Testifying before Congress, Air

Force General Richard Ellis explained why this once discarded plan for attacking an enemy's missile capability had suddenly reappeared in strategic war planning. A shift against America in the area of strategic capability, said Ellis, had emboldened the Soviets to undertake their recent adventures in Africa and Asia: "Because of this, deterrence can no longer be neatly divided into subgroups, such as conventional and nuclear. It must be viewed as an interrelated, single entity." Secretary of Defense Harold Brown then told the NATO allies that a change in doctrine and force modernization were both necessary to improve American capability "across the full spectrum of threats with which we must all be concerned."

But it was Richard Nixon, sitting alone at his desk in San Clemente, who best summed up the feelings of his successors. In a remarkable book, *The Real War*, published in 1980, Nixon sought to expunge the record of détente (implying that it was foisted upon him by the "trendy" establishment) and wrote a new explanation of the Nixon Doctrine: "If we are relatively equal to the Soviet Union in nuclear arms, but the Soviets have 5,000 Cubans, or even 500 agitators and terrorists, where we have no countervailing force, then the balance of power on the scene is massively on their side." In this way, therefore, nuclear weapons superiority became part of America's response to revolution.

Cold War II had begun. Defense spending rose from $108 billion in 1977 to $142 billion in 1980. After his defeat in the 1980 election, Carter sat down with the National Security Council to draw up a list of policy recommendations for the long view. They were notable for several reasons, not least for their similarity to many things Reagan had been saying, and for which Carter had condemned him as reckless and divisive. At the top was the need to make it clear to Moscow that an intrusion into Iran with conventional ground forces would immediately precipitate "a worldwide confrontation. . . . No one could guarantee that in such a broad conflict both sides would remain restricted to the use of conventional forces." Right behind was the need to convince Europeans that they would have to discipline themselves, do more to defend themselves, and repudiate the growing trend toward "neutrality" in Cold War II. To fight that struggle, moreover, it would be absolutely necessary to develop, in concert with the allies, a well-conceived strategy for "economic warfare" to punish the Soviets for any aggression. And, most prophetic of all,

Carter asserted, "We need to have some tangible buildup of our Caribbean military forces, as a clear but quiet signal to everyone that we will protect our interests in that region."

These proposals, recommendations of a defeated Democratic President, were all put into action by Republican Ronald Reagan. Much of the press's attention during the 1980 campaign was on the "New Right," a melange of fundamentalist religious groups seeking political salvation in "old time" American ideals and virtues, a disenchanted "silent majority" filled with both genuine and imagined grievances at the liberal establishment, and a coterie of neo-Populist Senators from rural areas. While many were Republicans, many were also refugees from the Democratic party of the New Deal. Reagan also attracted a number of Truman-era Cold War "liberals," who found that they had much in common with the Reagan people, at least on foreign policy.

The gyrations of this latter group, self-titled neo-conservatives, represent a dramatic intellectual shift, and, though less widely appreciated, a link with the pre-World War I era that goes well beyond Henry Kissinger's personal vision of a coming Doomsday. The most sophisticated review of the Carter Human Rights Campaign from this perspective was that of political scientist Paul Seabury. Writing in the June 23, 1981, *Wall Street Journal*, Seabury reached back to Britain's mid-nineteenth-century pre-eminence and its world responsibility. At the peak of British power, Prime Minister Benjamin Disraeli and his liberal critic, the human rights advocate William Gladstone, explained Seabury, debated what to do about the appalling "Bulgarian Massacres," perpetrated by the Turks. Ten thousand died, and there were those, first among them Gladstone, who declared that they should welcome a Tsarist expedition to punish the Sultan of Turkey. Disraeli ignored them, and instead deployed the fleet "to check the spread of Russian power."

Disraeli was right, concluded Seabury, and Gladstone wrong:

> Still, idealists would charge that power politics once more had prevailed over considerations of human decency. The case affords us reflection on the relations between human rights and national interests.

> Disraeli saw that vital interests of a *liberal* empire were threatened by the outward thrust of an ambitious and very unliberal Czarist empire.

. . . While corrupt, tyrannical, and at times savage, the Sultan's regime per se posed no threat to Britain, or for that matter, to Europe. An aggressive Russia did.

Seabury was a strong supporter of Reagan Human Rights nominee, Ernest Lefever, who, he said, was not only a man in Disraeli's mold but a strong disciple of the "great American theologian Reinhold Niebuhr . . . a humane Augustinian Christian." Lefever's connections with the Nestlé Company and the promotion of a disputed baby-formula to the Third World, however tenuous, forced the Administration to withdraw his name. It was about the only defeat Reagan would suffer on Capitol Hill in the first half of his term.

Seabury's use of the term "*liberal* empire" provides an important insight into the men who abandoned life-long allegiances to the Democratic party to join the Reagan team. Several would still deny that America was any kind of empire, just liberal. However that may be, the interweaving of concern about the decline of standards (a rubric that covers just about everything they dislike about the 1960s: defeat in Vietnam, permissiveness, pornography, the counterculture, and George McGovern) and the loss of American power and prestige provides a loose bond between Reagan's apparently disparate supporters. Few New Right leaders would have the patience to follow Seabury back along historical trails to Benjamin Disraeli, or search out Reinhold Niebuhr as an antecedent for Ernest Lefever. But these things did matter to the neo-conservatives.

To them the success of the "*liberal* empire" depends first on a strong ideological footing, the basis for what Americans think about themselves. A former socialist in the early twentieth-century Progressive movement, Niebuhr taught a generation of liberals to come to terms with what would later be called the "totalitarian temptation." What was different about the 1980s, in this view, was the nature of the internal danger. The 1960s had seen a flowering of post-New Deal liberalism withered by Vietnam protest movements and the guilt-ridden elder generation's "appeasement" of the radicals.

The major theme that engages the attention of both the New Right and the neo-conservatives is repentance. President John Silber of Boston University, for example, writes in the *New York Times* on September 2, 1982, that 700,000 young Americans have flouted the law in refusing to register for the draft: "This represents a serious challenge to democratic government. We must not allow a small minority to thwart the people's will as expressed in an act of Congress."

Not once in the article does President Silber explain the actual threat to national security that evaders pose. That may be implied, of course, but other concerns predominate. Passage of a draft registration act was an assertion of "will," an indication that the state was returning to health. The central issue is self-discipline. Traditionally, military service has been recommended—for rich and poor alike—as a means of bringing a man to himself. The draft question thus links a conviction that American military strength is waning with its remedy, and ties an equally pervasive feeling that parental (and societal) appeasement has resulted in a sickly generation, lacking patriotic stamina and deprived of moral fiber, with traditional democratic answers.

Concerned to expose the Soviet Union as a "failed" society, and certainly no example for Third World nations in economic development, neo-conservatives then face the problem of convincing Americans that the Russians do present a serious danger. And this brings them back to the problem of self-discipline and will. Not only draft evaders but corporate leaders have been responsible for the decline. "The leaders of 'big business,' " writes the newest Nixon in the *Real War*, "once were a bastion of support for American strength, just as they once were vigorously independent." But business, like government, has become bureaucratized, a synonym apparently for neutered: "There are few big business leaders I would have put in the ring with a healthy Brezhnev." And Richard V. Allen, Reagan's short-term National Security Adviser, would denounce businessmen, not for an absence of hormones but because they lusted for Communist markets after "supercharged . . . vodka parties and the promise of hundreds of millions in orders."

The Soviets realize that even with American help their system will not allow them to outproduce the United States, argues Nixon in the *Real War*,

> They also know they can only hope to overwhelm us militarily if our guard remains down long enough to let them get a decisive advantage. But in our will they sense a weakness that could offset the margin of safety our other strengths give us. The Soviets know their multiplication tables. Looking at Sir Robert Thompson's equation [a British

expert on guerrilla war who advised Nixon about Vietnam], national power equals manpower plus applied resources, *times* will, they understand that if the will factor is zero the whole equation is zero.

George F. Will, perhaps the ablest journalistic champion of the Reagan philosophy, saw early on that a conflict was brewing between "Libertarians," who wanted an Administration dedicated to the free market, and the emphasis upon discipline required for national security. There was no room for "Libertarian" thought in the Reagan administration, he would write. Well-meaning folk, with their rigid adherence to free market economics and Adam Smith neckties, the "Libertarians' " odd notions about the danger of the national security state to the individual's right to choose what was best mistook conservatism's mission in the late twentieth century. Government had grown too big, yes, and was stifling initiative, but that was quite a separate problem if you please from controlling trade with the Communist world, and from tending to national security responsibilities where government had been far too lax.

Almost every issue in the Reagan administration would be imbued with national security considerations, from the "Family Life" questions to the immense spending proposals for defense. Carter had reached out with his "born-again" Christian spirit in an attempt to get a handle on repentance but succeeded only in grasping the nettle of national discontent. The New Frontier style of liberalism had posited the greatest danger as an outside force, nibbling away at the edges of the Free World. Carter sensed the shift in attitude, but Reagan converted it to political advantage.

At Notre Dame University in 1977, for example, Carter said that the United States was at last free of "the inordinate fear of communism . . . the fear that led to the moral poverty of Vietnam." Against the background of Iran and Afghanistan, repentance had taken on a new meaning. Americans were in a mood only to repent defeat and the shame of the hostage humiliation. It was an introspective mood, to be sure, but it was concerned with the soft rot eating away at the center. Reagan had been waiting for the shift. "When 50,000 Americans made the ultimate sacrifice," he said in a speech that spurred his supporters on in Massachusetts, "to defend the people of a small, defenceless country from Communist, godless tyranny, that, my friends, is an act of moral courage, not an example of moral poverty."

The New Deal political system that had dominated the American scene since the Great Depression postulated a "majority party" committed to moderate reform, Keynesian in orientation, kept from excess by a "loyal opposition" of Republicans. The Democrats under Carter seemed confused. One reading of the 1980 election returns would be that the electorate voted for "shock therapy," voted to jolt the system back onto its proper foundations. Reagan's frequent references to Roosevelt and the New Deal would certainly support such an argument. The Roosevelt he voted for in his youth, Reagan would tell a television interviewer, had pledged to cut government spending. The New Deal was only intended to be temporary medicine for a sick patient. Those around FDR, however, had in mind something else, either fascism or "modified communism." "Well, I don't believe that was really in Roosevelt's mind, and, I think that, had he lived, and with the war over, we would have seen him using Government the other way."

He would have used government, presumably, to oppose the goals of errant liberals and to combat Communism in any form, at home and abroad. He would also have repudiated the autarchic economic policies of New Deal "fascism," and returned to Wilsonian economic internationalism. Some New Deal "veterans" were outraged at these remarks, but Reagan's offhand commentary on Roosevelt's travail hit a sensitive spot with neo-conservatives concerned about the unresolved New Deal quandary (actually Wilson's original problem) of the frontierless democracy. So many modern problems were subsumed under that decades-old debate.

Carter was not entirely to blame, of course. Before him, détente was an obvious failure, not least because it gave Europe and Japan an impression of a desperate America, and a desperate Nixon, who turned up on the Great Wall of China to praise men he had made a career of anathematizing to win re-election in 1972, and then in Moscow to avoid the searching questions of Watergate investigators. Adjustments in Cold War policy were necessary, indeed overdue, but Nixon made détente appear dictated by weakness, the nation's and his own, by a lack of resolve and by economic expediency. In this view, therefore, German *Ostpolitik*, a long-standing concern, was more likely to become "neutralism," opening the way for the moral disarmament of Western Europe.

To correct this impression, the Trilateral Commission had been created. Composed of leading citizens, opinion-shapers, and economic policymakers from the United States, Western Europe, and Japan, the Commission undertook to repair the political damage done to America's image by Vietnam and its aftermath, and to the world economy by Nixon's abrupt, unilateral, economic policies. "[T]he overriding goal," said its founders, "is to make the world safe for interdependence. . . ." It publishes reports on a variety of subjects of interest to the "Free World" and has devoted special attention to the presumed "Crisis of Democracy." Because of its internationalist ideology, and elitist membership, the Trilateral Commission was a favorite target for the New Right. Both Jimmy Carter and Zbigniew Brzezinski were Trilateralists. Indeed, Carter was vetted for the Presidency by Commission members. Reagan's only serious rival for the nomination, George Bush, was also a Trilateralist, an albatross that weighed him down in the primaries.

Nevertheless, the "Crisis" discussed by Commission author Samuel P. Huntington bore more than a slight affinity for concerns that would later be expressed by the New Right "moral majority," and for themes taken up by Ronald Reagan on his way to the White House. Surveying what he labeled the democratic surge of the 1960s, Huntington concluded that, while it was not new—there were echoes of the Jacksonian and Progressive eras—this time it had quite got out of hand:

> Al Smith once remarked that "the only cure for the evils of democracy is more democracy." Our analysis suggests that applying that cure at the present time could well be adding fuel to the flames. Instead, some of the problems of governance in the United States today stem from an excess of democracy. . . . Needed, instead, is a greater degree of moderation in democracy.*

The predominance of ideological concerns, the determination to deal with the decay of will power, also informs the work of the Committee on the Present Danger. The underlying assumption of the Committee has its root in 1930s' concerns about Nazi power. The Soviet threat is the same, argue members, only more dangerous because the Russians have nuclear weapons and are willing to use them. Its founders were veterans of "Team B," an outside group that George Bush called in when he was director of the CIA to re-evaluate intelligence estimates of the Soviet military build-up. Team B's chairman was Richard Pipes, who would become Reagan's top Soviet

*"The Crisis of Democracy" (New York, 1975), p. 113.

expert on the National Security Council. Under his direction, Team B concluded that the Soviet threat had been underestimated and that SALT-II would lock the United States into a permanent state of inferiority.

Pipes made headlines early in 1981 by predicting that war was inevitable unless the Russians changed their internal system. Common to other members of the Reagan administration as well was the Harvard expert's view that the Soviet Union had entered into a crisis from which there were only two exits, one back toward full Stalinism and war and the other toward "liberal economic reform ... something resembling a mixed economy." American policy could shape Russian choices by a new "containment" strategy that rewards moderation. But the first step must be to "rebuild" America's nuclear Big Stick.

American military power had waned, believed Committee members, to a point where the Soviets could (despite—and probably because of—all their internal difficulties) achieve effective superiority, and, under that cover, move almost at will into all areas of the world: into Europe under the guise of neutralism, into Africa behind revolutionary leaders and Cuban mercenaries. Interviewed in the *Boston Globe* for August 4, 1981, Eugene Rostow, co-founder of the Committee, along with Paul Nitze, and the Administration's first arms negotiator, freely admitted that no one had the slightest idea what there was to negotiate with the Russians. What could be negotiated until the United States had fully re-armed?

Things got so bad in the Carter years, he explained, that it was "pure luck" war missed America: "There was steady erosion of our position in all sorts of ways. But the worst didn't happen. It was a great demonstration of that great truth that the Lord takes care of drunks, dogs, women and the United States of America." Mark Twain's old-fashioned humor is thus appropriated for very serious purposes. "We have no choice but to re-arm," Rostow continues, "when you have one nation in the world, the Soviet Union, that is out to achieve Empire."

Mark Twain's irreverent regard for received truth has no place, however, in Rostow's grim world. Here instead is a *Star Wars* "for keeps" world, the showdown between Darth Vader and Luke Skywalker, where the costs of containing the Empire must be paid, and where only the truly worthy will be permitted to understand and use the Force. Himself a recanting author of a study favoring *A New*

Isolationism, Johns Hopkins political scientist Robert Tucker drew out the implications of America's situation. "In abandoning isolationism in the 1930s," he now asserts in *Foreign Affairs*, "we responded not only to a perceived threat to our physical and economic security. We also recoiled from the prospect of a world in which America's political and economic frontiers would become coterminous with her territorial frontiers, a world in which societies that shared our institutions and values might very possibly disappear —in sum, a world in which the American example and American influence would become irrelevant." On that darkened globe, America could no longer realize its original promise, "since a hostile world from which America was shut out would inevitably affect the integrity of the nation's institutions and the quality of its domestic life."

How many Vietnams, how many Irans, would it take to reduce America to such a precarious situation? The Soviet Union need not launch a nuclear first strike to win Cold War II; all it needs is the unchallenged capability to do so. In the scenarios imagined by Rostow and Nitze, war would be likely to erupt out of a confrontation over country "Z." If the Russians continue outspending the United States on defense, so the argument develops, one day the superpowers will find themselves, not surprisingly, committed to opposite sides in Z's civil war. Much hinges on the outcome: control of vital energy resources, possibly, but also something even more valuable— credibility. In answer to a formal request from the legitimate government, Washington prepares to send in its (at last) newly organized and outfitted, Rapid Deployment Force. Long delayed by the objections of overly fastidious liberals, and those confused by Jimmy Carter's stop-and-start approach to defense, the RDF has not yet been tested—and now it is probably too late. (Here it is necessary to interject into the scenario a comment from *The Real War* that described another reason for the delay in mounting an appropriate response to Soviet aggression: misplaced idealism that had allowed American policies "to become hostage to the parochial passions of African leaders who have no appreciation of or concern for the issues at stake there between East and West.")

The Washington-Moscow "hotline" lights up, an urgent message is coming in from the Soviet leader. Soviet prestige is also at stake, asserts the new premier, who, to make matters worse, has just emerged from a Politburo meeting where his colleagues have complained that his policy toward China is too soft. He is not in a mood to trifle. Unless the United States backs down, he will order a nuclear strike against American land-based missiles. Russian superiority has given the Soviets the crucial option of "limited" nuclear war, the counterforce choice, because they will be able to launch such a strike, receive what is left of the American strategic attack, and still be able to destroy the nation's cities. Under those conditions, the President would have to make a very unpleasant decision, perhaps in less than thirty minutes. He must decide whether the country can survive humiliation any better than nuclear holocaust. The only chance of avoiding this predicament is to start now to re-arm. Rostow puts it this way: "The only conceivable course for the US is to rearm in the interest of peace. You could say, is that a paradox? No, it isn't."

The re-establishment of American superiority at the top will, as John Kennedy once imagined, cause the Soviets to restrain their urge to keep gnawing away at the foundations of world order. So clearly etched in studies developed at the Hudson Institute, the RAND Corporation, and the Georgetown Institute of Strategic Studies, fuzziness appears whenever one attempts to identify country Z. Then one must ask, what is it exactly that the United States proposes to defend? Asked about the risks of making Saudi Arabia a regional policeman, given what had happened in Iran, President Reagan responded casually, "We will not permit it to become an Iran." Country Z remains an abstraction, much like the darting luminous green outlines on an arcade computer game.

Such thoughts do not disturb Eugene Rostow's composure. Speaking of the European disarmament movement, the CPD founder finds that it is real enough, but it is caused by the sudden discovery of Russian power: "Yes, Europe is very much alarmed because people have become conscious of the nature of Soviet policy and the weight of weapons behind it. Therefore, they're naturally afraid. It's sensible, it's reasonable, it's inevitable. And those facts have to be dealt with." Dealt with, however, so that they do not lead to European self-abnegation and, ultimately, the permanent neutralization of the Continent.

It is world order that is country Z, an abstraction to be sure, but the ultimate purpose of the liberal state. Only by maintaining a favorable environment outside its borders can liberalism survive. Or, as neo-conservative social critic Irving Kristol puts it,

It is an inescapable fact that the American economy is a vital organ of a larger world economy. The one cannot survive, and certainly cannot prosper, without the other. The wealth of nations today is indivisible. Our economic growth will henceforth be as dependent on our foreign policy as on our economic policy. And if we fail to establish the conditions for such growth, our democracy will itself unravel, as economic pressures give rise to political polarization, at home and abroad. . . . What few seem to realize is that a prospect of economic growth is a crucial precondition for the survival of any modern democracy, the American included.*

Ideological concerns, both Tucker and Kristol confirm, do not exist in a vacuum. In July 1980, as the American Presidential campaign really got under way, *Business Week* magazine reported with alarm on "The gradual succession of Europe from the U.S.-dominated Atlantic Alliance." Shaken by the impression of weak leadership in Washington, and moved by a new definition of their economic interests, European leaders were perfectly willing to risk American wrath by arranging their own "summit" series with Russian leader Leonid Brezhnev. European leaders, according to *Business Week*, were being "blown eastward" by four winds: weak leadership in Washington, the decline of U.S. power, the fall of the dollar, and increased East-West trade.

These winds threatened the U.S. corporate stake in Europe, a stake that had now reached $150 billion. American investments remit tens of billions of dollars in critically needed dividend and royalty payments to parent companies: "Any move by Europe toward economic neutralism that throws up nationalistic barriers to trade and investment or any turning away from the U.S. as an economic partner threatens these crucial economic ties." Former Secretary of State Henry Kissinger, who hoped to have a somewhat larger role in a new Republican administration, was quoted as saying that unless European perceptions of America were changed, and soon, "we will see a de facto growth of the neutralism of our allies." The current distancing of Europe from the U.S., he added, was "one of the greatest foreign policy crises in our history—probably the greatest."

Discounting election hyperbole, the special report ended with words and phrases that might have been taken from any of the

---

*Quoted in Nixon's, *The Real War*, p. 240.

sources or writers listed above: "Unless Washington can again show the strength that brought America the leadership of the alliance in the first place, an increasing neutralism in Europe is likely to do for U.S. business what it has already done for U.S. prestige." An "excess of democracy," or at least an exaggerated set of "promises" from the Kennedy era to the present, had also created a situation where the nation's security interests came second—politically and economically —to what had been demanded by minorities or pressure groups. During the years of America's decline, observes Robert Yost of the Computer Sciences Corporation, in the July 14, 1980, issue of *Business Week*, defense spending slipped steadily from 6 percent of the Gross National Product in 1973, to 5.3 percent in 1977, and 5 percent in 1979. "The level of GNP for defense, and particularly the trend in this level, reflects more than defense capability," says Yost. "It reflects national will. And the perception of that will may itself be a key factor in deterring conflicts."

Events in Eastern Europe—where the Cold War began—gave the new administration an opportunity to test the hypothesis that American "weakness" was responsible for most of the world's ills. When the dissident Solidarity union challenged Polish authorities, who then imposed martial law on the country, the stage was set for a demonstration of rediscovered will and strength of character. Or so it seemed.

Reagan had begun his administration with a denunciation of Soviet duplicity, a historic necessity, he suggested for Godless Marxist regimes. He had never seen a shred of evidence that the Soviets had retreated an inch from their goal of world revolution: "The only morality they recognize is what will further their cause, meaning they reserve unto themselves the right to commit any crime, to lie, to cheat." They lie, also, to cover the abysmal failures Communism has recorded over the years inside the Soviet Union, political and economic, failures that compel Russia to practice repression at home and equally brutal expansionist diversions.

Poland was also to be the example of the false promise of détente, an investors' paradise populated in fact by serpents who tempted capitalists into lending the Communist government over $25 billion. It might be painful to withdraw from Poland, but, said some of Reagan's advisers, ideals could not be compromised. Besides, if controls were to be put upon a runaway *Ostpolitik*, now was the time, and Poland was the place to do it. Alas, the Polish debacle would demonstrate instead flaws in the central hypothesis. To begin with, the Polish crisis created an awkward personal predicament for Reagan. During the campaign he had promised midwestern farmers to end the grain embargo imposed by Carter during the initial phases of the Afghan occupation. Now he was stuck. Every time he proposed that the Western Europeans support economic measures against the Soviet Union, he was charged with hypocrisy. Second thoughts also prevailed about forcing Poland to default on its loans. After the Iranian debacle, which cost up to $100 billion, the Polish "revolution" (with its implications for the rest of Eastern Europe) looked to be the trigger of a gun pointed at Western capitalism, something that could easily set off a new Great Depression. Dedicated to exposing the tyranny of the Soviet system in the satellites, the Reagan administration nevertheless acted to prevent a Polish default on its foreign loans.

Reagan did not escape the wrath of some neo-conservatives on the Polish issue. The President has said that he welcomes the signs of an impending break-up of the Soviet empire from within, charged Norman Podhoretz, yet when presented with an enormous opportunity to do something to speed up the process, he turned it down: "One remembers easily enough that Carter instituted a grain embargo and a boycott of the Moscow Olympics [over Afghanistan], but one is hard-pressed even to remember what the Reagan sanctions were." The ultimate insult, this, to put Reagan on a plane with Jimmy Carter. "[T]he Administration seemed more worried about hurting a few bankers than about hurting the Soviet empire."

Yet if Podhoretz found that the Administration, quoting George Will, loved commerce more than it loathed Communism, Reagan came across quite differently in Western Europe. His Hollywood image had predisposed European leaders toward a different kind of skepticism of the new President, and, in a sense, he lived up to those expectations. At a summer 1981 Summit of Western leaders and Japan's Prime Minister, Reagan called for a unified policy on loans and credits to Russia and Eastern Europe. He was especially anxious, as well, to curtail trade in high-technology items. These measures would accomplish, it was supposed, two essential purposes: (1) they would demonstrate once again America's moral leadership, its right to lead the alliance; and (2) they would expose Soviet economic failings to the world. Afterwards, Reagan traveled to London to speak to Parliament, where he delivered a ringing version of his remarks at the Summit, denouncing Russia and Soviet society and calling for the West to take the offensive in non-military measures of undermining the wicked regime.

He was cheered by Conservatives, led by Prime Minister Margaret Thatcher, whose own policies were designed to get Britons to stand on their own feet again. They shared a common interest in monetarist domestic policies, and a conviction that "leftist" pabulum had weakened moral fiber as well as economic muscle. But the consensus stopped there. When the Europeans, faced with high unemployment rates (which they blamed on American efforts to bring down domestic inflation), went ahead with shipments of needed materials to complete a natural gas pipeline from the Soviet Union to NATO countries, the Administration reacted by imposing restrictions on American companies and any subsidiaries participating in the enterprise. Prime Minister Thatcher, who had fought a mini-war in the South Atlantic to prevent the Argentines from taking over the Falkland Islands, now proved that she could also stand up to the Americans: "The question is whether one very powerful nation can prevent existing contracts being fulfilled; I think it is wrong to do that." She also told the House of Commons it was unwise for the Americans themselves to make this attempt: "I think it is harmful ultimately to American interests because so many people will say there is no point in making a contract to secure materials, machinery and equipment from the U.S., if at any time they can just cancel the contract."

Americans were more than a little put out with Thatcher. The Falkland Islands war came at a good time for the Tories, boosting Conservative ratings at a time when the economy was in the doldrums, but it undercut Reagan's efforts to form a conservative bloc in the Americas dedicated to halting the spread of "Sandinist-type" revolutions in El Salvador and Guatemala. It was not a left-wing Labour leader who joined Thatcher to condemn American arrogance but the mordant relic of the imperial past, Enoch Powell, Unionist MP for South Down, who had no use for patient lectures. Powell was deeply offended by Vice President George Bush's statement about the pipeline measures. "We've heard a lot of protests," said Bush, "from our European allies. I am sorry. The United States is the leader of the free world, and under this administration we are beginning to act like it." Bush's attitude was, said Powell, that Americans were a "unique society," put together from all nationalities, races and interests on the globe, put together by God to show the rest of the world how to live.

> The manic exaltation of the American illusion has its dark counterpart, its depressive phase. I found the following a remarkably apt description of the American nightmare. The words are those of the Executive Director of a New York-based group called the Committee for the Free World: "Do we wish, if we can, to preside over the beginning of the break-up of the Soviet empire, or do we wish to accommodate ourselves to the idea that we may one day find ourselves all alone in a sea of grim and envious and unfree people?"

Official French and German statements about the pipeline diplomacy were hardly less blunt. By midsummer 1982, the Reagan administration had retreated a few steps toward the center. Early threats of strong action against Cuba for its interventionism in Central America had been toned down, though reports of CIA-activities against the Nicaraguan "Sandinist" regime replaced these warnings in the headlines. An understanding with China that arms shipments to Taiwan would gradually be phased out broke with past Reagan declarations. Neo-conservatives complained, a barometer of drift, that the Administration's Middle Eastern policies, and growing criticism of Israeli Prime Minister Menachem Begin's determination to annex the West Bank territories, amounted to Carterism without Carter. Begin stressed that the Lebanon War to root out PLO (Palestine Liberation Organization) terrorists was really America's battle, too, but, while Washington officials may indeed have appreciated the result (and the demonstration that American weapons did seem to work better than the Russian-supplied arms of the opponents), the Administration shied from the spotlight as its principal beneficiary. Finally, Reagan took cognizance of the furor his proposed $1.5 trillion defense spending plan had created in Europe by reacting to "peace demonstrations" with a major speech on arms limitation, and by submitting his own START program for Russian consideration.

Many observers felt the change was the result of Alexander Haig's resignation as Secretary of State and his replacement by the less temperamental George Shultz. At his confirmation hearings, Haig had warned that Russian military prowess could eventually paralyze Western policy, and, portentously, "There are more important things than maintaining the peace." Actually, Haig's tenure had been punctuated with as many shots across the bow of his supposed enemies in the White House as in the Kremlin, and he had opposed forcing a showdown over the pipeline. Be that as it may, Shultz managed to negotiate a face-saving "agreement" on loans and credits to the Soviet Union that ended the impasse within the alliance.

By all accounts George Shultz wears his ideology more lightly than his predecessor did, as befits one whose expertise is in international economics as opposed to strategic grand-designing. He would agree, for example, with a *Wall Street Journal* comment of December 29, 1981, that "East-West crises are acquiring the distressing habit of becoming West-West crises." George Shultz's counterpart at Defense, Caspar Weinberger, a former colleague as well in the Bechtel Corporation, also had disagreements with Al Haig. But Weinberger's worldview is based upon a somewhat different reading of the problem posed by habitual "West-West crises."

Sounding again themes from the 1930s, Weinberger offered a criticism of modern appeasement, quoting for ironic effect the words of the Great Appeaser, Neville Chamberlain, that "weakness in arms strength means weakness in diplomacy." Addressing the Royal Institute of International Affairs in London, the Secretary asked if Europeans had learned from that experience that they must "stay resolved" and demonstrate "the will to respond, in concert, to a new global challenge." A few weeks later, Weinberger told interviewers at *Business Week* magazine that what concerned him the most about European reluctance to act decisively in the Polish situation was that it might trigger an isolationist backlash in America. "It's a worry because isolationism is never far from the surface in the U.S., and anything that feeds it at all is an unfortunate thing."

Isolationism translates, in this view, to an inevitable increase in state "intervention," as efforts at self-containment become inevitably preludes to government efforts at redistribution of existing wealth. At bottom, then, is a fear that the inward soul-searching that accompanied defeat in Vietnam threatens the very heartbeat of "liberal" society. Here is the connection between "foreign" and "domestic" policy. "In recent years," writes Norman Podhoretz,

> most liberals have been far more preoccupied with how to redistribute wealth than with how to create it; with how to protect the environment against the depredations of industrial enterprise than with how to foster technological development; with how to make people more secure than with how to encourage them to take risks. . . .

No battle rages for the soul of Ronald Reagan, but Shultz and Weinberger do represent, if only because of the institutional roles they find themselves living out, the growing unease about the covenant with power in the twilight of the American Century, and the uncertain options for the future.

Shultz's appointment coincided with a number of events, beginning with a financial crisis in Mexico, that highlighted "West-West" difficulties, the limitations of American power, and the North-South division. Set against the background of a world depression, these could topple the bastions of order as if they were ramshackle dwellings along Charles Dickens's desolate London street Tom-all-Alone's, in a "crash and a cloud of dust." "As several more houses are nearly ready to go, the next crash in Tom-all-Alone's may be expected to be a good one."

The world around *Bleak House* quavered on the edge of revolution, but in the Reagan administration's scenario the "next crash in Tom-all-Alone's" could come only from an outside force. In the Caribbean, from Cuba. Reagan has long concerned himself with Mexico's economic problems and, more to the point, their likely impact on the United States. Members of his Administration, as well as vintage Cold Warriors, have talked openly of the peril to American equilibrium should Cuban-inspired revolutionists successfully exploit Mexican difficulties. The most visible path for a Cuban incursion into Mexico would be through Central America; and the most likely way north economically would be to exploit the aftermath of the sudden decline in world oil prices. If that happened, Mexico would release to the United States a flood of refugees, and to all the world a deluge of defaults. The "hostages" Iran had held would be as nothing compared with these.

Another default posed unimaginable dangers. At a meeting of the International Monetary Fund's directors in early September 1982, the industrial nations were solemnly warned that they must increase its resources or face disaster. The behavior of the commercial banks, said the Fund's managing director, Jacques de Larosière, in curtailing loans to Eastern Europe after the Polish crisis and to Latin America because of Argentine and Mexican debt difficulties has pushed everyone closer to the abyss. Larosière's plea for a 50 percent increase in contributions to the Fund received a warm response, largely because it seems unwise to be against the idea at such a time, and also because in their jittery state members welcome being told what they must do. But the American Secretary of the Treasury, Donald Regan, said that there were limits to what the United States would be able to contribute:

> Other nations have to realize that even the United States has its limitations. We cannot do everything. We cannot be the defender of the Western world, as we know we are, and have high defense expenditures and at the same time run the domestic social programs that we have been running and give as much financial aid abroad as we have.

Unemployment inside the industrial countries had reached postwar highs; inside the United States it neared 11 percent, a post-Great Depression high. Across the European continent and in America, the total approached 35 million. Perhaps the most candid statement by an Administration leader, Regan's remarks were all but an admission that neither supply-side economics nor traditional Republican budget conservatism could alter the facts of life in the late twentieth century. The game was up. Americans had been told that their domestic situation could not be improved until the great "hangover" from the 1960s responded to Reaganomics. What they had to learn for themselves, apparently, was that the great runaway inflation and the recessions that followed were directly traceable to Lyndon Johnson.

Vietnam was far more traumatic to Americans than the Boer War was to Edwardian England, but the real comparison of our times to then, and the fate of declining empires, is not Henry Kissinger's vision of excessive zeal and ambition among client states, but the economic rivalry that grew up between Germany and England and the naval arms race. The Soviet Union is no economic competitor, but it is a threat to American supremacy in that arena, at least as the perception grows that Moscow, as President Reagan put it in a speech to the National Association of Evangelicals on March 8, 1983, was the "focus of evil in the modern world."

Richard Nixon's inability to transcend the ideology of Cold War I with détente, and his inability to make a break with the Cold War rationale for Vietnam even as he de-escalated, produced a credibility gap that Reagan and his advisers now seek to fill with the rhetoric of Cold War II. As his domestic difficulties deepened, and the Nuclear Freeze Campaign mounted in the fall of 1982, Reagan struck back in El Salvador. Alexander Haig had raised goose bumps with his descriptions of Soviet-Cuban inroads into the Caribbean area, but he had failed to put it in the broader perspective George Shultz now strived to achieve, with greater success.

State Department-inspired articles began appearing that featured the consequences of instability throughout the Central American region, as well as the connection between the dangers there and Mexico's welfare—and, in its broadest context—relations with the entire Third World. *Business Week* featured a story on February 7, 1983, entitled "The Third World Threat to World Recovery." In 1980 and 1981, it began, the main engine of growth in the world economy was the Third World. Developing countries accounted for more than 40 percent of U.S. exports in 1982, and 28 percent of all exports of the 24 industrial nations that make up the Organization for Economic Cooperation and Development.

Although the Third World nations had come to realize that the Soviet Union was long on promises and short on action, the more strident leaders of developing countries continued attacks on the West that elevated the danger of default, economic turmoil, and, although the article did not say it, Communism. "The Non-Aligned Movement, whose coordinating committee met in Managua, Nicaragua, in mid-January, denounced the international economic system as an "irrational" structure dominated by the "North." Thus confronted, Reagan "bowed" to reality and increased IMF resources by $45 billion, "reversing his Administration's opposition to increasing the lending capacity of international agencies." But it was also clear that the lending capacity of the United States was nowhere near enough to support the bankers in the event of a massive default on the more than $640 billion outstanding in commercial loans to the Third World, much of it concentrated in Mexico and Latin America.

In Vietnam America spent more than $100 billion in a failed effort to stop the spread of Communism in Asia; yet it now appeared that defense spending was a cheaper way to halt the menace in Central America; and certainly cheaper than a collapse and default. "We believe that the government of El Salvador is on the front line in a battle that is really aimed at the very heart of the Western Hemisphere," Reagan told the San Francisco Commonwealth Club, initiating a campaign to gain Congressional support for doubling American aid—"and eventually at us." Appearing before a Senate subcommittee, reported *Time* on March 14, 1983, Secretary of State Shultz delivered a bleak prediction that, if things continued to go as they were, El Salvador's troubles would eventually reach Mexico, "with which we have a long border."

Once again Mexico was the wedge. The long border that Shultz spoke of had concerned Wilson exactly seven decades earlier, and, in the same way; it was not merely a territorial line, it was also an economic and an ideological frontier. Ironically, Mexico's troubles had been worsened by the sharp decline in oil prices, so much so that, reported *Business Week*, American exports had declined by $5 billion to Mexico alone, costing the U.S. 100,000 jobs. Even more serious for Mexico, the principal and interest on its 1982 debt came to 129 percent of its export earnings.

In contrast to the few warnings issued about the Vietnam build-up in the Kennedy years, El Salvador was often on the front page. Despite this difference, however, and despite the steady accusations of officially sanctioned terrorism, the sound of falling dominoes seemed louder as the Administration made considerable progress in impressing Congress of the need to double aid for the war against the insurgents. Reagan insisted that there was no plan to "Americanize" the war, but, for all the criticism among neo-conservatives for the dreadful mistake of "nation-building" in Vietnam, his advisers were hard at work persuading the government of El Salvador that it must demonstrate genuine progress toward democracy by holding early elections.

That was the real parallel with Vietnam. That was the reason Americans originally went to Saigon in 1954. The risks were very great, and according to White House "sources" time was very short in El Salvador. But that was only the least of the risks. From the Administration's point of view there was the risk of a "policy of minimalism," that, having to proceed cautiously so as not to alarm Congress or trigger a "teach-in" movement, it would find itself in another endless war. A Republican version of "All the way with LBJ" would be the worst disaster of all.

If El Salvador fell, agreed the dean of Cold War Democrats in the Senate, Washington's Henry Jackson, the Rio Grande would no longer be a secure boundary. The "invasion" of Mexico by ideological shock forces would, given the catastrophic state of the Mexican economy, put the danger so close to home that the governors of Florida, Texas, and California would demand that troops be brought home from Europe to guard the frontiers. Could America stand by and do nothing, or do just enough to keep the other side from winning, asked columnist David B. Wilson, while the Latin poor became "front-line Hessians of the Soviet empire, Moscow surrogates like Castro's Cubans and Nicaragua's Sandinistas?"

Romantic notions of Latin American revolutionaries, Reagan and his advisers complained, stimulated anew by the "activist" wing of the Church, disguised the truth, ignored "the facts of history and the aggressive impulses of an evil empire. . . . The real crisis we face today is a spiritual one; at root, it is a test of moral will and faith." Alarmed that the nation had lost the will to shape its own future—in the image of its founders—Reagan reached back to Puritan roots. "Don't get cynical," he told supporters in 1976 after a losing effort in pursuit of the Republican nomination, "look at yourselves and what you were willing to do and recognize that there are millions and millions of Americans out there that want what you want, that want it to be that way, that want it to be a shining city on the hill."*

One hundred and thirty years earlier, Herman Melville wrote an allegorical tale of Captain Ahab's fiery hunt for the white whale. *Moby-Dick* was not a commercial success. Nor did it receive much critical acclaim in Melville's lifetime. Ahab's ship, the *Pequod*, bearing the name of a vanquished Indian tribe, set forth from the ancient Puritan homeland on Christmas Day, manned by a crew from all the races of the world, captained not by a tyrant, but by a strangely disfigured seagoer who holds an "election" to determine the crew's willingness to join him in striking through the mask that conceals the meaning of the white whale to mortals. After a journey around the world, Moby-Dick is sighted. Now, nature and God must yield their secrets. On the final day of the hunt, the whale eludes his pursuers in the long boats, and submerges under the *Pequod*. Surfacing suddenly, the white whale destroys Ahab's last ship. The captain's harpoon is powerless to save his ship—or himself.

Woodrow Wilson had accepted the original covenant with power reluctantly, with a pledge that it would be used only to prevent America from being shut out of the room where decisions affecting future world peace were to be made. Over the years his successors transformed that commitment, ambiguous as it was, into an unshakable faith in Ahab's harpoon. And so the *Pequod* sails on to its destined meeting place with the mysterious leviathan. It waits in an eternity of silence.

*Lou Cannon, *Reagan* (New York, 1982), p. 226.

A Note on Sources and Suggestions for Further Reading

I have footnoted the text very sparingly, hoping thereby to enhance the sense of dialogue between author and reader. Each chapter is really an "essay," or think-piece, and together they form a cluster around the principal themes of the liberal state, its supporters, and the use of power. As such, the essays are intended to be exploratory rather than exhaustive, provocative more than persuasive. In their construction, nevertheless, I have drawn upon more than twenty years of research, using the manuscript sources of leading figures, the printed record of Congressional hearings, and public documents. What follows is a brief list of suggested readings the reader may find useful to pursue arguments in the text, or alternative points of view.

Diplomatic historians have not yet discovered a new paradigm to replace traditional methodology, sometimes referred to scornfully as what one clerk said to another. Efforts to apply the computer to the study of foreign policy have so far not convinced anyone there is a crying need to re-tool before we go on, but diplomatic historians have incurred a growing debt to colleagues in political science and military history. A starting point, in reference to this book, would be Alan Wolfe's *The Limits of Legitimacy: Political Contradictions of Contemporary Capitalism* (New York, 1977) and Michael Howard's *War and the Liberal Conscience* (New Brunswick, N.J., 1978). Geoffrey Barraclough's "classic," *An Introduction to Contemporary History* (Baltimore, 1967), has helped to relieve many historians of the burden of ethnocentrism, a particularly welcome occurrence, especially for students of diplomatic history.

CHAPTER ONE.   A companion essay to this chapter is my "Woodrow Wilson and the Mexican Revolution," which appears in Arthur S. Link, ed., *Woodrow Wilson and a Revolutionary World* (Chapel Hill, 1982). In this heavily documented, monographic style, essay, I explore many of the same themes from a somewhat narrower angle. The predicament liberalism faced as Wilson came onto the scene was not unique to America, that is what made the solution so imperative. My impressions have been formed by Peter Weiler, *The New Liberalism: Liberal Social Theory in Great Britain 1889–1914* (New York, 1982), and the recent translation by Grete Heinz of Eckart Kehr's essays on Germany, *Economic Interest, Militarism, and Foreign Policy* (Berkeley, 1977). No President left a fuller record of his thoughts than Wilson, and the appearance of *The Papers of Woodrow Wilson*, edited by Arthur S. Link, David W. Hirst, John E. Little, *et al*, 37 vols. to date (Princeton, 1966–), allows the historian to follow the unfolding of Wilson's policy with something approximating "precision." Theoretical works of great value are Arno Mayer, *Wilson vs. Lenin: Political Origins of the New Diplomacy* (Cleveland, 1964) and N. Gordon Levin, Jr., *Woodrow Wilson and World Politics* (New York, 1968). Mayer is also the author of the masterful, *Politics and Diplomacy of Peacemaking: Containment and Counterrevolution at Versailles 1918–1919* (New York, 1969).

CHAPTER TWO.   Much of the best new work done on New Deal diplomacy in the 1930s and the question of legitimacy (or appeasement) has been by British scholars. Two books, C. A. MacDonald, *The United States, Britain and Appeasement 1936–1939* (New York, 1981) and David Reynolds, *The Creation of the Anglo-American Alliance, 1937–1941* (Chapel Hill, 1982), are particularly worthwhile. Similar themes are pursued, also, in James R. Leutze, *Bargaining for Supremacy, 1937–1941* (Chapel Hill, 1977). Some years ago scholars from Japan and the United States collaborated on a bi-national approach: *Pearl Harbor as History: Japanese-American Relations, 1931–1941*, edited by Dorothy Borg and Shumpei Okamoto (New York, 1973). Research for my essay in that volume, "The Role of the Commerce and Treasury Departments," provides part of the foundation for this chapter, which is also something of a companion piece to another essay, "New Deal Diplomacy: A View from the Seventies," which is in Leonard P. Liggio and James J. Martin, eds., *Watershed of Empire: Essays on New Deal Foreign Policy* (Colorado Springs, 1976). The Roosevelt "approach" is thoroughly explored in Robert

Dallek, *Franklin D. Roosevelt and American Foreign Policy, 1932–1945* (New York, 1979), but Robert Sherwood, *Roosevelt and Hopkins: An Intimate History* (New York, 1948) is still impressive as an over-all introduction.

CHAPTER THREE. This chapter owes much to the work of, and conversations with, scholars who have made their way into the dark maze of Soviet policymaking. Two articles by Albert Resis, "Spheres of Influence in Soviet Wartime Diplomacy," *Journal of Modern History* (September 1981), 53:417–39, and "The Churchill-Stalin Secret 'Percentages' Agreement on the Balkans, Moscow, October, 1944," *American Historical Review* (April 1978), 83:368–87, hopefully presage a general work on this subject. The first attempt to survey domestic "interest groups," and their impact on Stalin's foreign policy by William O. McCaggs, *Stalin Embattled, 1943–1948* (Detroit, 1978) presents us with a much more complex view of the Soviet dictator's problems than American historians are accustomed to hearing about. David Carlton, *Anthony Eden* (Bloomington, Ind., 1982) contains new material on the British attitude toward Eastern Europe. How the battle over Eastern Europe looked from Charles de Gaulle's viewpoint is one of the subjects covered in François Kersaudy, *Churchill and De Gaulle* (New York, 1982). What Churchill was up against with FDR is described in William Roger Louis, *Imperialism at Bay: The United States and the Decolonization of the British Empire, 1941–1945* (New York, 1978). In a category by itself is Christopher Thorne's comprehensive account, *Allies of a Kind: The United States, Britain, and the War Against Japan, 1941–1945* (New York, 1978).

CHAPTER FOUR. Historians have yet to integrate successfully the testimony of Truman administration officials before the Senate Foreign Relations Committee taken in Executive Session, with other documents available to them. In the formative years of the Cold War, 1947–50, these hearings, made available only since 1973, are of crucial importance. For this chapter, two of especial significance are *Legislative Origins of the Truman Doctrine* (Washington, 1973) and *Military Assistance Program: 1949* (Washington, 1974). Far more than biography, Ronald Steel's *Walter Lippmann and the American Century* (Boston, 1980) delivers what the title promises. The best over-all introduction to American policy in the Cold War remains Walter LaFeber, *America, Russia, and the Cold War* (New

York, 1976). On the difficulty of harnessing military power for political ends in the Cold War, see Martin Sherwin, *A World Destroyed: The Atomic Bomb and the Grand Alliance* (New York, 1975) and Gregg Herken, *The Winning Weapon: The Atomic Bomb in the Cold War, 1945–1950* (New York, 1980). Problems of implementing containment are discussed in John Lewis Gaddis, *Strategies of Containment: A Critical Appraisal of Postwar American National Security Policy* (New York, 1982). Background for this chapter can also be found in Lloyd C. Gardner, *Architects of Illusion: Men and Ideas in American Foreign Policy, 1941–1949* (Chicago, 1970).

CHAPTER FIVE.   The Korean War and America's Far Eastern policy have been under close scrutiny in recent years. Some of the new approaches are presented in, Dorothy Borg and Waldo Heinrichs, eds., *Uncertain Years: Chinese-American Relations, 1947–1950* (New York, 1980). On China, also see Michael Schaller, *The U.S. Crusade in China, 1938–1945* (New York, 1979). The Washington origins of the Korean War are dissected in, William Stueck, *The Road to Confrontation: American Policy toward China and Korea, 1947–1950* (Chapel Hill, 1981). The war's internal origins, that is, inside Korea, are the subject of Bruce Cumming's *The Origins of the Korean War: Liberation and the Emergence of Separate Regimes, 1945–1947* (Princeton, 1981). The transformation of an "Atlanticist" into an Asian "specialist" is one of the key themes in Ronald W. Pruessen's fine *John Foster Dulles: The Road to Power* (New York, 1982).

CHAPTER SIX.   The spate of books now available that offers a reassessment of the Eisenhower years began, interestingly enough, with a book on Richard Nixon, Gary Wills's *Nixon Agonistes: The Crisis of the Self-Made Man* (Boston, 1970). Dulles has not yet had his due as a policy "thinker." A preliminary effort in that direction is the author's "Economic Strategy, 1945–1960," which will appear in Norman Graebner, ed., *The Theory and Practice of National Security, 1945–1960* (tentative titles). How the postwar "dollar gap" became the deficit "balance of payments" dilemma is recounted in Fred L. Block, *The Origins of International Economic Disorder* (Berkeley, 1977). An excellent short study of the development and theory behind the Common Market movement is R. C. Mowat, *Creating the European Community* (London, 1973). It should be read with, Richard Mayne, trans. of Jean Monnet, *Memoirs* (New

York, 1978). Suez prompted the writing of "thrillers." Two of the best are Miles Copeland, *The Game of Nations* (New York, 1969) and the much more recent, Donald Neff, *Warriors at Suez* (New York, 1981). Books on other aspects of liberation are Madeline Kalb, *The Congo Cables: The Cold War in Africa from Eisenhower to Kennedy* (New York, 1982) and Richard Immerman, *The CIA in Guatemala* (Austin, Texas, 1982).

CHAPTER SEVEN. Keeping up with new books on Vietnam is already an impossible task. A convenient introduction is George M. Herring, *America's Longest War* (New York, 1980). Changes in the way liberals see themselves can be gleaned from Arthur M. Schlesinger, Jr., *The Imperial Presidency* (New York, 1974). Deeper soul-searching, and a very fine overview, is George W. Ball, *The Past Has Another Pattern: Memoirs* (New York, 1982). The memoir style from another perspective is exemplified in Maxwell Taylor, *Swords and Plowshares* (New York, 1972). Although it deals primarily with the earlier years, Ronnie Dugger's *The Politician: The Life and Times of Lyndon Johnson* (New York, 1982) is essential reading on Vietnam. For those in a hurry, the essence of Vietnam decision-making is brilliantly summarized in Larry Berman, *Planning a Tragedy: The Americanization of the War in Vietnam* (New York, 1982). European constraints on Vietnam policy are explored from the French angle by John Newhouse, *De Gaulle and the Anglo-Saxons* (New York, 1970), and Alexander Werth, *De Gaulle* (New York, 1966). Another special study, James Clay Thompson, *Rolling Thunder: Understanding Policy and Program Failure* (Chapel Hill, 1980), puts to rest the mythology of not-enough-bombs on not-enough-targets as the reason for America's defeat. The "backlash" on the right has begun, however. Guenter Lewy's *America in Vietnam* (New York, 1978) is a thoroughgoing critique of both policymakers and anti-war protesters, while Norman Podhoretz, *Why We Were in Vietnam* (New York, 1982), tweaks liberal noses by throwing up to dissenters the record of their past statements.

CHAPTER EIGHT. The Nixon era has become the battleground of memoir writers. Kissinger's massive (still an understatement) volumes, *The White House Years* (Boston, 1979) and *Years of Upheaval* (Boston, 1982), are hardly to be "equaled." Yet Nixon's *RN: The Memoirs of Richard Nixon* (New York, 1978) is more candid and, in some ways, less self-serving. H. R. Haldeman, *The*

Ends of Power (New York, 1978) and John Ehrlichman, *Witness to Power* (New York, 1982) have had their say, but the full story of the Byzantine atmosphere in the Nixon White House came in Seymour M. Hersh's study of Kissinger, *The Price of Power* (New York, 1983). An excellent contemporary account of détente is Henry Brandon, *The Retreat of American Power* (New York, 1973), while the catastrophic "fall-out" from Vietnam is detailed in William Shawcross, *Sideshow: Kissinger, Nixon and the Destruction of Cambodia* (New York, 1979).

CHAPTER NINE.   Few books classified as "instant" history last long. An exception probably will be, Thomas Ferguson and Joel Rogers, *The Hidden Election: Politics and Economics in the 1980 Presidential Election* (New York, 1981), which summarizes a great deal of what has happened in the last two decades. A very similar analysis from the conservative viewpoint is Kevin P. Phillips, *Post-Conservative America: People, Politics, and Ideology in a Time of Crisis* (New York, 1982). A full discussion of the United States and *Ostpolitik*, from 1949 to the present, is badly needed. In the meantime, James Oliver Goldsborough, *Rebel Europe* (New York, 1982), poses some of the central questions. Barry Rubin, *Paved with Good Intentions: The American Experience and Iran* (New York, 1980), is likely to remain the primary source for many a year. Nuclear weaponry and policy strategy, the ultimate covenant with power, have drawn much attention. Mary Kaldor, *The Baroque Arsenal* (New York, 1981) provides an overview, while John Prados, *The Soviet Estimate: U.S. Intelligence Analysis and Russian Military Strength* (New York, 1982), placed alongside of Robert Scheer, *With Enough Shovels* (New York, 1982), will disturb the most complacent volunteer in Cold War II. Jimmy Carter's *Keeping Faith: Memoirs of a President* (New York, 1982) reflects, even in its title, Carter's uncertainty about what he was doing, confirmed by Hamilton Jordan's *Crisis: The Last Year of the Carter Presidency* (New York, 1982). Tensions inside the Carter administration are reflected in the memoirs of two antagonists: Cyrus Vance, *Hard Choices* (New York, 1983) and Zbigniew Brzezinski, *Power and Principle* (New York, 1983). Reagan's self-assurance, on the other hand, emerges clearly from Lou Cannon's *Reagan* (New York, 1982). Though not so sweeping, perhaps, George F. Kennan's *The Nuclear Delusion* (New York, 1982) may equal Henry Adams's *Education* as an American "classic."

Index

Acheson, Dean G., on threat to liberalism from Germany and Japan, 45–46; destroyer-bases deal, 49; 51, 55, 66, 71, on Truman Doctrine amendments, 94; on NATO rationale, 98; 99, on NATO successes, 100; Truman Doctrine and Korea, 107–8; Asian consultants, 111–12; defense perimeter speech, 113–14; likelihood of "Communist" attack in 1950, 116; on impact of Korea, 118; resents George Kennan's advice, 119; on Chinese intervention, 123; 126, and Schuman plan, 134; 135, 139, 141, on Ho Chi Minh, 152–53; and Berlin crisis 1961, 160; and defense of Richard Nixon, 184–85
Adenauer, Konrad, 185
Afghanistan, 200
Africa and common market, 134
Agent theory of revolution, 19
Alanbrooke, Lord, 56, 59
Algeria, 188
Allen, Richard V., 216

Allende, Salvador, 205
Anderson, John, 211
André, Philip, 134
Anglo-American Trade Treaty of 1938, 41
Angola, 206–7
Anti-colonialism, 104
Appeasement, 36, 37, 42
Argentina, 224
Armstrong, Hamilton Fish, 71
Aswan Dam, 142–43
Atlantic Charter, 55, 56, 68, 74–75, 128
Atomic bomb and "diplomacy," 73, 88, 104, 114–15, 118
Attlee, Clement, 92, 123, 129
Auchinloss, Gordon, 16
Austerity, threat to liberalism in postwar era, 95–96
Austin, Warren, 119
Austria, 137

Baker, Ray Stannard, 25–26
Bakhtiar, Shahpour, 209
Balfour, Arthur, 15
Ball, George W., 165–66